The Alien Abduction Phenomenon

I0212276

ALSO BY PAUL MEEHAN AND FROM MCFARLAND

*Alien Abduction in the Cinema: A History
from the 1950s to Today* (2023)

Space Exploration on Film (2022)

The Haunted House on Film: An Historical Analysis (2020)

Tech-Noir: The Fusion of Science Fiction and Film Noir
(2008; paperback 2018)

*The Ghost of One's Self: Doppelgangers in Mystery,
Horror and Science Fiction Films* (2017)

The Vampire in Science Fiction Film and Literature (2014)

Horror Noir: Where Cinema's Dark Sisters Meet (2011)

Cinema of the Psychic Realm: A Critical Survey (2009)

The Alien Abduction Phenomenon

Science, Evidence and the Unknown

PAUL MEEHAN

Exposit

Jefferson, North Carolina

ISBN (print) 978-1-4766-9553-2
ISBN (ebook) 978-1-4766-5578-9

LIBRARY OF CONGRESS CATALOGING DATA ARE AVAILABLE

Library of Congress Control Number 2025011038

© 2025 Paul Meehan. All rights reserved

*No part of this book may be reproduced or transmitted in any form
or by any means, electronic or mechanical, including photocopying
or recording, or by any information storage and retrieval system,
without permission in writing from the publisher.*

Front cover image: © andrey_l/Shutterstock

———

Printed in the United States of America

Exposit is an imprint of McFarland & Company, Inc., Publishers

Ⓢ

Exposit

*Box 611, Jefferson, North Carolina 28640
www.expositbooks.com*

Table of Contents

Preface

You're driving down a lonely stretch of road at night. Maybe you're on your way somewhere, or perhaps you've had a sudden urge to take a drive to no particular destination for no particular reason. You idly wonder why there is no other vehicular traffic on this usually well-traveled thoroughfare. The night around you is unusually quiet and the very atmosphere seems heavy and oppressive.

For some odd reason you pull off onto a side road as if some outside force is guiding you. The car seems like it's no longer under your control. You come to a stop in a deserted clearing where you perceive a large, dimly-lit object resting on the ground. The car's engine and headlights turn off by themselves.

The next thing you know you're back on the road. A sign informs you that you're twenty miles further along the roadway, but you have no memory of driving this distance. When you arrive at your destination you find that there are two hours of missing time that you can't account for.

In the aftermath of this odd experience you acquire an irrational dread of the stretch of road you traveled that night. You start to have nightmares about being kidnapped by a group of strange beings and examined on an operating table. You begin to wonder if something very strange really happened to you that night. You become hypervigilant, sleeping with the lights on and a weapon under your pillow. Over the ensuing years you are summoned to several other nighttime close encounters with these mysterious beings in lonely places that you can only vaguely remember.

The above scenario is a template for a generic narrative of alien abduction using details culled from numerous reports. These stories have a disquieting edge that is reminiscent of ghost stories or other-worldly encounters with supernatural beings. As one of the characters in the movie *Close Encounters* observes, contact with an alien intelligence is like "Halloween for grown-ups."

More recent abduction research has revealed what is perhaps an even more disquieting scenario. Abductees relate stories about human/alien hybrids who resemble normal people on the outside but who possess the aliens' powers of mind control and are secretly working to implement their program to establish hegemony over our planet. Toward this end the hybrids are conducting various clandestine operations in our everyday world. They are no doubt responsible for bizarre reports of mysterious Men in Black, bogus social workers, strange job interviewers, shadowy highway workers and phantom clowns.

While there is only circumstantial evidence for any of this, it should be noted that private researchers with limited resources have uncovered these revelations. No government on Earth has ever undertaken a well-funded study of the phenomenon to either prove or disprove the veracity of these claims. While there appears to be a renewed interest in unidentified flying objects (UFOs) and unidentified aerial phenomenon (UAPs) by the U.S. intelligence and military communities at present, there is still no real will to pursue an investigation of alien contact.

My own involvement with UFOs began sometime around 1975 when I was living in a ground-floor apartment on University Avenue in the northwest Bronx. One afternoon I heard people yelling outside and ran out to investigate. On my way to the front door I felt an unusual tingling as the hair on my arms stood up like when there is a lot of electricity in the air during a thunderstorm. I raced out into the street but saw nothing; however, a neighbor told me that a UFO had been observed flying slowly and at a low level over the Jerome Park Reservoir located just a few blocks away. The object was described as football-shaped, with a row of very bright white lights and a red light in the middle. The witness also described their impression of passengers inside the UFO who were peering out, "like the monorail ride at the World's Fair." Needless to say, this event sparked my interest in the phenomenon. I had always been a science fiction buff, but now I began to research accounts of real-life encounters with these enigmatic craft and the beings who piloted them.

A few years later I was a student studying cinema in the Film and Theater department at Hunter College in Manhattan. One day I struck up a casual conversation with a fellow student when somehow the subject of my interest in UFOs came up. She gave me an odd, somewhat conspiratorial look and proceeded to relate the following story.

She told me that at one time she had worked at a department store with a friend, a man who was heavily involved in the New York theatrical scene. One day while they were working together, he asked her, "Do you want to see something?" He then proceeded to loosen his shirt to reveal a purplish-blue bruise-like mark about one inch wide that extended underneath his entire armpit. Then he showed her another identical mark under his other arm. She likened these to stretch marks, livid scars that are often seen on the abdominal areas of women during pregnancy, only these were darker in color.

Her story was that the friend had been driving one night, somewhere in the northeast, perhaps in upstate New York, Connecticut, or Massachusetts (she was vague about the exact location). He was in the vicinity of a nuclear power plant (possibly the Indian Point nuclear facility in Westchester County) when he observed a large, luminous UFO directly overhead. His vehicle came to a complete stop and he lost consciousness. When he awakened sometime later the craft was gone and he discovered the underarm scarring, but he had no memory of anything that had occurred.

This tale had many of the earmarks of a "classic" abduction narrative, such as the roadway locale, missing time amnesia and unusual bodily markings. These story elements, however, were not well known to the general public during the mid–1970s. Another curious factor was the event's occurring in the vicinity of a nuclear power plant, as UFO sightings at nuclear plants and weapons sites continue to be a source of concern to military and intelligence analysts. For instance, there was a dramatic sighting of an enormous UFO hovering above the Indian Point nuclear reactor on July 24, 1984, during a wave of sightings in the Hudson Valley between 1983 and 1986.

My informant was good enough to provide me with the phone number of her friend. I called the number several times but was never able to contact him. For that matter, I never saw or spoke with my fellow Hunter student again.

Since that time I have been fascinated with UFOs and the abduction phenomenon. A solution to the mystery of an alien presence in our world may have momentous consequences for the future of humankind.

Introduction

Something Is Out There

On July 26, 2023, a hearing was held by the U.S. House of Representatives Committee on Oversight and Accountability on the subject of Unidentified Aerial Phenomena (UAPs), formerly known as UFOs. A panel of three witnesses testified under oath concerning various aspects of the phenomenon, but the most controversial claims were voiced by whistleblower David Grusch. Grusch, a decorated Afghanistan combat veteran, was a former Air Force intelligence officer who had worked at the National Geospatial-Intelligence Agency (NGA) and the National Reconnaissance Office (NRO). He had served as the representative of the NRO to the Unidentified Aerial Phenomena Task Force from 2019 to 2021.

In this capacity, he said that he had reviewed documents that claim that the U.S. government has an ultra-secret, black-budget UFO retrieval program, beginning with a craft that had crashed in Mussolini's Italy in 1933 and was obtained by the U.S. government at the end of World War II. He further testified that this clandestine program is in possession of materials from other crashed UFOs, including the bodies of non-human biological entities. According to Grusch, this project was so covert that individuals had been murdered in order to keep the secret.

Grusch was deemed to be a credible witness, owing to his impeccable credentials as a military officer and intelligence official, but his claims were considered highly controversial by members of Congress and the press. It was noted that he had no firsthand knowledge of these programs but had only reviewed documents concerning them.

Also on the panel were former Navy pilot Ryan Graves, who

testified that his F/A-18 squadron had encountered UFOs that appeared as dark gray or black cubes inside a clear sphere and that an anomalous object had a near collision with two fighter jets in 2014. Graves addressed the potential threat that these objects posed to aerial navigation. A fellow former Navy aviator on the panel, David Fravor, testified that, while he was stationed on the aircraft carrier U.S. *Nimitz* in 2014, he had witnessed an object performing maneuvers that were impossible given the current state of aviation technology.

In the aftermath of the hearing, Senate Majority Leader Chuck Schumer and a bipartisan group of senators introduced an amendment to the current annual defense spending bill that would compel the relevant agencies to hand over UAP records to a review board that would be charged with disclosure of UAP records to Congress. Senators Kirsten Gillibrand and Marco Rubio joined in demands for further transparency from these executive branch agencies.

Just weeks later, on September 14, NASA released a 36-page report generated by a panel of 16 "experts" that analyzed 800 UAP reports over a period of nine months and came to the conclusion that there was insufficient evidence to suggest that UAPs were extraterrestrial in origin, although this remained a possibility. The agency reportedly spent a whopping $100,000 on the report, which attempted to debunk a number of recent cases while claiming that the data needed to explain the vast majority of sightings one way or the other do not exist.

There was much speculation in the press and in the blogosphere concerning the motives of the government in conducting these hearings and issuing reports after denying the reality of the phenomenon for many decades. Some felt that Grusch's testimony had been manipulated by covert intelligence agencies to create the false impression that the United States was in possession of alien technology in an effort to intimidate our adversaries. Cynics groused that these sensational revelations constituted a distraction from political issues during a contentious presidential election cycle. Journalists probed Grusch's background, revealing a past history of psychiatric problems, which could have been an effort to discredit him.

The United States government has had a long involvement with the phenomenon dating back more than sixty years. The Air Force initiated their first UFO study, Project Sign, in January of 1948. Their initial conclusion, contained in a report dubbed the "Estimate of the

Situation," was that the unidentified craft were of extraterrestrial origin. The report was passed along to Chief of Staff General Hoyt S. Vanderberg, who disagreed with its conclusion and ordered all copies to be burned. Project Sign was superseded by Project Grudge, which was formed in December of 1948 and attempted to debunk all sightings by casting aspersions on those who reported them.

Grudge in turn was succeeded by Project Blue Book in March of 1952, a study that lasted until it was terminated in December 1969. Blue Book collected and analyzed over 12,000 reports before concluding that UFOs were not a threat to national security and that there was no evidence that they were of extraterrestrial origin. Critics of the project noted that it was given a low priority and very limited resources by the Air Force and was more of a public relations operation than a serious study of the phenomenon. The Air Force contracted a scientific study conducted by physicist Edward Condon at the University of Colorado beginning in 1966 that reached similar conclusions after reviewing only 59 cases in detail. The Condon study was later critiqued for its anti–UFO bias, but the Air Force relied on its findings to terminate Blue Book in 1969.

Thus ended the U.S. government's two decades–long official involvement with UFOs, although conspiracy theories have persisted about clandestine UFO programs conducted without the public's knowledge or congressional oversight. The best known of these is Majestic 12, or MJ-12, which purportedly consisted of 12 prominent military and intelligence officials that was formed in the wake of the alleged crash of a flying saucer and the retrieval of alien bodies from Roswell, New Mexico, in July 1947. Documents that detailed the formation of MJ-12 surfaced in 1984 under dubious circumstances and are widely considered to be hoaxes. According to *New York Times* journalist Ralph Blum in his book *Out There*, the Defense Intelligence Agency (DIA) initiated its own secret, albeit informal, investigation known as the "UFO Working Group" in 1987 under the direction of Army Colonel Harold E. Phillips, which did little more than jawbone about the subject and conduct minimal investigations. Blum's book has been shown to contain numerous factual errors that call the existence of the Working Group into doubt.

There matters stood until December 16, 2017, when the *Times* revealed that there actually *were* secret government UFO research programs. The Advanced Aerospace Threat Identification Program (AATIP) was established by the Defense Intelligence Agency in 2007 to determine if the phenomenon constituted a threat to national security. The program was operational until 2012, when it was succeeded by the Unidentified Aerial Phenomenon Task Force (UAPTF), which continued the study by the CIA and the U.S. Navy.

After more than six decades the best and brightest stars in the intelligence and scientific communities have failed to solve the UFO conundrum. The subject is so mired in various prejudices, negative mindsets and science fiction tropes that it may not even be amenable to study by the authorities in any meaningful way. For example, Luis Elizondo, who at one time was director of the AATIP program, resigned from the project because certain senior government officials expressed a belief that the phenomenon was demonic in nature. Elizondo felt that the philosophical beliefs of these individuals precluded any objective evaluation of the data and resigned his position in the program in protest. He reportedly experienced reprisals from higher-ups that damaged his career and reputation for expressing his opinions.

As for the scientific and academic establishment, they steadfastly maintain that there is no evidence for the existence of UFOs and aliens even in the face of sightings by trained observers such as pilots and other military personnel, radar/visual cases, analysis of ground traces and other forms of evidence. Part of their attitude is due to what has been termed the "giggle factor," a prejudice that arises from what is considered to be the absurdity of pop culture concepts like "flying saucers" and "little green men" (cue *The X-Files* theme music here). This arrogant viewpoint can be summed up in the phrase "it can't be, therefore it isn't," which serves to remove the subject from any serious consideration.

The scientific/academic establishment grouses about a lack of hard evidence for the phenomenon, while punishing any of their ilk that dare to contradict their orthodoxy. Cases in point include the sad fate of University of Arizona atmospheric physicist Dr. James E. McDonald, whose professional reputation was destroyed over his advocacy of UFOs, a factor that ultimately led to his suicide; historian Dr. David Jacobs, who was passed over for a full professorship at Temple University for his research into alien abductions; and Dr. John Mack, who nearly had his tenure revoked by Harvard University due to his abduction studies. Science demands hard evidence but ridicules and punishes those who dare to think outside the box. Perhaps the study of UFOs and abductions lies beyond the scope of present-day scientific analysis.

As a result, UFO research has been largely conducted by non-scientists and interested amateurs from a number of diverse fields. These researchers, who constitute what is known as ufology, have limited resources with which to conduct their investigations. They frequently endure ridicule from the press and other skeptics. This is especially true of abduction researchers, who are on the cutting edge of UFO investigations. Historically, most studies of the phenomenon have concentrated on analyzing the properties of the UFOs rather than scrutinizing their occupants, but this approach has its limitations. Abduction researcher Budd Hopkins expresses the shortcomings of this methodology in these terms: "We were trying to collect sightings. That's like trying to get the license plate on the getaway car without having figured out what the crime was."[1] Former UK government UFO investigator Nick Pope continues the automotive analogy thus: "If the Queen called at your house, you would probably not be interested in the car in which she arrived. You would want to know why she was visiting you!"[2]

In the many decades since the beginning of the modern UFO era in 1947, the U.S. government has only investigated one abduction case. The University of Colorado study examined the 1968 experience of police sergeant Herb Schirmer without drawing any firm conclusions. An abduction conference was held at the Massachusetts Institute of Technology (although not under the auspices of MIT) in 1992 that assembled a group of the most prominent non-governmental researchers and abductees to share their viewpoints, but this was a one-off event. Since that time, abduction studies have been conducted by individual researchers who have disparate opinions about the phenomenon.

During the early years of the modern UFO era in the 1950s, the Hollywood movie industry exploited the most sensational aspects of alien visitation in a series of saucer movies that played upon Cold War era anxieties and paranoia. Films such as *The Thing from Another World*, *Invaders from Mars*, *The War of the Worlds* and *Invasion of the Body Snatchers* painted extraterrestrials as hostile invaders bent on the domination of humankind. An alternate view of alien interaction was offered by a group collectively known as the "contactees," individuals who claimed to be in communication with benevolent "space brothers" that arrived on Earth from utopian worlds bearing messages of peace and warnings about the prospects of nuclear war. While the 1950s-era contactee movement had largely faded by the end of the decade, their mindset has experienced a resurgence in the 21st century and continues to muddy the waters surrounding notions of alien intentions. The decade also witnessed sightings of mysterious "occupants" or "humanoids" in connection with UFO landings.

The abduction phenomenon began to emerge during the 1960s and 1970s in a series of enigmatic liaisons that resembled neither the horrific prognostications of the alien invasion films nor the contactee's meetings with benign space brothers. The science fiction paradigm for interaction with aliens revolved around the concept of "contact." In this scenario, benign extraterrestrials would initiate open contact with humanity and invite us to become the fledgling member of an interplanetary federation of worlds. This narrative assumes that we are on a rough cultural and technological parity with the aliens, which does not appear to be the case. Instead, the intelligence behind the abductions has chosen to remain secretive while conducting enigmatic forays around the edges of our reality and treating captive humans like experimental animals. Thus, the science fiction conceit of open contact with a higher civilization on more or less equal terms has yet to be realized and will likely never be realized.

Some examples of the contact theme in science fiction film include *Close Encounters of the Third Kind*, in which a group of scientists and government officials establish a covert liaison with extraterrestrials; *Contact*, wherein a single human emissary communicates with an alien intelligence; and *Star Trek: First Contact*, where the crew of the starship *Enterprise* travels back in time to witness the initial meeting between humankind and the Galactic Federation. Interestingly, many science fiction luminaries, including the late Ray Bradbury, Isaac Asimov, Gene Roddenberry and Arthur C. Clarke, have been or are openly hostile to reports of UFOs and contacts between humans and aliens.

As the decades wore on, no answers to the abduction mystery were forthcoming. Although there was evidence of the reality of UFOs as "nuts and bolts" machines that included radar returns, ground traces, etc., no unequivocal physical evidence of the abductors has surfaced to date. Skeptics have formulated various psychological explanations for these events, including highway hypnosis, sleep paralysis and hallucinations, but although some of these theories have merit (and will be discussed in a later chapter), they cannot account for all aspects of the phenomenon. Researchers have advanced some exotic explanations of their own, including the notion of UFOs and abductions as part of a control system designed to effect societal change initiated by secretive human groups, the manifestation of phantom-like Jungian archetypes and alien encounters that take place within a paraphysical "imaginal realm."

By the 1990s abduction studies had been advanced to new levels of sophistication and respectability by dedicated researchers such as Budd Hopkins, Dr. David Jacobs, Dr. John Mack, Raymond Fowler and others. Although there were some disagreements among the investigators as to methods of study and the motivations of the ufonauts, some disturbing patterns began to emerge. Sperm, ova and fertilized embryos were being extracted from the abductees and manipulated by the advanced scientific techniques of the abductors. The aliens appeared to be engaged in a program to produce human/alien hybrid beings that resembled normal people but retained the aliens' psychic mind control abilities. These creatures were thought to be part of a multi-generational program to eventually wrest planetary hegemony from our species.

Abductees related stories of their encounters with these hybrids that took place not on board a UFO but in everyday, quotidian settings. There were tales of the mysterious Men in Black who called upon witnesses at their homes and attempted to intimidate them into silence while confiscating any evidence of their sightings. Even more bizarre were accounts of frightening "phantom clowns" and "bogus social workers" who attempted to lure children away from their parents. Strange "job interviews" were being conducted in connection with abductions and traffic was reportedly being re-routed during highway events by shadowy "highway workers."

There is a Dionysian element of irrationality and fantasy surrounding the study of the phenomenon, but a careful analysis can hopefully discern the signal within the noise.

CHAPTER ONE

Flying Saucers, Contactees and Occupants

The modern UFO era began on June 24, 1947, when mountain pilot Kenneth Arnold spied a formation of fast-moving objects in the skies near Mt. Rainier in Washington State. Arnold gave an interview to members of the press on the following day in which he described the herky-jerky movements of the disc-shaped objects as being similar to that of a saucer skimming over the surface of water. When the story reached the Associated Press wires, an anonymous headline writer dubbed the craft "flying saucers," a vaguely ridiculous term that would surround the phenomenon with an aura of ridicule. A spate of saucer sightings followed in the wake of Arnold's press conference that mostly occurred in the Western United States. The most significant of these were the alleged crash-retrieval event at Roswell, New Mexico, over the July 4 weekend, and a UFO sighting near Maury Island in Puget Sound that yielded materials supposedly ejected from the craft.

During the 1950s, post–World War II technological breakthroughs would alter the American cultural landscape in ways that were conducive to a national paranoia. The most anxiety producing innovation was the advent of nuclear weapons, which quickly developed from the atomic bombs dropped on Japan in 1945 to the much more destructive potential of the hydrogen bomb that stoked fears of worldwide annihilation. Advances in rocket science would lead to the invention of the Intercontinental Ballistic Missile (ICBM) a delivery system that could rain atomic death anywhere on the globe. Postwar rocketry would also provide the means for earthlings to travel to other worlds for the first time, which presented another series of potentially threatening unknowns, for if we could travel to other planets, the denizens of these realms could return the favor and send their spaceships to visit us.

Prior to the deep space probes of later decades, little was known about the other planets in our Solar System. Ideas about our sister worlds were largely driven by the notions of science fiction writers who envisioned them as the abodes of extraterrestrial life. In the works of writers such as H.G. Wells, Edgar Rice Burroughs and Ray Bradbury, Mars was thought to be a desert planet that was the abode of a dying, decadent race. Conversely Venus, whose surface was forever obscured by a heavy layer of clouds, was conceived of as a world of tropical jungles teeming with life. Such other planets as Mercury, Jupiter, Saturn and even the Moon were believed to harbor life and alien civilizations. It would be decades before American and Soviet interplanetary probes disabused these ideas by proving that no life existed elsewhere in our system.

In the meantime, the press had a field day heaping derision on those who reported sighting the flying saucers, labeling them as being drunk, crazy or hallucinating, and the military was similarly busy

A 1950s-era flying saucer is pictured in this illustration from the 1956 MGM movie *Forbidden Planet*. The domed disc configuration is frequently reported by witnesses.

publicly debunking them. The saucers, however, had insinuated themselves into our popular culture, in large part due to the Hollywood motion picture industry that seized upon the money-making potential of the paranoid concept of alien invasion. Photogenic disc-shaped craft would appear in a number of classic sci-fi flicks of the period such as *The Day the Earth Stood Still, Invaders from Mars, This Island Earth, Forbidden Planet* and *Earth vs. the Flying Saucers.*

During this period the Air Force's Project Blue Book continued to collect UFO sighting reports, but new venues for witness accounts appeared with the advent of "civilian" study groups that collated sighting data outside the auspices or influence of the government. The first of these, the Aerial Phenomenon Research Organization (APRO) was founded by researchers Jim and Coral Lorenzen in 1952. This was followed by the National Investigations Committee on Aerial Phenomena (NICAP) in 1956, formed by prominent UFO author and proponent Major Donald Keyhoe. These groups would be instrumental in gathering and curating witness reports in a forthright and independent forum before the public.

As the phenomenon continued to gather steam and public interest in it grew, witness accounts became more bizarre and outlandish. In addition to reports honestly submitted by respectable citizens that contained corroborating evidence in the form of physical traces, there were individuals who suffered from mental illness who claimed to have occult communications with beings from other planets, and attention seekers who deliberately fabricated hoaxes. About halfway through the decade, disturbing reports of humanoid "occupants" observed in the vicinity of landed craft also began to filter in from Europe and elsewhere.

But a new breed of witnesses would also emerge during the '50s who claimed to have all the answers to the UFO enigma by virtue of their direct communications with saucer pilots. These individuals would come to be known collectively as the "contactees." While their accounts resembled fourth-rate science fiction tales, their narratives presented a comforting take on an otherwise threatening phenomenon.

First out of the box was George Adamski, who operated a burger stand on Mount Palomar—the site of the Palomar Observatory, an astronomical research facility in North County (San Diego area) currently operated by Caltech. Adamski set up a toy telescope on his property, pretended he was an astronomer connected to the observatory and bestowed the bogus title of "professor" upon himself. On November 20, 1952, Adamski claimed he had made contact with a Venusian saucer pilot in a desolate spot in the California desert. The alien, whose name was Orthon, had long blond hair and was dressed in an outfit resembling an aviator's flight suit. Orthon informed Adamski, using a combination of telepathy and sign language, that he had come to Earth to warn us that radioactive fallout from nuclear testing was affecting the other planets in our solar system. The contactee was permitted to peek inside Orthon's landed flying saucer. The contactee also took one out of focus photograph of the Venusian craft when it took off. The only other evidence of this alleged contact was a set of Orthon's footprints that supposedly bore a set of indecipherable hieroglyphics.

Adamski would co-author a book about his contact experience with British writer Desmond Leslie entitled *Flying Saucers Have Landed,* which was published in 1953. He followed this up with *Inside the Space Ships* in 1955, in which he chronicled further meetings with aliens from Mars, Venus, Jupiter and Saturn, all of whom resembled ordinary humans. These liaisons reportedly took place in bars, cafes and other public places in the Los Angeles area. Adamski also reported on conversations he had with an elder being he referred to as "The Master" while on board one of the spacecraft. The Master instructed his apt pupil about the nature of the advanced utopian societies on other worlds and their mission to eliminate the threat of Earth's atomic weapons. Adamski was told that he had been anointed to convey the aliens' message of peace, love and nuclear disarmament to an unbelieving public. The contactee was also taken for a ride to the Moon in a flying saucer, where he observed its cities and inhabitants from orbit using a viewing apparatus.

Thus, the template for the contactee belief system was established. The aliens resembled ordinary earthlings and were able to move among us incognito. They had come bearing a message of interplanetary brotherhood from technologically advanced societies in order to save us from ourselves. Adamski and the other contactees were to act as emissaries bearing this gospel from outer space to the masses. Contactee philosophy offered up a heady admixture of California bohemianism and Cold War atomic jitters that sought to resolve two of the most anxiety-producing issues of the times in one fell swoop. Those mysterious, potentially threatening flying saucers were piloted by benevolent beings that had come to our planet to alleviate the menace posed by the specter of global thermonuclear war.

It wasn't long before a new crop of alleged saucer witnesses emerged to get on the contactee bandwagon. Highway mechanic Truman Bethurum reportedly encountered the diminutive crew of an alien ship one night while he was working in a remote part of the California desert. As related in his 1954 book *Aboard a Flying Saucer*, the little fellows escorted him to their landed craft to parlay with their captain, a woman of unearthly beauty named Aura Rhanes. Ms. Rhanes claimed to be from a planet named Clarion, which was within our solar system but was perpetually occluded from us because its orbit always positioned it on the other side of the sun. Clarion was the typical utopian paradise, free of war, hunger and want, and the Clarionites were visiting Earth to prevent us from destroying the planet with our wicked ways.

Another contactee, Daniel Fry, made his extraterrestrial contact while working at the White Sands Proving Ground, a missile range in New Mexico where he worked as a rocket technician for the Aerojet Company. In his 1954 book *The White Sands Incident*, Fry related his close encounter with an alien craft shaped like a flattened spheroid that reportedly took place on July 4, 1949. As he approached the landed craft he was greeted by a disembodied voice that identified itself as belonging to an entity called "A-lan." The voice informed him that the craft was being remotely controlled by a "mother ship" in orbit high above the Earth, and asked Fry if he wanted to take a ride. Once he was on board, A-lan related a cautionary tale about an atomic war between the lost continents of Atlantis and Lemuria that had nearly destroyed all life on Earth that was an obvious metaphor for Cold War tensions. Fry reported that he traveled from New Mexico to New York in thirty minutes in A-lan's spaceship.

Orfeo Angelucci was a mechanic who worked for the Lockheed Aircraft Corporation in Burbank, California, when he allegedly experienced his alien encounter on May 23, 1952. As he recounted in his 1955 book *The Secret of the Saucers*, while driving through Los Angeles, he saw a saucer land in a nearby field and felt compelled to enter it. Once inside, a voice claiming to be a "space brother" began to expound upon the aliens' mission to save earthlings from imminent disaster from nuclear war, etc. On subsequent occasions he would meet alien emissaries named Neptune, Lyra and Orion, as well as Jesus Christ himself, who informed Angelucci that he had been an extraterrestrial in a former life. In comparison with the accounts of other abductees, Angelucci's contact narrative emphasized the spiritual over the technological aspects of his experiences with the saucer people.

Contactee Howard Menger, who hailed from New Jersey, came to be known as the "East Coast Adamski." In his 1959 book *From Outer Space to You*, Menger claimed that alien beings from Mars and Venus had taken him on an excursion to the Moon, where the spacecraft landed and the contactee was treated to a sightseeing tour of a lunar city. According to Menger, the Moon had a breathable atmosphere similar to Earth's. Unlike his West Coast counterparts, he attempted to provide physical evidence for his contact claims in the form of a "space potato," which supposedly had five times the protein of a terrestrial vegetable, a "free energy motor" that was nothing more than a prop and piano melodies supposedly composed by a Saturnian. He even released a record album of these alien tunes entitled *Music from Another Planet*.

The contactees were all publicity hounds who authored books and pamphlets and appeared on national television shows expounding on their experiences with the space brothers. They became part of a popular social movement and formed organizations to spread their philosophy to a wider audience. Adamski founded the Adamski Foundation, Truman Bethurum formed the Sanctuary of Thought and another contactee, George Van Tassel, established the College of Universal Wisdom. Van Tassel also organized an annual event called the Giant Rock Spacecraft Convention in the desert near Landers, California, that drew thousands of fledgling contactees, true believers and curiosity seekers every year. He also constructed a domed structure at the site called the "Integratron" that could supposedly recharge the human cell structure and extend people's lifespan many times over.

To the chagrin of serious UFO researchers such as Major Donald Keyhoe of NICAP and the Lorenzens at APRO, the contactees were looked upon as authorities who possessed firsthand knowledge of the flying saucer phenomenon. Their lurid, half-baked accounts of encounters with space people tended to muddy the waters around the subject, creating a confusion that irked scientifically-minded investigators. The contactees introduced occult concepts such as "channeling," in which alien voices supposedly spoke through an earthly medium, along with mystical notions such as psychic healing, reincarnation and past lives. Some of them were even charlatans who bilked people out of money with far-out investment schemes allegedly inspired by the advanced technical knowledge of the space people.

The end result of the contactee movement was to ramp up the ridicule factor surrounding the UFO phenomenon. A secondary consequence was to establish the iconography of space visitors as normal sized, handsome males with shoulder-length blond hair. Oddly, this imagery would persist in a number of sightings of ufonauts, especially in the United Kingdom. Referred to as "Nordics" by researchers, these long-haired types have variously been regarded as a separate race of alien beings or as human-looking hybrids.

The contactees may have derived their inspiration from Robert Wise's classic saucer movie *The Day the Earth Stood Still*, which was released in 1951, two years before Adamski penned his initial contact account. In the film, Klaatu (Michael Rennie), a saintly, benevolent alien, lands his flying saucer in Washington, D.C., accompanied by his menacing robot cohort, Gort (Lock Martin). Running afoul of military authorities after being taken into custody, the alien escapes and assumes the identity of "Major Carpenter." He takes refuge with widow Helen Benson (Patricia Neal) at her boarding house in order to study earthlings while incognito. Klaatu hails from a utopian planet free of war and suffering and has come to Earth to warn us about the dangers of nuclear testing, but before he can deliver his message he is hunted down and killed by the military. He is eventually brought back to life by the robot and conveys an ultimatum to a group of assembled scientists and dignitaries, stating that, unless the nations of the world abandon their warlike ways, the celestial powers that be will act to destroy the Earth. After delivering this doomsday screed, Klaatu re-enters his saucer and ascends into the heavens. A thinly-veiled science fiction take on the death, resurrection and ascension of Jesus Christ, similarities with contactee narratives are obvious.

As the 1950s wore on, the contactee movement began to wane due to a number of factors. One of these was a breakdown of their credibility due to a series of exposés. In December 1957, for instance, Adamski received a letter on State Department stationery purportedly sent by an official named "R.E. Straith" of the "Cultural Exchange Committee" encouraging the contactee's work. The problem was that neither the identity of Straith nor his committee could ever be verified because Adamski had been the victim of a clever prank. The UFO gadfly Jim Moseley and his partner in crime Gray Barker had forged the letter on some State Department stationery they had obtained from a friend. Another hoax was perpetrated by an attorney named Jules St. Germain, who mailed George Van Tassel some bogus photos of a saucer and its occupant and later embarrassed the contactee by exposing the subterfuge on the Long John Nebel TV show. Daniel Fry offered to take a lie detector test to prove the veracity of his contact claims but wound up failing the test. Howard Menger would recant his story and assert that his book was "fact/fiction" written as part of a U.S. government sociology experiment.

Another reason for the decline of the classic contactee movement was the advent of American and Soviet space probes. Beginning in 1959, the American Pioneer and Russian lunar probes had orbited and impacted on the Moon and sent back images of the lunar surface. In particular, the Soviet *Luna 3* orbiter had returned the first pictures from the Moon's far side in October of 1959. None of this imagery revealed the cities or alien inhabitants of the Moon that were reportedly witnessed by Adamski, Menger and others. Subsequent probes to Mars and Venus during the 1960s found that these worlds were equally devoid of life or extraterrestrial civilizations.

While the classic contactee movement of the 1950s faded, it would assume new forms in the following decades, when the saucer clubs devolved into cults. In 1973 a French musician named Claude Vorilhon claimed to experience a series of contacts with an alien named Yahweh who claimed that extraterrestrial geneticists called the "Eloihim" created life on Earth by manipulating DNA. Vorilhon renamed himself "Raël" and founded an organization called the International Raëlian Movement, headquartered in Geneva, Switzerland, that would eventually attract thousands of followers. In 2002 a Raëlian biotech firm called Clonaid generated worldwide attention when it announced that they had engineered the birth of the first cloned human, a baby named Eve. The Raëlians did not allow any independent verification of the cloning, however, and the birth of a clone is generally regarded as a hoax. The Raëlian cultists practice free love and the peculiar symbol of their religion consists of a Nazi swastika embedded within a Jewish Star of David.

In 1975 a Swiss farmer named Billy Meier claimed to be receiving telepathic messages from aliens called the Plejaren, who hailed from a planet called Erra which he alleged is located in the star cluster known as the Pleiades. Like Adamski, Meier backed up his contact claims with photographs and home movies of saucer-shaped craft he refers to as "beamships." Meier founded a non-profit organization called the Free Community of Interests for the Border and Spiritual Sciences and Ufological Studies that was designed to bolster his contact allegations. He claims to have traveled back in time to meet the historical Jesus and considers himself a spiritual leader in the tradition of Moses, Buddha and Mohammad. Analysis of his UFO photos have shown that they are faked and critics have noted anti–Semitic sentiments expressed in his doctrines.

The most tragic example of the dangers of the contactee belief system, however, was evidenced in the demise of the Heaven's Gate cult. Founded in 1975 by ex-musician Marshall Herff Applewhite and his partner in crime Bonnie Lou Nettles (a.k.a. "The Two"), the group made national headlines when they convinced around 20 people in Waldport, Oregon, to sell all their worldly possessions and join the cult with the promise of being taken aboard an alien spaceship. When the group seemed to disappear, the media speculated that they had left the planet, but in reality they had merely been sequestered by the cult.

During the next several decades, the charismatic Two went underground while leading a ragtag band of followers on the fringes of society. Nettles died in 1985, but Applewhite carried on, solidifying the cult's organizational and financial status. In 1996 the Heaven's Gate group rented a mansion in Rancho Santa Fe, near San Diego, California. When an amateur astronomer claimed to detect a "companion" object in the tail of the Hale-Bopp comet that was passing near the Earth in 1997, Applewhite declared that it was an alien spaceship and commanded his disciples to kill themselves so that their souls would ascend to a higher level and be taken aboard the craft. Between March 22 and March 26, there were 39 cult members (including Applewhite) who committed ritual suicide at the mansion in an event that made headlines around the nation. Ironically, the initial report of the comet's traveling companion was debunked by astronomers, who railed against the scientific illiteracy of the cultists. Heaven's Gate has the dubious distinction of being the first contactee group of the Internet age. The cult supported itself by designing web pages and utilized the new technology to solicit new members.

Despite a legacy of disinformation, criminal fraud and mass suicide, the contactee mindset is still viable in the 21st century. Several books written by retired *Los Angeles Times* journalist Phillip H. Krapf, who shared a Pulitzer Prize for his reportage on the 1992 L.A. riots, are a case in point. In his 1999 book *The Contact Has Begun*, subtitled *The True Story of a Journalist's Encounter with Alien Beings*, Krapf relates how he was beamed aboard an enormous starship operated by an extraterrestrial race called the Verdants, who are preparing to initiate open contact with the nations of the Earth. The author describes a three-day-long sojourn aboard the ship while undergoing an orientation and indoctrination procedure designed to prepare him for becoming one of the Verdant's envoys during the complex process of establishing contact. An ancient, hyper-intelligent and spiritually advanced species from a utopian society, the Verdant's intent is to admit our world into the Intergalactic Federation of Sovereign Planets (IFSP). This event will usher the troubled nations of the Earth into a golden age of peace and harmony, and will allow the human race to take its place among the myriad interstellar civilizations.

Krapf describes the alien craft as a kind of Holiday Inn in space, with comfortable lodgings, views of outer space and delicious meals delivered via alien room service. The aliens have familiar names like Gus, George, Emily and Gina that are helpfully inscribed on name tags just like in a convention on Earth. An alien woman even offers to have sex with him, but he declines. He is told that the Verdants have discovered the location of Heaven in the universe and have communicated directly with God. The aliens' plan was for Krapf to be part of an elite corps of "Ambassadors," prominent scientists, religious and spiritual leaders, journalists and assorted influencers who would announce the impending contact to the general public, beginning in the early 2000s. Krapf published a follow-up book, entitled *The Challenge of Contact*, in 2001, but after more than two decades this promise of extraterrestrial contact has not been fulfilled.

One wonders what motivated Krapf to potentially compromise his credibility as a journalist by spinning such an outrageous yarn. Perhaps it was merely a ploy to sell books and become a minor UFO celebrity. His stories of benevolent aliens, imminent contact, extraterrestrial spirituality, a utopian future and the admission of humanity into an intergalactic community of worlds are all congruent with classic contactee concepts dating back to the 1950s. The difference here is that Krapf is a much more seasoned writer than Adamski, Bethurum et al., and is able to describe his alleged experiences in more vivid and original detail.

British researcher Nick Redfern, who writes on a variety of paranormal topics, offers a revisionist take on the contactee movement in his 2010 book *Contactees: A History of Alien-Human Interaction*. His thesis is that the contactee's experiences were generated either by visions of entities produced by an overflow of the psychedelic substance DMT that occurs naturally in the human body, or by geomantic energies in the form of quasi-intelligent plasmas that create the illusion of liaisons with space brothers and sisters. These esoteric phenomena are thought to interface with human consciousness to create hallucinatory states that explain the "enigma" of the contactees. In this way, Redfern attempts to legitimize their encounters as being genuine mystical occurrences while ignoring their obviously fictional origins. Oddly, he also advances the theory that abduction cases are bogus events staged by shadowy government agencies that are designed to study human reactions to purported alien contact experiences.

Abduction researcher Kathleen Marden is the niece of well-known abductee Betty Hill (see Chapter Two) who has authored several notable books about the phenomenon. In her 2022 book *Forbidden Knowledge: A Personal Journey from Alien Abduction to Spiritual Transformation*, Ms. Marden chronicles her transition from scientifically oriented abduction researcher to mystical truth seeker. Much of the book is dedicated to the pronouncements of one Kevin J. Briggs, a medium who claims to channel communications from a diverse group of extraterrestrials called the "Council of Eight." They represent six races who are emissaries from a Galactic Federation tasked with furthering humanity's spiritual development so that we may take our place as a member of the Federation. The Council consists of individuals such as Ort the Arcturian, Jark the Reticulan, and their leader, Rah, "a ninth dimensional Annunaki Watcher." The dubious practice of channeling alien intelligences harks back to the séance rooms of the Spiritualist movement and was adopted by contactees like George Van Tassel and others as a means of directly communicating with extraterrestrials. The theme of humanity being conducted into a Federation of planets is also a well-worn contactee and science fiction trope.

The contactee mindset is a comforting myth of the establishment of a harmonious relationship between humankind and a mysterious "other" that has intruded upon our collective consciousness. As such, the myth has deep resonance within the human psyche, especially when contrasted with the uncertainties presented by the enigmatic abduction phenomenon. It's much more soothing to conceive of benevolent E.T.s who are here to resolve our many problems and usher us into a golden age of peace and enlightenment than to contemplate the presence of abductors who treat their subjects like laboratory animals and whose motivations remain obscure and troubling.

Returning to the 1950s, a new paradigm of alien contact would emerge that was entirely different from that of the contactees: cases in which humanoid beings were reported in connection with UFOs. Reports of what would come to be called "Occupants" began to surface mainly in Western Europe and North and South America, but the majority of humanoid sightings took place in France in 1954. From the onset many researchers rejected these accounts from serious consideration due to concerns over the ridicule factor posed by the notion of "little green men," but there were also more profound psychological factors that inhibited their ability to perform a rational analysis. While ufologists could study the myriad characteristics of UFOs, contemplating the beings that piloted them was simply too threatening for many investigators. Occupant reports were primarily investigated and collated by the French journal *Lumieres dans la Nuit*, the British publication *Flying Saucer Review* and the American Aerial Phenomenon Research Organization (APRO).

The Occupant cases had several features in common. While a smattering of reports described oversized (six to seven foot) ufonauts and a few others featured normal-sized beings, the majority of sightings were of diminutive humanoids between three and four feet in stature. Like human astronauts, in many cases the Occupants wore what were described as "diving suits" along with space helmets and protective apparatuses that ostensibly enabled them to breathe and survive in Earth's atmosphere and environment. They were observed collecting specimens of earthly fauna and flora and gathering samples of soil, water and minerals. Scant interest was shown in observing humans or

This poster for *The Man from Planet X* (1951) depicts the image of a diminutive Occupant-type alien complete with space helmet and breathing apparatus.

their works, and when people witnessed them performing their tasks, their reaction was to quickly scamper back into their vehicles and depart. Sometimes they would immobilize overly curious observers with a paralyzing ray as they fled.

An early European case that was reported to Project Blue Book via the CIA in 1952 was witnessed by Oscar Linke, the former mayor of the small German town of Gleimershausen and his daughter Gabriella. While walking home through a wooded area near the town of Hasselbacht at twilight, Linke and his daughter observed two humanoids dressed in shiny metallic clothing that were stooped over and appeared to be looking at something on the ground. One of the ufonauts wore a device like a "lamp" on the front of its body that lit up periodically. When the two beings became aware that they were being watched, they raced into a large object shaped like a "frying pan" parked in a forest clearing that promptly rose into the air and sped away.[1]

Another humanoid sighting was reported from Santana dos Montes in Guanabara State, Brazil, on January 3, 1953. Hospital worker Mauricio Ramos Bessa was driving home on a rural road when he encountered a luminous, oval-shaped craft hovering in front of his vehicle. He watched as two dwarfish (4 to 4½ feet tall) humanoids dressed in shiny, gray clothing exited the UFO. One of them carried a cylinder which was used to scoop soil from the road. At this point Bessa began to experience a severe headache along with blurred vision and did not clearly observe the entities re-entering the object, but as soon as the craft departed his head stopped aching and his vision cleared.[2]

The most rigorously investigated Occupant case from the French wave of 1954 was that of Marius Dewilde, who lived in the town of Valenciennes near the Belgian border. At about 10:30 p.m. on the evening of September 10, Dewilde was alerted to the presence of something in his garden by the barking of his dog. Taking a flashlight, he went outside to investigate and encountered two small entities walking toward a dark mass parked on railroad tracks adjacent to his home. The creatures were about 3½ feet tall and were wearing "diving suits" and enormous helmets covering their heads. When he tried to accost the figures he was blinded and paralyzed by an energy beam emanating from the object on the railroad tracks. When he regained his sight and the use of his limbs, he observed the object ascend and fly out of sight. Dewilde reported his sighting to local authorities who launched an investigation by the Air Police, the Department of Territorial Security and the local gendarmerie. Wooden ties on the railroad tracks were found to have been damaged by a heavy object and gravel on the roadbed was calcinated as if subjected to a very high temperature.[3]

A farm at Isola in northern Italy was the scene of another Occupant sighting on November 14, 1953, where a farmer observed the landing of a cigar-shaped craft. While he watched from concealment, three diminutive humanoids attired in "diving suits" emerged from the UFO and approached some cages containing rabbits. Thinking that the dwarves were going to pilfer his livestock, the farmer fetched his rifle and aimed it at the interlopers, but found that his weapon would not fire and he became paralyzed and unable to speak. He watched the beings take several cages of rabbits into their vehicle, and when the craft departed the paralysis left him and he was able to fire his rifle once more.[4]

The most well-known and historically important Occupant case occurred in Socorro, New Mexico, on April 24, 1964. Patrolman Lonnie Zamora was chasing a speeding car on the edge of town when he heard a roaring sound and observed a flame in the sky about half a mile away. Fearing that an explosion had taken place, Zamora stopped chasing the speeder and drove toward the commotion. As he approached he observed a featureless, white oval-shaped object resting on the arroyo on four landing gear and caught a brief glimpse of two small figures wearing white coveralls near the object. One of the beings appeared to turn around to look at him and seemed startled. While approaching closer on foot, Zamora lost sight of the Occupants, who had presumably entered the landed craft, and he watched as a flame emerged from the underside of the object as it rose into the sky and flew away.

Zamora's sighting was investigated by Project Blue Book scientific consultant Dr. J. Allen Hynek, and an FBI agent, Air Force Intelligence officers and the Lorenzens from APRO. The UFO had left landing traces in the form of four depressions in the desert soil left by the craft's landing gear. Vegetation was charred and smoldering at the intersection of the four depressions. Patrolman Zamora had an impeccable reputation and his testimony was not in doubt. This case is credited with converting Dr. Hynek from being a UFO skeptic to having an agnostic view of the phenomenon.[5]

Another well-known Occupant sighting was that of Maurice

Masse, who experienced a close encounter on his farm near the French village of Valensole on July 1, 1965. While tending to his lavender plants early that morning he came upon a football-shaped object resting on six legs that he first assumed was a helicopter. As he moved closer to investigate he observed two small humanoids that were examining a lavender plant. Masse described the creatures as being the size of an eight-year-old child, with huge hairless heads about three times the size of an adult's head. When one of the beings noticed the farmer, it pointed a cylindrical device at him that rendered him paralyzed. Moments later the two Occupants got back in their machine and flew away. Interestingly, when researchers showed Masse a color picture of a model of Lonnie Zamora's UFO, he insisted that it was the same craft he had encountered in his lavender field.[6]

The Occupant cases continued into the 1970s. On the night of November 4, 1973, Mr. Roger S. of Goffstown, New Hampshire, observed a strange light in his kitchen emanating from his backyard. Thinking there was a fire on his property, he peeked out the back door, where he saw two humanoids wearing seamless, glowing silver suits and conical headgear collecting items from the ground in his backyard and placing them in a silver bag. Stunned by the sight, Roger went into his bedroom to fetch his handgun, then opened the back door and commanded his trained dog to attack the intruders, but the animal refused to approach them. Overcome with fear, Roger watched as the humanoids continued to pick up objects from the yard before walking away into the woods, where they were lost from sight. The witness called the local police to investigate, and some children next door stated they saw two luminous "ghosts" in Roger's backyard.[7]

Another European case took place in the Belgian town of Vilvorde during mid–December of 1973. The witness, Monsieur V.M., woke up at 2 a.m. to answer the call of nature when he heard an odd sound and observed a diffused, greenish illumination coming from his garden. Peering outside, he saw a small humanoid (1 meter 10 centimeters in height) dressed in a luminous green outfit and wearing a fishbowl-type transparent helmet on its head. A tube extended from the rear of the helmet into a backpack that covered the creature's shoulders. The entity was facing away from the witness while holding a device resembling a vacuum cleaner or metal detector, which it was passing over objects in the garden. When V.M. directed a flashlight beam onto the humanoid, it reacted by turning toward him and fixing him with a regard before walking straight up the wall in an apparent feat of antigravity.[8]

On the afternoon of February 14, 1977, French commerce clerk M. Severin was walking to his home near Petit-Île, France, when he was struck by a luminous ray from a car-sized, white object hovering over a nearby cornfield. He then observed a small humanoid that seemed to be scraping something on the ground, and as he watched the creature was joined by two others who descended a ladder from inside the UFO, one of whom held a bag in its hand that was presumably a container for a soil sample. The ufonauts were between 1 and 1.2 meters tall and were dressed in white, metallic-looking outfits. When a fourth being started to descend the ladder it became aware of the witness, whereupon all of the humanoids quickly scampered back inside the craft, which ascended into the sky. Severin reportedly suffered from headaches and vision problems after the incident.[9]

A case that was investigated by New York abduction researcher Budd Hopkins involved a liquor store owner named George O'Barski. Sometime in the middle of January 1975, O'Barski closed up his shop in lower Manhattan and began to drive to his home in North Bergen, New Jersey, at around one or two a.m. While taking a short cut through North Hudson Park, which was deserted at that time of night, he observed a round, brilliantly-lit UFO that descended to hover above a playing field about 60 feet away from his car.

He watched in amazement as about ten 3½-to-4-foot-tall beings disembarked from the craft, each one holding a spoon-like implement and a small bag with a handle, and began scooping up dirt and putting it inside the bags. When the task was completed, the little humanoids re-entered their machine, which promptly took off into the night. O'Barski described the beings as wearing light-colored, one-piece uniforms with hoods or helmets that covered their heads. Upon investigation, Hopkins discovered that a heavy glass door at a nearby apartment complex was inexplicably shattered on the night of the incident.[10]

Some common elements in the cases cited include diminutive humanoids wearing "diving suits" and protective helmets, the collection of soil, plant and animal samples, and the paralysis of witnesses caused by a device wielded by the ufonauts. In all cases, the Occupants had no interaction with humans except for immobilizing them while they went about their business of taking specimens. Unlike the contactee narratives, there was no communication between the witnesses and the alien beings, and in contrast to the contactee's uncorroborated claims, several of the Occupant cases were investigated by military, intelligence and civilian authorities. The Occupant phase of sightings took place roughly between the mid–1950s and the mid–1970s, after which they seem to have ceased as the abduction phenomenon became more prominent.

It is possible that the Occupant sightings were staged events that had little or nothing to do with the ostensible purpose of collecting biological samples, but were rather designed to create the false impression that they were astronaut-scientists who were conducting a survey of Earth's biosphere. These studies could have taken place in extremely remote locations where they would not have been observed instead of in backyards, farms or other places frequented by potential witnesses. In many cases they wore what appeared to be space suits and helmets similar to what earthly space explorers wore. Witness George O'Barski claimed that the humanoids he observed reminded him of the Apollo astronauts taking rock samples on the Moon, and this is precisely the notion that the event was meant to convey.

Hopkins notes that "[i]t seems absurd on the face of it to imagine that the entire episode occurred because a UFO crew, whoever they may be, actually needed soil from North Hudson Park. Could the mission instead have been a species of theater, a display of imagery designed to communicate certain basic information? ... It has been suggested that the entire enterprise involves ... a 'consciousness-raising' effort by subtly imparting the idea of their presence to 'mere earthlings' without unduly alarming us."[11] This scenario would apply to the majority of Occupant cases as well.

In addition to the Occupant sightings, another type of close encounter had the appearance of being staged. Beginning in the 1960s there were numerous reports of UFOs interacting with cars, trucks and aircraft. Most of these incidents involved vehicles driving down lonely stretches of roadway in rural areas late at night. The UFOs reportedly made engines stall, engulfed the witnesses in cones of light, exhibited other electromagnetic effects, and in some cases even wrested control of the vehicles away from their drivers. There were also incidents in which cars were levitated from the road, events that presaged later abduction reports of automobiles and their passengers being lifted up and taken inside of a hovering craft. Many witnesses reported suddenly

Vehicular encounters appear to have been deliberately staged, possibly as a dry run for future highway abductions (Dreamstime).

encountering UFOs as they rounded a bend in the road, as if it was prepositioned there for maximum dramatic effect.

Commenting on this aspect of the phenomenon, Blue Book scientific consultant Dr. J. Allen Hynek observed that "[i]n case after case, reports contain the phrase 'after rounding a bend in the road'.... When there is open country on either side of the road, one can't help but wonder why."[12] Similarly, researcher Richard Hall, the former acting director of the NICAP investigative group, speculates that "[v]ehicle confrontation cases ... seem to be deliberate, planned encounters with humans for purposes unknown ... the bewildering observations indicate some measure of deception, staging, or psychological games by the intelligences behind UFOs to veil their true purposes or intentions from us while they carry out some secret 'game plan.'"[13]

Both the Occupant cases and the vehicle encounters appear to have been designed to announce the alien presence in a roundabout way by seeding the idea into humanity's collective consciousness via tabloid articles, accounts in UFO books, science fiction movies and other media. At the same time these staged events obscured close encounters that the UFO intelligences took great pains to keep secret—alien abductions.

CHAPTER TWO

The Abduction
Phenomenon Emerges

A new paradigm of alien contact began to emerge during the 1960s. The contactee movement, along with its concept of benevolent, human-looking space brothers, had become discredited. Data from the 1954 European Occupant sightings was slowly making its way across the Atlantic to American researchers. Witnesses began describing a new type of interaction with alien beings, one that was secretive, enigmatic and terrifying.

In stark contrast to the actions observed during Occupant sightings, in which the ufonauts avoided direct contact with humans, paralyzed witnesses and took off in their craft rather than interact or communicate, narratives began to emerge in which people became the main focus of the aliens' activities. Humans were reportedly being taken inside UFOs against their will and subjected to enigmatic medical procedures. Telepathic communications between the beings and those they abducted became a staple of the experience. Gone were the "diving suits," space helmets and breathing apparatuses worn by the Occupants; the beings were suddenly able to tolerate Earth's atmosphere and environment without utilizing any protective gear.

One hallmark of the abductions involved the experience of missing time. Witnesses frequently reported an instantaneous shift in their perception of events that left inexplicable gaps in their memories. Sometimes there was no recollection of even seeing a UFO or of time lost during the experience. Unlike the various antics of the Occupants, who may have been deliberately play-acting to reveal their presence to witnesses, the abductors took great pains to conceal their activities by manipulating the memories of the abductees.

An example of the missing time phenomenon was cited by abduction researcher Budd Hopkins in a case involving a New Jersey couple who had spent a weekend at the Jersey Shore and were returning home at around five o'clock in the afternoon. Suddenly, without any transition in their consciousness, it was nighttime and they found themselves in an unfamiliar field far from the main highway with no memory of how or why they got there. This case also provides an example of *translocation*, the anomalous transportation of a vehicle from one place to another without having being driven there. There was no sighting of a UFO or aliens, yet some inexplicable experience had occurred, which was in all probability an abduction event.[1]

While researchers only became aware of abductions during the 1960s, it's unclear as to exactly when they began. Hopkins claimed to have cases dating back to the 1930s and '40s, but provided no details. British researcher Jenny Randles, however, cites a probable abduction that took place in England in September of 1942, during the Second World War. The witness was Albert Lancashire, who at the time was a soldier on sentry duty at a secret radar base near Newbiggin, Northumbria, in northern England. His post was located on the North Sea coast, where Lancashire observed a light over the sea that coalesced into a black cloud. Thinking that he was observing a German secret weapon, he stepped outside to have a better look and was struck by a yellow beam of light that caused him to lose consciousness. He awoke on the ground outside his sentry post with no memory of what had occurred. Decades later he claimed that his memory of the event returned during a series of dreams in which he remembered awakening in a room where he saw an Asian woman lying on a bed. He was given a pair of "goggles" to wear over his eyes. A "man dressed in white" was also in the room.[2]

An intriguing case that was reported to Blue Book involved a retired schoolteacher who reported that her car was followed by a UFO for several miles while driving down a Nevada highway late one night in 1955. There was also a suggestion that the witness had experienced a period of missing time that masked an abduction event. The incident was reported to the Air Force, who rejected it as unreliable because the eyewitness had previously reported a sighting. At the time it was thought that the observation of a UFO was such a rare event that reports of multiple sightings were improbable, if not impossible, so the Air Force made no further attempt to investigate. In subsequent decades, however, it was learned that multiple abductions are commonplace.[3]

An incident involving Brazilian farmer Antonio Villas-Boas, however, is considered to be the historic first case of alien abduction by researchers. According to his testimony, on the night of October 15, 1957, he was plowing the ground with a tractor on his family's ranch located near the town of São Francisco de Salles in the state of Minas Gerais when a UFO shaped like an elongated egg swooped down and landed nearby. The tractor's engine died and when Villas-Boas tried to flee he was restrained by three beings who forcibly subdued him and carried him inside their machine. The ufonauts were small humanoids who wore tight-fitting outfits with helmets that covered their heads. Their helmets were large, covering an area twice the size of a human head and had three tubes that fitted into the backs of their outfits.

Once inside, the creatures conducted him into a brightly-lit room, where they undressed him. One of the beings spread a colorless, odorless liquid over his skin with something resembling a sponge and collected samples of his blood and skin. He was then taken to another room that was empty except for a large couch, where smoke or a vapor issued from small tubes in the wall that made him nauseous. After some time had elapsed a naked female being was ushered into the room. The creature was shorter than Villas-Boas, had platinum blond hair on her head, slightly slanted eyes, thin lips, high cheekbones, a sharply pointed chin and bright red pubic and underarm hair. Her figure was slim, well-proportioned, and generally attractive.

The female wasted no time in making erotic advances to Villas-Boas, whereupon he became sexually excited, possibly as a result of being exposed to aphrodisiac substances while onboard the craft. They had sexual intercourse twice, but in the aftermath of their lovemaking the woman began to reject him, which led him to believe the aliens had only used him as a "stallion" to improve their breeding stock. A short while later the door to the room re-opened and the female was led out, but before she left she pointed to her belly, then pointed her finger skyward. One of the ufonauts took him back to the outer room where he was handed his clothes and allowed to dress himself. He was then conducted on a brief tour of the exterior of the craft before being directed to descend a ladder, and once he was on the ground he watched the

UFO depart into the heavens. He calculated that he had been aboard the craft for about four hours and fifteen minutes.

After reading some articles on UFOs published in the Brazilian weekly newspaper *O Cruzeiro*, Villas-Boas wrote letters about his experience to the publication's reporter João Martins, who arranged for him to travel to Rio de Janeiro for an interview on February 28, 1958. Dr. Olavio Fontes, a physician and the Brazilian representative of the American research group APRO, was also in attendance. After listening to the abductee's story, Martins informed Villas-Boas that his story would not be published in the newspaper because it was too unbelievable and could not be corroborated. Dr. Fontes examined the witness and concluded that he had suffered from symptoms of radiation poisoning and reportedly experienced nightmares and anxiety in connection with his experience.

Researcher Peter Rogerson claims that the Villas-Boas case was a hoax inspired by an article in a November 1957 issue of *O Cruzeiro* that related a similar close encounter narrative without citing further specifics. This begs the question as to why João Martins refused to publish Villas-Boas' story if it was so similar to one that had already appeared in his newspaper. Rogerson also asserts that the witness cribbed narrative elements from the contactee stories of George Adamski, again without providing details. During the 1958 interview Villas-Boas was shown drawings of one of Adamski's "Venusians," and flatly declared that the picture bore no resemblance to the beings he had encountered. In addition, the craft that he reported seeing looked nothing like the flying saucers of the contactees. Unlike the contactees, Villas-Boas did not receive a message from the aliens, embark on a mission to save the Earth from nuclear war, write a book about his experience or seek to profit from it. A more outrageous hoax narrative was advanced by a CIA operative during the 1970s, who asserted that the abduction was an event staged by intelligence operatives as part of an experiment to study the public's reactions to extraterrestrial contact (more on this in a later chapter).

The Villas-Boas case is an outlier in some respects that differs from later abduction accounts in a number of specifics. For one thing, his abductors did not impose amnesia about the event, which was recalled in great detail by the witness; for another, he was not subjected to a medical examination like future abductees. Unlike later accounts of Gray aliens, the entities wore space suits and protective helmets in a manner similar to the humanoids reported in the Occupant cases. The abductors had to resort to physical force to subdue the witness and bring him aboard their craft, whereas in subsequent close encounters the abductees were compelled to comply with their captor's commands by the aliens' use of a technique of mental domination. The entities communicated with each other and with the witness by means of a series of animal-like growls rather than via mental telepathy.

On the other hand, there are also a number of similarities with later abduction narratives. Villas-Boas described doorways inside the craft that appeared out of a blank space of wall and then closed up again while not showing any trace of an opening. This "fluid metal" technology is a feature that has been reported in numerous UFO sightings. The female alien he encountered seems to presage accounts of human/alien hybrid beings that populate abduction reports in later decades. Villas-Boas' narrative also underscores the aliens' continuing interest in human sexuality and reproduction.[4]

The case that propelled the phenomenon into popular consciousness, however, was that of New Hampshire couple Betty and Barney Hill. On the night of October 19, 1961, they were returning from an impromptu weekend trip to Canada driving down U.S. Highway 3 through the White Mountains on their way to their home in Portsmouth. They noticed a bright "star" that seemed to be following their vehicle that would eventually resolve itself into a huge, brightly-lit, disc-shaped object with a row of windows that hovered over the road ahead. Looking through binoculars from a distance of about 80 feet, Barney observed several humanlike figures at the windows, including a ufonaut that stared directly at him. Fearing that they were about to be captured, Barney got back in the car and floored the accelerator in an attempt to escape.

At this point they both heard an odd beeping sound and became unusually drowsy. Some time later they heard the beeping sounds once more as they seemed to awaken from a trancelike state. They arrived home at about 5 a.m., two hours later than expected, but were not aware of the temporal discrepancy at that time. In the days following the incident Barney discovered that the shoes he had worn that night were inexplicably scuffed on their tops. He also found an unusually tender spot in his groin area.

In the aftermath of their weird experience Betty began experiencing a series of vivid nightmares in which she encountered strange beings. Six days after the incident, Betty sent a letter to Major Donald Keyhoe, director of the NICAP civilian UFO investigative organization, who referred the case to their field investigator, Walter Webb, who interviewed the Hills toward the end of October. Betty also contacted an intelligence officer from Pease Air Force Base, Major Paul W. Henderson, who dutifully forwarded a report to Project Blue Book. Although the report indicated that an unidentified radar return had been detected in the area around the time of the Hills' sighting, Blue Book declined to investigate further.

Barney began to experience terrifying flashbacks about the encounter and sought treatment for ulcers and chronic high blood pressure, which led his physician to recommend hypnotherapy. They were referred to Boston psychiatrist Dr. Benjamin Simon, who used hypnosis to treat World War II soldiers with post-traumatic stress disorder. Dr. Simon began his treatments in 1963, placing Barney and Betty under hypnosis separately while not allowing them to recall the details of their sessions until their therapy was concluded.

Under hypnosis Barney recalled that he had inexplicably driven off the highway onto a side road where they were met by a group of small humanoids who placed them in a trance-like state and

The abduction of Barney Hill (played by James Earl Jones) is re-enacted in the NBC-TV telefilm *The UFO Incident* (1975).

escorted them inside a landed UFO. Barney, who seemed to have been put into a deeper trance, remembered less of the experience than Betty and kept his eyes closed during most of the abduction. He was dragged inside the craft by the ufonauts, scuffing the tops of his shoes, and taken to a room where he was undressed. A cup-like device was placed over his groin that collected a sperm sample.

Betty remained conscious during the abduction and was undressed in a separate room, where she was examined by beings she referred to as the "Examiner" and the "Leader," who took samples of her hair and skin. She was then subjected to a painful procedure that was supposedly a "pregnancy test" in which a long needle was inserted into her navel. After the examination she had a conversation with the Leader about the aliens' point of origin and was shown a "star map" of their home system that she was able to draw during a subsequent hypnosis session.

When their examinations were completed, the couple was placed back in their vehicle, where they watched the UFO take off and disappear into the sky. Barney then backed their car down the side road onto Route 3. They heard the second set of beeping noises as their memories of the abduction faded and they continued on to their home in Portsmouth.

Dr. Simon allowed the Hills to listen to the tapes of each other's hypnotic sessions once their therapy was completed. Despite the fact that they both vividly re-experienced the terror of the abduction, Dr. Simon expressed the belief that their experience was not a real event but rather a form of psychological aberration. His opinion, however, did not persuade the Hills that their ordeal had been imaginary. Besides, there were corroborating factors such as Barney's scuffed shoes and a circular pattern of genital warts, which appeared in the area where a sperm sample had been taken, that had to be surgically removed.

Unlike the contactees, the Hills did not seek publicity or financial gain from their close encounter, but after their story was revealed by a reporter for a Boston newspaper in 1965, they decided to go public. Author John G. Fuller wrote a bestselling and accurate account of the abduction entitled *The Interrupted Journey*, which was published in 1966. An NBC-TV telefilm adaptation of the book, *The UFO Incident* aired in 1975 and featured emotionally riveting performances by James Earl Jones and Estelle Parsons as the Hills. The star map that Betty had drawn under hypnosis was analyzed and the home system of the abductors was allegedly identified as the twin stars Zeta 1 and 2 Reticuli, sun-like stars located about 40 light years from Earth.

The Hill case was at first not highly regarded by researchers, partly because of negative associations with the contactee's tall tales of alien encounters. Unlike the contactee hucksters, however, the Hills were solid citizens who were highly regarded in their community. Betty was a well-respected social worker, while Barney, who worked for the post office, was deeply involved with the civil rights movement at the local chapter of the NAACP and was appointed to the New Hampshire Commission on Human Rights. Still, there was a prejudice against sightings of alien beings that were just too threatening or considered too ludicrous to contemplate. Atmospheric physicist Dr. James McDonald, one of the foremost scientific proponents of the UFO phenomenon, expressed the opinion that the Hill case would set the study of UFOs back ten years.

In succeeding decades skeptics would attempt to debunk their experience as being a hallucination, a fantasy, or false memories recovered under hypnosis. According to one theory, their sighting was triggered by the light from an aircraft warning beacon on nearby Cannon Mountain. A recent book by Matthew Bowman entitled *The Abduction of Betty and Barney Hill: Alien Encounters, Civil Rights and the New Age in America* (2023) postulates that their experience was the result of fear of racial persecution in connection with their interracial marriage (Barney was African American) during the volatile years of the Civil Rights movement during the 1960s. The psychological mechanism by which the couple's racial anxieties could have led to the generation of a terrifying fantasy of alien abduction remains problematical, however.

The Hill's account offered a novel paradigm of alien contact, the features of which would be replicated in similar experiences subsequently reported by other abductees. This pattern would include the consciously remembered sighting of a UFO, followed by a period of missing time amnesia that occluded the actual abduction. Memories of the event would manifest themselves in dreams or nightmares, and later would be remembered under hypnosis. The abductors were usually described as small humanoids with large heads and eyes that wrapped around the sides of their heads that established the iconography of the "Gray alien." They communicated with each other and with the abductees via mental telepathy rather than verbal speech. There was a differentiation between the beings Betty referred to as the Leader and the Examiner, who were larger than the smaller humanoids that abducted them, and who were in charge of the operation.

An obscure case that was reported by Brazilian APRO representative Dr. Olavio Fontes was in all probability an abduction, although it was not classified as one at the time. The incident took place in late November of 1961 (no exact date is specified), about a month after the Hill abduction. The single witness was Cavalhiero Mendes, a retired police officer who was a real estate agent at the time of the event. Mendes was staying at a place called Pinhal Beach on business, scouting out beachfront properties for sale as vacation homes.

He was staying alone at a small beach house, trying to sleep one night when he felt an irresistible urge to go outside. At about 9:30 he left the house and walked toward the beach, where he observed a large, bright light about 900 feet away. Mendes was drawn inexorably toward the glow, and as he approached more closely, he saw that the light was emanating from a disc-shaped object resting on the sand. Then two humanoid figures emerged from the back of the object and began to advance toward him. He couldn't make out any facial details due to the bright light coming from the craft, but they seemed to be wearing headgear that resembled football helmets.

Mendes wanted to flee, but he received a telepathic message from the beings, telling him that he couldn't resist them and that he was unable to move. When he attempted to retreat he found he was paralyzed and rooted to the spot. As the creatures came closer Mendes lost consciousness, and the next thing he knew he had walked away from the area where the craft had been and was back at the beach house. The time was now 11:30 and he had experienced two hours of missing time. His only fragmentary memory was of someone scraping skin from his forearm.

In the aftermath of his experience Mendes began feeling depressed and anxious. He eventually contacted two members of the Brazilian military who had investigated UFO sightings. Both of them recommended that he undergo hypnotic regression to recover his lost memories, but Mendes steadfastly refused. The case had a number of features indicating that an abduction had taken place, including missing time amnesia, a confrontation with humanoid beings and a vague memory of having a skin sample taken. All of these features were similar to what the Hills had experienced just weeks earlier.[5]

The only abduction ever to be investigated by the U.S. government took place on the night of December 3, 1967, when policeman Herb Schirmer was on patrol near the outskirts of Ashland, Nebraska, at about 2:30 a.m. At the intersection of Highways 6 and 63, he observed a disc-shaped craft that rose up into the sky when he trained his cruiser's headlights on it. Schirmer duly noted that he had seen a "flying saucer" in his police report for that night, but was aware there was a half hour gap in his timekeeping. Returning home, he found he had a headache, a red welt on his neck, and a buzzing in his ears that prevented him from sleeping.

Schirmer's experience came to the attention of investigators at the University of Colorado's UFO research project (a.k.a. the Condon Committee), which was ongoing at the time. A polygraph examination was administered that indicated Schirmer believed he was telling the truth, and he was subjected to a battery of psychological tests that revealed no mental abnormalities. He was also hypnotized by University of Wyoming psychologist Leo Sprinkle, with inconclusive results. The Committee's conclusion was that Schirmer's experience was not objectively real, but was merely a form of psychological delusion.

Unsatisfied with the Committee's results, Schirmer was hypnotized a second time, which revealed more details about what had occurred that night. Under hypnosis, he recalled that a group of 4½-to-5-foot-tall humanoids disembarked from the craft and approached his police cruiser. The entities had gray skin, flat noses, slit-like mouths and eyes with cat-like pupils. They were wearing one-piece, silvery gray uniforms emblazoned with the emblem of a winged serpent, which is the symbol of Quetzalcoatl, a deity worshipped in ancient Mesoamerica.

The ufonauts fired a ray at Schirmer that incapacitated him and he was taken inside the ship to converse with their leader using a mix of telepathy and English speech. He was told that the crew drew electricity from power lines to fuel their craft and that radar could sometimes disable their machines. The aliens hailed from a "nearby galaxy," and had been visiting our planet for a long time. They had established covert bases in several locations on Earth, including underground and undersea bases in Florida, Argentina and Alaska. The leader took Schirmer on a brief tour of the UFO and was shown a viewing screen that displayed three "war ships" in flight in outer space. Schirmer was told that they would return to visit him two more times before giving him a mental command to forget about the close encounter, and he was returned to his police car with a period of missing time as he watched the UFO take off.

Perhaps the Leader's most interesting revelation, however, was that the aliens were abducting humans in order to gradually make their presence known. According to Schirmer's hypnotic testimony, "to a certain extent they want to puzzle people. They know they are being seen too frequently and they are trying to confuse the public's mind. He is telling me they want everyone to believe some in them." This disclosure appears to explain the ufonaut's apparently enigmatic behavior as a strategy of deliberate deception and misdirection.[6]

An abduction that allegedly took place in 1967 but did not come to light until the 1970s would eventually provide material for four books by researcher Raymond Fowler. As revealed in Fowler's 1979 book *The Andreasson Affair*, on the evening of January 25, 1967, Betty Andreasson was at her home in Ashburnham, Massachusetts, with her parents and seven children. Suddenly the house lights flickered and went out and an anomalous light was seen shining through the kitchen window. While Betty moved her children to safety in the living room, her father, Waino Aho looked out of the window and observed a group of beings he described as looking like "Halloween freaks" approaching the house with an odd jumping motion, "like grasshoppers."

All members of the household except Betty were paralyzed and lost consciousness. In ufological parlance they were "switched off," a phenomenon in which only selected individuals experience an abduction while other witnesses are placed in a state of suspended animation. As Betty watched, a group of entities entered the home by passing right through the solid matter of the kitchen door. The creatures were small humanoids with gray skin, slanted eyes and large, pear-shaped heads who were wearing identical dark blue uniforms. Instead of being frightened by the apparitions, Betty was calm and felt an aura of friendliness emanating from the intruders.

Their leader, who was slightly taller than the others, addressed Betty by name and identified himself as "Quazgaa." Following the leader Betty was transported through the door into an oval object shrouded in mist in the backyard. An abduction event ensued during which Betty was subjected to various "medical" procedures, including having a long needle inserted into her navel to "measure her for procreation," using a technique similar to the one Betty Hill had described years earlier. She described other bizarre experiences, including being placed in a transparent "immersion chair" that was filled with fluid and being shown the image of a huge bird that was consumed by fire like the mythological Phoenix. This complex event seems to have been overlaid with symbolic imagery that derived from Betty's devout Christian faith and may have emerged from her subconscious.

In his 1977 book *Situation Red: The UFO Siege*, researcher Leonard Stringfield relates an enigmatic event that took place in January 1968. The anonymous witness related that he was driving a tractor trailer along a desolate stretch of the M-28 highway in the Upper Peninsula of Michigan during a snowstorm. The truck's windshield wipers became clogged with snow and the driver got out of the truck at about 12:15 a.m. to remove the excess snow from the wipers when the area all around him was suddenly illuminated by an extremely bright light. After a few seconds the light subsided and was replaced by a pale green cone of luminosity that enveloped both the witness and his vehicle.

He noticed that he felt warm inside the cone and that the snow no longer seemed to be falling on him. The next thing he knew he found himself standing about 20 feet away from the truck with no recollection of how he had gotten there. It was still snowing, and although the snow was five to seven inches deep, there were no footprints leading to or from the truck, and he was oddly dry and warm. When he returned to the tractor trailer he found that its diesel engine was stalled and cold and had to be restarted, and that the time was now 5 a.m. He had lost nearly five hours of missing time and now had a severe headache and suffered from nausea, conditions that persisted for the next four days. The witness was at a loss to explain the period of amnesia when he was apparently in a warm, dry place somewhere outside the truck for almost five hours. Because there was no sighting of a UFO or aliens, this event was not immediately recognized as an abduction.[7]

Another abduction reportedly took place in Westmoreland, New York, on May 2, 1968, to a young woman named Shane Kurz. Ms. Kurz recounted that she had been watching the motion of UFOs in the sky from her home before falling into a deep sleep. The next morning she was awakened by her mother, who was concerned because she found

Shane lying on top of the bedspread in her dressing-gown and slippers, with her legs and clothing caked in mud. In addition, there was a trail of muddy footprints leading from the outside into the house. In the wake of her unremembered experience, Shane suffered from migraine headaches, an unexplained weight loss, and her menstrual periods stopped for a year.

These symptoms eventually led Shane to seek regression hypnosis to unlock the hidden memories of that night. Under hypnosis she remembered being drawn toward the window, where a telepathic voice compelled her to go outside. She was induced to cross a muddy field toward a saucer-shaped craft and was levitated inside, where she found herself in a room that resembled an operating theater. A group of Gray aliens stripped her naked and subjected her to a series of medical examinations, including the harvesting of her ova using a long needle, a procedure that may have had an effect on her menstrual cycle afterward. She was then swabbed all over her body with a thick liquid substance as a prelude to having sexual intercourse with the leader of the ufonauts, who she described as being a slender humanoid. She was then released to return home, but remembered nothing of her ordeal.

In the aftermath of her experience Shane found that she had a long triangular mark on her abdomen. The liquid that was smeared all over her body might have been an aphrodisiac because she reported that she enjoyed having sex with the alien leader. A similar procedure was described by Antonio Villas-Boas, who had a fluid applied to his body prior to having intercourse with a female entity. Another abduction resembling the Kurz affair was experienced in Somerset, England, in October 1973 by a witness referred to by the pseudonym "Mrs. Verona," who reportedly was paralyzed and forced to have sex with an alien being. Several months prior to her abduction, Shane had a liaison with a mysterious person who may have been a human/alien hybrid, an event that will be discussed in a later chapter.[8]

Several of the cases cited above exhibit an uncanny phenomenon researcher Richard Boylan refers to as the "travel urge," and notes that abductees may travel long distances to make the rendezvous. One person felt compelled to cross three state lines to a remote area of the Sonoran desert where the abduction took place. Abductees sometimes feel the urge to undertake a trip, such as the impromptu journey to Canada by Betty and Barney Hill. In his book *Incident at Devil's Den*, Terry Lovelace relates how he and a friend felt they had to take a day-long road trip from Whiteman Air Force Base in Missouri to a remote spot in Devil's Den State Park in Arkansas where they were abducted. Abductees often report that they are compelled to perform certain actions, such as the travel urge, as if they have been placed in some kind of hypnotic trance in which they are under the control of their abductors. In the Calvahiero Mendes case and the Shane Kurz abduction the individuals involved were induced to leave the houses in which they were sleeping and walk toward a UFO where they would be captured.

The compulsion to yield to the travel urge can be overwhelming. Researcher Raymond Fowler cites a case reported to him by a witness named John, who was awakened at about 1 a.m. with an irresistible impulse to leave his house. This was highly irregular, as he was separated from his wife at the time and should never have left his daughter alone in the house late at night. John got into his car and drove to

Abductees are often drawn to a deserted abduction site in what has been termed the "travel urge" (Dreamstime).

a desolate spot where he was abducted.[9] Similarly, David Jacobs delineates the experience of an abductee called Patti Layne, who described how she was compelled to leave her dorm room at a small Pennsylvania college to drive to some nearby mountains one night. She felt that "I had to get out.... I wanted to get out and I knew I had to go by myself.... I just had to find this place in the mountains and I would feel better."[10] Driving out into the night, she soon found herself on a lonely dirt road in the mountains where an abduction took place.

Later that year, on the night of August 7, two staffers at the Buff Ledge Camp on Lake Champlain near Burlington, Vermont, were abducted from the campsite. As recounted in NICAP field investigator's 1994 book *Encounter at Buff Ledge*, maintenance man Michael Lapp and counselor Janet Cornell (pseudonyms) were lounging on a dock on the lake at about 8:10 p.m. While preparing to swim, they noticed a bright light in the distance that quickly approached them and resolved itself into a large, disc-shaped, luminous craft. The UFO maneuvered until it hovered directly over their position and shone a bright light down that enveloped the couple, who then lost consciousness.

The next thing Michael remembered was waking up on the dock at about 9:00 p.m. as their fellow campers returned from a swimming event at Burlington. Two of the returning campers and a staff member observed the UFO as it disappeared into the distance. Neither Michael nor Janet remembered anything about what had happened during their period of missing time, and did not discuss their strange experience with each other. Ten years later, after Michael began having disturbing dreams about being abducted, he contacted J. Allen Hynek's Center for UFO Studies, who dispatched researcher Walter Webb to investigate. Michael and Janet had not seen each other during the ensuing decade, but once she had been located, Webb arranged to have both of them hypnotically regressed separately by therapists in Boston.

A complex abduction experience was described by both subjects during their hypnotic sessions. Both of them recalled being floated up into the UFO on a beam of light, where they encountered four short beings with oversized bald heads, large eyes that extended around the sides of their heads and bluish-green skin. The ufonauts subjected them to medical examinations using probes that were placed at various parts of their bodies, scraped samples of their skin and took samples of their bodily fluids.

Michael remembered that the disc-shaped craft rendezvoused with a much larger vessel that appeared to be somewhere in outer space at a considerable distance from the Earth. The couple was conducted into the larger craft, where Michael observed a group of humans, some of whom were clothed and others were naked, gathering in a hazy environment. He also remembered being shown vision screens that displayed projections of rapidly changing data that his abductors told him was information he would be using for some future task. The imagery of a smaller, disc-shaped craft docking inside the hanger bay of a much larger ship would be replicated in the well-known abduction of Travis Walton just a few years later.

The year 1973 would witness a dramatic uptick in abductions, with a significant number of them taking place in the month of October. Researcher Kevin Randle, who was a field investigator for the Aerial Phenomenon Research Organization (APRO) at the time, would author a book in 1988 entitled *The October Scenario* in which he explored a cluster of abduction events he had personally investigated during this time period. According to Randle, there were at least 60 credible instances of landings, occupants and abductions reported during the October '73 "wave." His book contains an impressive catalog of landings and humanoid sightings that were recounted during this relatively brief interval of time.

The most well-known of these events took place on October 11 when two men, Charles Hickson and Calvin Parker went fishing that night from an abandoned shipyard pier on the Pascagoula River in Mississippi. The pair observed a blue light that quickly moved toward their position and resolved itself into an oval-shaped UFO that landed nearby. Three robot-like entities emerged from the craft and floated over to the two men, whereupon Parker fainted from the shock while Hickson remained conscious during the ordeal. The creatures were described as being about five feet tall, with gray, wrinkled skin, slit-like mouths and lobster-like claws instead of hands. Their heads had no visible eyes and sported sharp pointed, antenna-like appendages where their ears and nose would be on a human head. Hickson and Parker were floated inside the vehicle in a paralyzed state, where Hickson described being scanned by a device resembling an eye as he floated above the floor. Parker, who remained unconscious during the proceedings, remembered nothing about being inside the ship.

When the ufonauts had finished examining the men, they floated the two witnesses back to the pier as the UFO departed and Parker regained consciousness. In the aftermath of their bizarre close encounter the men were in a highly agitated state and decided to report their experience to the Jackson County Sheriff's Department. The men's credibility was greatly enhanced when law enforcement officials recorded them discussing the event with each other while alone together using a voice activated recorder that taped their conversation and documented the men's mental anguish and sincerity. Hickson and Parker were then transported to Keesler Air Force Base in Biloxi, where they were examined by a team of military doctors.

In the meantime the men's story had been picked up by the news wires and had caused a sensation. Researchers and journalists rushed to the scene to conduct investigations, including former Project Blue Book scientific consultant J. Allen Hynek, Jim and Coral Lorenzen of APRO, along with APRO's Research Director James Harder, who would conduct hypnotic regression sessions with the men. Both Harder and Hynek stated that they believed the witnesses to be sincere. Later that month a lie detector test was administered to the abductees that seemed to support their veracity, but skeptics pointed out that the UFO had not been observed by motorists on an adjacent highway or workers on a nearby bridge, while some witnesses would come forth who reported seeing the craft at a later date. Hickson claimed he experienced subsequent contacts with aliens and wrote a self-published book about his later encounters entitled *UFO Contact at Pascagoula* in 1983.[11]

An abduction that reportedly transpired on the night of October 16–17 involved the kidnapping of a single mom and several of her children from their home in a small town in Utah. Pat Roach was asleep on a couch in her living room when she was awakened by her youngest child, Kent, who was frightened by seeing a "skeleton" in the house. The loud barking of a dog at a neighbor's home woke up the other children, and Pat, thinking that a prowler was trying to enter their house, called the police who responded to her call but found no prowler and quickly left. Some of her children, however, insisted that "spacemen" had come into the house and taken the family on board a "spaceship."

Nothing happened for another two years until Pat read an article about UFO abductions in *Saga* magazine and contacted the publication. The case was referred to APRO, who sent Randle and James

Harder to investigate and conduct hypnotic regression sessions with Pat and her children. An abduction narrative would emerge, in which Ms. Roach and several of her children were taken aboard a craft parked in a nearby field by a group of beings. The ufonauts were described as being a little over four feet tall with slender builds, large slanted eyes and claw-like hands. They were wearing fluorescent outfits with belts across their chests that reminded Pat of military uniforms. Pat and four of her children were floated inside the craft and into a large, bright, round room containing high-tech, computer-like machines. Ms. Roach was stripped naked and placed on an examination table and subjected to the by now familiar needle-in-the-navel procedure. She also reported that the beings extracted and recorded her thoughts and memories using other needle-like probe devices. The most startling detail to emerge, however, was the sighting of a normal human being who was assisting the aliens with their gynecological procedures. This individual was described as being a bald, middle-aged man about 55 years old who wore horn-rimmed glasses and black clothing, and had his hand in a rubber glove. He reportedly tried to calm the abductee by using a reassuring bedside manner.

Pat was placed in a trance state during which she was compelled to answer questions about her personal life. She expressed the observation that the beings "limited time," but provided no further explanation about this unusual concept. Her impression was that they needed to extract information about human psychological makeup from her. The aliens acted in a highly efficient manner, but Pat had nothing but contempt for their cold-blooded methods of information gathering. Two of Pat's children fully corroborated the substance of their mother's experience and provided additional details. Her six-year-old daughter Debbie stated she had seen a line of people, including some local boys from the neighborhood that she recognized, waiting to get on "the machine." Another odd facet of the experience involved Debbie, who suffered from a serious illness, was told by one of the aliens that she wouldn't be sick anymore and was reportedly healed of her affliction in the aftermath.[12]

Arguably the most curious aspect of the affair concerned the human being who was assisting the ufonauts with their medical examinations. It would eventually be revealed during subsequent abduction accounts that certain abductees willingly cooperated with the aliens by helping them with their tasks. For instance, Betty Andreasson related how she helped calm a female abductee during an embryo extraction procedure and even drew a detailed picture of the incident. A number of abductees interviewed by David Jacobs also reported that they were compelled to assist the abductors by interacting with other abductees.

At around the same time, on the night of October 16, another kidnapping was transpiring in Northern England that was briefly touched upon in an earlier passage. An Italian émigré living in England named Mrs. Verona (a pseudonym) was obliged to visit a sick acquaintance and began a late night drive down a lonely stretch of road toward the town of Wellington at about 10:45 p.m. A light appeared in a nearby field and her car engine and headlights suddenly failed. When she got out of her vehicle to have a look, a force struck her on the shoulder and pushed her to the ground. A robotic entity then seized her and she lost consciousness.

She awoke inside a room in a landed craft where she found herself totally naked and strapped to an examination table. Three normal-sized humanoids wearing face masks and clothing that resembled surgical gowns conducted a medical exam and took nail parings and a blood sample. A cup-like suction device was placed on her genitals, whereupon she experienced an uncomfortable pulling sensation. The entities left her alone in the examination room for a time, but then one of them returned and placed a small pin on her thigh that paralyzed her. While she was in this helpless state, the being forcibly had sexual intercourse with her. When the act was completed her assailant removed the pin and she lost consciousness once more.

When she awoke she was standing next to her car fully clothed but in a state of confusion. She was able to drive home and arrived at about 2:30 a.m. and related her ordeal to her sympathetic husband. Mrs. Verona remembered most of her experience without hypnosis and reported it to British UFO researchers four years later. As previously noted, the sexual aspect of the abduction has similarities with the incidents reported by Shane Kurz and Antonio Villas-Boas.[13]

A businesswoman named Susan Ramstead left her apartment on the evening of October 19 to attend a seminar. While driving through a rural area she sighted a UFO in a cornfield, her car stopped and she experienced a period of missing time. Three years later she decided to explore her missing time experience under hypnosis. She recalled being taken inside the craft by a group of small, large-eyed humanoids along with a being she identified as a female who had breasts and wore a long skirt. She was compelled to remove her clothes and lie on a table, where the creatures took blood and skin samples and inserted the familiar long needle into her navel. Additionally, a cold metal tube attached to a machine was placed between her legs and entered her genital area.

As in the Pat Roach case, Ms. Ramstead reported that the aliens recorded her thoughts. Using telepathy, her captors forced her to relive the most emotionally intense incidents from her life history, both positive and negative, that were recorded by a machine. She experienced a feeling of extreme terror at the thought that the aliens were going to take her on a one-way trip to their home world as a specimen, but her fears would prove to be unfounded. When the beings had completed their procedures she was allowed to dress herself, was returned to her car and given a hypnotic command to forget the incident.[14]

Just one day after the Ramstead affair, on October 20, a college student named Leigh Proctor left her dorm to spend a few days at home with her family, who lived on a farm in a rural area (location not specified). When she didn't arrive, her worried parents contacted the local sheriff, William H. Shaller, who launched an investigation. Ms. Proctor's abandoned car was discovered on the side of a road with the hood up and the motor still running and Leigh's wallet, money and ID on the car's front seat. Fearing foul play, the police conducted sweeps of the surrounding countryside, but found no clue as to her whereabouts. On the fourth day (October 24), Leigh walked into Shaller's office in a disheveled and disoriented state. She remembered most of her bizarre experience consciously but agreed to be hypnotized to provide further details.

Under hypnosis she remembered driving down a deserted stretch of highway when her car engine died and her headlights went out. When she exited the vehicle to find out what was wrong, she was seized from behind by three five-foot-tall humanoids with large eyes who seemed to be wearing masks that obscured their features. The beings forced her into a UFO, where she recalled being strapped to a table in a brightly lit room for long periods while her abductors performed blood tests, skin scrapings, a rectal exam and other procedures. As in the Pat Roach and Susan Ramstead cases, the beings hooked the abductee up to a machine and interrogated her in order to record her thoughts. At times she occupied a room where she was given water and tasteless food and allowed to sleep. On October 24 she awoke to find that she was no longer aboard the craft, but in a nearby cornfield where she was able to find her way to the sheriff's office.

In the aftermath of her ordeal, Leigh Proctor suffered a mental breakdown, dropped out of college and moved out of her parent's home into a dingy apartment in town. Following up on the case, Sheriff Shaller found that she had purchased a .38 handgun. Thinking that she intended to use the gun to commit suicide, she explained to him that she intended to use the weapon on the aliens instead, who had told her they would return because "they were sure that she would want to see the baby." Note that this reference to human/alien hybridization took place over a decade before this narrative theme would become a feature of the abduction accounts related in Budd Hopkins' seminal 1987 work *Intruders*.[15]

The last major abduction event of the fall 1973 wave occurred in the early morning hours of November 2. Lyndia Morel, who worked as a masseuse at the Swedish Sauna in Manchester, New Hampshire, left her workplace at about 2:45 a.m. and began driving to her home in nearby Goffstown. While driving down Route 114 she noticed an anomalous light that appeared to be pacing her car. As the light came closer it resolved itself into a globe-shaped UFO whose surface was covered with a hexagonal pattern. There was also an oval window on the upper left-hand exterior of the craft. As it approached more closely Ms. Morel felt that the object was taking control of her vehicle. Then she became aware of a humanoid creature staring at her through the window of the UFO.

She described the creature as having wrinkled gray skin, two prominent dark eyes and a slit-like mouth. The eyes seemed to be taking control of her body and drawing her toward the craft while sending her a telepathic message not to be afraid. At this point she believed she was about to be captured and experienced a period of amnesia. When she regained her senses she pulled into the driveway of a house, ran to the front door and began pounding on it frantically. By the time the residents came to the door the object had disappeared. An investigation of the case was conducted by a scientific consultant for APRO, who intimated that an abduction had taken place but details were never released to the public. Oddly, the globular UFO with a honeycombed surface bore an uncanny resemblance to the alien spaceship featured in the 1953 science fiction film *It Came from Outer Space.*[16]

The 1973 wave of UFO sightings, landings and abductions would be the last such cluster of these events. Researchers have long noted that periods of intense UFO activity seems to come in waves, referred to as "flaps," interspersed with intervals of relative inactivity. Previous waves in the United States occurred in 1947, 1952 and 1967–68, while another flap took place in Western Europe in 1954. No concrete explanation for these waves and troughs of UFO activity has ever been put forth, nor has another flap transpired during the last half century since 1973.

Abductions continued to be reported throughout the 1970s, including a couple of cases from Europe. During the evening of March 23–24, a young man named Harald Andersson (a pseudonym) was out for a walk near his home in Lindholmen, just north of Stockholm, Sweden, when he heard a voice in his head that compelled him to walk to a certain location where he was blinded by an intense light that emanated from above. He reacted by throwing himself on the snowy ground while trying to shield his eyes from the powerful glare. His next memory was standing on his doorstep confronting his wife, who was upset when she noticed he had a burn mark on his cheek and a wound on his temple.

The witness consulted Dr. Ture Arvidsson at the Danderyd Hospital during April and May of that year. Dr. Arvidsson hypnotized Andersson in an effort to pierce the veil of his amnesia about the incident. Like Betty and Barney Hill, Andersson re-experienced the abject terror of his ordeal under hypnosis. He described how, after he threw himself on the ground, he was levitated aboard a hovering UFO. On board the craft he tried to fight off a group of tall, hooded entities as they attempted to place a device on his forehead. He was unsuccessful as the beings forcibly pressed the instrument against his head, causing him to experience a burning sensation. The creatures intimated that they would return to see him again, whereupon he passed out and his next memory was finding himself at his front door.

Andersson experienced some odd after-effects as a result of his abduction experience. He began to undergo occurrences of telepathy and psychokinesis, have premonitions of future events and to affect electrical equipment just by going near it. This latter type of activity, which has been termed "electrical sensitivity syndrome," would be noted in the aftermath of subsequent abduction events, as would a reported increase in psychic capabilities. The witness also experienced an interval of missing time amnesia and was subjected to the travel urge that guided him to the spot where the abduction took place. Some corroboration of the event was provided by an independent witness who observed a conical beam of light shining down from an overhead object at the site of Andersson's abduction.[17]

On October 27, 1974, as John and Susan Day and their three children were driving near the town of Aveley in Essex, a dense green mist or fog appeared on the road ahead of them. Driving into the strange cloud, they experienced feeling cold and noted an anomalous silence and odd lights while they were inside. It seemed like they were only enveloped in the fog for a couple of seconds, but when they returned home they found that it was over two and a half hours later than it should have been, and they had no memories of the period of missing time. Subsequently, the family experienced recurring dreams about having been examined on operating tables by "gnomes" during this event, dreams which are memories of a typical abduction.

This was the first British case to be investigated using hypnotic regression which took place three years after the event. Under hypnosis they recalled that their car was levitated into a UFO where a complex abduction transpired. John, Susan and their ten-year-old son Kevin were all subjected to medical procedures conducted by dwarfish, animal-like creatures with hairy faces and taller, more human-like entities that seemed to be in charge of the operation. The taller beings lacked facial features and may have been wearing masks. After his examination John was taken on a tour of the ship, where he was shown a laboratory and a control room and had images of the aliens' home world projected into his mind. At the same time Susan underwent a similar physical exam and was also conducted on a tour of the craft. She was shown images of the Earth from space on a viewing screen that zoomed in on her home in England.

When their abductors had finished with them, the family members were placed back in their car and continued on their way home with no conscious memory of what had transpired. After recovering their memories, John claimed that the "Watchers," as he called the aliens, had been responsible for the evolution of the human race using genetic engineering and interbreeding. At one time they were more involved with the affairs of humankind, and identified themselves as the gods of Greek mythology, but over time they withdrew from their role as our divine mentors.[18]

During the early morning hours on August 13, 1975, Air Force Sergeant Charles Moody got off duty at Holloman Air Force Base and traveled to a desert area near Alamogordo, New Mexico, to watch the Perseid meteor shower—but encountered a disc-shaped UFO instead. Moody got into his car, but the vehicle would not start as he watched a group of shadowy human forms through a window on the craft. At this point he felt a numbness come over him and the next thing he knew he was sitting in his car watching the UFO depart. Returning home at about 3 a.m., he found it was an hour and a half later than it should have been. Moody conferred with a USAF flight surgeon, who suggested he use self-hypnosis to recover his memories of the event. After several weeks he was able to recall being taken into the craft by a group of five-foot-tall humanoids with oversized bald heads, large eyes and mask-like features.

He was escorted to a room on the UFO where he was taken to their Leader, with whom he communicated using telepathy. Although he did not remember physically resisting his captors, he was told that he sustained minor injuries during an initial scuffle with the ufonauts. The Leader then passed a rod-like device over his body to repair any damages. Then Moody was taken on a tour of the ship, where he was treated to a view of the craft's propulsion system. The Leader told him that they had come to our world in peace, and that they would initiate contact with humanity within three years. The next thing he knew he was sitting in his car with amnesia about his close encounter.

When Moody reported for duty the next day, he found he was suffering from back pain and a burning rash on his lower body that caused him to go on sick call. Knowing that something strange had happened to him, he eventually contacted APRO and an investigation was launched. Moody was a participant in the Air Force's Human Reliability Program and was carefully screened by a psychiatrist who declared him free of any emotional disorders, a fact that greatly enhanced his credibility. After he contacted UFO researchers, he was shipped overseas by his military superiors before further hypnosis sessions could reveal more details about his sighting.[19]

One of the best-known abductions took place on the evening of

November 5, 1975, when crew boss Mike Rogers and six loggers who had been thinning timber in the Apache-Sitgreaves National Forest in Arizona observed an illuminated, disc-shaped craft hovering above a nearby clearing. As Rogers stopped the truck to have a better look, one of the loggers, Travis Walton, got out and approached the object. His crewmates watched as a blue-green ray of energy struck Walton, knocking him backwards. Shocked by the sight, the men panicked and Rogers drove away down the forest trail as fast as he could, but when the men came to their senses they decided to return to the site to see if Travis was hurt. When they arrived at the clearing, however, there was no trace of Travis or the UFO.

The men reported the incident to law enforcement officials in the town of Heber, who organized extensive searches of the area conducted by deputies, volunteers and helicopters over the next few days, but Travis or his corpse could not be located. Suspecting that Walton had been murdered, the Apache County Sheriff's Office insisted that Rogers and his men undergo polygraph tests, which all of them passed except for one. Five days later, on the night of November 11, Travis reappeared and called his family from a pay phone at a gas station outside of Heber. He was found to be in a disorientated, incoherent state after his ordeal.

Unlike the majority of abductees, Walton remembered the details of the incident without being hypnotized, although he could only recall a very brief portion of his five day ordeal. As he recalled in his 1978 account of his close encounter, *The Walton Experience*, after being rendered unconscious by the energy beam from the UFO, he remembered waking up on an operating table surrounded by three small gray-skinned creatures that seemed to be performing a medical procedure on his body. The beings had oversized craniums, vestigial facial features and prominent eyes. Alarmed, Travis leapt to his feet and confronted the creatures, whereupon the three humanoids quickly fled from the room.

Left to his own devices, Walton wandered around the ship for a while until he was approached by a normal-looking man wearing blue coveralls and a transparent helmet. The "man" escorted him out of the smaller saucer into a large hanger-like area where several other disc-shaped craft were parked. He was then led into a small room where three more human-like beings were waiting and a device resembling an oxygen mask was placed over his face that caused him to lose consciousness. This brief sequence of events was all he could remember about his experience.

The Walton abduction was investigated by Jim Lorenzen of APRO, and funding for various medical and psychological tests was provided by the *National Enquirer* tabloid. Eminent scientific researcher Dr. J. Allen Hynek of the Center for UFO Studies also interviewed Travis and stated his opinion that the case was not a hoax. Along with the Hill and Pascagoula events, Walton's experience would become one of the most publicized abductions of all time and would provide the basis for the 1993 film *Fire in the Sky*.

On the night of January 6, 1976, three women, Mona Stafford, Elaine Thomas and Louise Smith traveled from their home in Liberty, Kentucky, to a restaurant in Lancaster, about 30 miles away, to celebrate Ms. Stafford's birthday. They left the restaurant at about 11:15 and were headed home on Route 78 when they encountered an enormous, domed, disc-shaped UFO. All three women experienced severe eye pain when an extremely bright light engulfed their vehicle. They lost control of the car, which was traveling at 85 miles per hour, and they seemed to be driving down a long, dark, straight section of road without any familiar landmarks, which was odd because all of the roadways in the area are curved. Their next memory was arriving at Ms. Smith's home at 1:25 a.m. with about an hour and a half that they couldn't account for.

After the incident all three women suffered from headaches and eye and skin inflammation, along with red welts on their bodies and severe emotional distress. When an article about the event appeared in a local newspaper, the case came to the attention of UFO investigators from both APRO and CUFOS. All three women eventually underwent hypnotic regression that revealed they had all been abducted. They reportedly underwent a series of bizarre experiments at the hands of a group of four-foot-tall humanoids with gray skin and large, dark eyes. While Ms. Smith's memory of the event was fragmentary, Ms. Stafford recalled being restrained on a table in a superheated room with her arms and legs constricted in an excruciating position while an "eye" observed her suffering. Ms. Thomas revealed that a noose was placed around her neck that tightened around her throat whenever she tried to think or speak.[20]

Unlike most abduction accounts, the usual physical/medical

examination procedures appear to have been de-emphasized in favor of a psychological experiment involving the measurement of the abductee's reactions to fear, pain and stress. These procedures are reminiscent of the sadistic experiments carried out by Nazi doctors like Josef Mengele in concentration camps during the 1940s. All three women suffered lasting physical and psychological aftereffects in the wake of their horrifying ordeal.

On August 22 of that year, four men, Jim and Jack Weiner (who were identical twins) and their friends, Chuck Rak and Charlie Foltz, were on a fishing trip in the Allagash Waterway, a remote area in Baxter State Park in Maine. The four men were doing some night fishing on Eagle Lake in a canoe when a large, spherical UFO approached that shone a bright light down on them. The next thing they knew they had returned to their campsite, where they watched the UFO depart and found that about two hours of their time was unaccounted for.

This case was not investigated until 1989, when memories of their experience began to surface in dreams and the men consented to be hypnotized. The incident was investigated by researcher Raymond Fowler in his 1993 book *The Allagash Abductions*. Under hypnosis, the men remembered being levitated out of their canoe into the hovering sphere inside a cone of light. Their clothing was removed as the men waited their turns to be examined while sitting on a bench inside the craft. Their abductors were the by-now-familiar Gray humanoids with large, dark eyes and spindly bodies. All of the men were subjected to physical examinations, while Jim Weiner recalled being placed in a machine that made him feel as if his body was being dismembered. Samples of saliva, blood, skin, feces, urine and sperm were collected by the beings. The four men were then returned to their canoe with two hours of missing time and no memory of the abduction.

Ten years later Jim Weiner began experiencing sleep problems and the perception of a forbidding alien figure in his bedroom. He eventually contacted Raymond Fowler who arranged for the men to be hypnotized. During the hypnosis sessions, it was revealed that Jim and Jack Weiner had been abducted during their childhood years, and Jack recalled another abduction that he had experienced in 1988. The four men all had art training and produced detailed drawings of the abductors and their medical procedures.

This case had a couple of curious postscripts. Chuck Rak, one of the four abductees, later recanted his testimony about being abducted, reportedly as part of a scheme to make money by claiming the case was a hoax and embarrassing researchers. The other three witnesses continue to stand by their account.

Jack Weiner later developed an anomalous lump on his leg that was referred to a surgeon, who removed it. Jack was informed that local pathologists were unable to identify the removed object and forwarded it to the Center for Disease Control for analysis. When Fowler requested copies of Jack's medical records, he discovered that the object had been forwarded to the Armed Forces Institute of Pathology in Washington, D.C., where it was analyzed by a United States Air Force colonel. No further information about the specimen could be obtained from the government.

The 22 cases enumerated above are in chronological order spanning a period from 1942 to 1976. This is not a catalog of all abductions occurring during this time frame, but it does include the most important and well-publicized cases (Hills 1961, Pascagoula 1973, Walton 1975) as well as a number of more obscure incidents that deserve more intense scrutiny. All of them took place at night in deserted places when the witnesses were fully awake and in a state of normal consciousness. A majority of these occurrences (14) transpired when the witnesses were engaged in driving or operating a vehicle. An episode of missing time amnesia was a feature in 18 of these events. Hypnosis was used to recover memories of the abduction in 13 of the cases, while six of them (Villas-Boas 1957, Andreasson 1967, Pascagoula 1973, Verona 1973, Moody 1975, Walton 1976) were remembered without hypnosis. In nine cases (Villas-Boas 1957, Hills 1961, Andreasson 1967, Kurz 1968, Roach 1973, Verona 1973, Ramstead 1973, Proctor 1973, Allagash 1976), the ufonauts reportedly performed reproductive procedures on the abductees. A majority of cases occurred in the United States, while three cases were reported from the United Kingdom, one from Sweden and two from Brazil.

Most of the abductions (15) involved single witnesses, while three of them (Hills 1961, Buff Ledge 1968, Pascagoula 1973) featured two witnesses, two cases (Day 1974, Kentucky 1976) had three witnesses, one (Allagash) had four and one (Roach 1973) had five. Three of the occurrences (Nevada 1953, Mendes 1961, Michigan 1968) involved instances of missing time amnesia indicative of an abduction event, although the witnesses were never hypnotized to recover memories of being inside a UFO. In six of the cases (Villas-Boas 1957, Hills 1961, Verona 1973, Ramstead 1973, Proctor 1973, Kentucky 1976), the UFOs interfered with vehicle engines or took complete control of the vehicle. Three incidents (Hills 1961, Kurz 1968, Andersson 1974) featured the travel urge, while six (Kurz 1968, Buff Ledge 1968, Andersson 1974, Day 1974, Kentucky 1976, Allagash 1976) involved the levitation of a person or vehicle inside a craft on a beam of light. In seven cases (Lancashire 1942, Hills 1961, Kurz 1968, Buff Ledge 1968, Roach 1973, Day 1974, Allagash 1976) memories were only recovered years after the abductions took place using hypnotic regression.

The circumstances of these events underscore the abductor's necessity for secrecy. The abductions take place on deserted stretches of roadway in the gloom of night, or in a locale where they can conceal their presence. If the location is not remote enough, they have the ability to mentally compel the abductees to travel to a more secure site where the abduction can take place. They can also assume physical control of the abductee's vehicle in order to guide it to an obscure spot where their actions will not be observed. In most cases they choose to impose amnesia on their human subjects to further conceal their actions. The degree of control they are able to exercise to manipulate human minds and physical objects borders on the preternatural.

One of their most impressive technological capabilities is the reported ability to draw people and automobiles (along with their passengers) inside a hovering craft using a beam of light or intense energy. This concept has long been featured in science fiction books and movies, where it is referred to as a "tractor beam." An example is Princess Leia's spaceship being pulled up into the hold of Darth Vader's massive Star Destroyer craft in the first *Star Wars* movie.

For the most part, the ufonauts communicate with the abductees using mental telepathy instead of spoken language. Barney Hill described communicating with the alien Leader thus: "He did not speak by word. I was told what to do by his thoughts making my thoughts understand."[21] Similarly, Michael Lapp, one of the abductees in the Buff Ledge case, reported that he heard his abductor's voice "in his head," and that the alien told him that "this is what you call telepathy."[22] Jim Weiner, one of the Allagash Four, was asked if his alien captors

Witnesses report that ufonauts can employ a "tractor beam" to lift entire vehicles inside their craft (Dreamstime).

communicated using verbal speech and replied, "No, but I know that's what they want me to do, so I figured that I might as well do it."[23]

The Betty and Barney Hill case established the iconography of what would come to be known as the "Gray" alien. Both of the Hills described their abductors as being small humanoids with oversized craniums and large eyes that slanted around the sides of their heads. Their skin color was an aluminum gray, and their heads were entirely hairless without eyebrows or eyelashes. The humanoids had spindly bodies, no discernible ears, broad, flat noses and slit-like mouths. These descriptors would become the stereotypical image of aliens not only in abduction reports but in popular culture as well. Other, more exotic alien types would become a feature of later abduction narratives.

In many cases the witnesses consciously remembered a UFO sighting before their memory of the abduction was blanked out. The most common feature of the experience was a physical examination with strange instruments and hi-tech equipment. Skin, hair and fingernail and blood samples were collected, and the abductee's bodies were sometimes scanned with an eye-like device. The abductor's main focus, however, was on the reproductive system, complete with the harvesting of sperm and egg cells. In the Pat Roach, Susan Ramstead and Kentucky abductions, the beings conducted painful psychological experiments on their human subjects and recorded their responses by "taking their thoughts." Villas-Boas, Susan Ramstead and Travis Walton observed what appeared to be human/alien hybrids that were the result of genetic engineering.

By the late 1970s Occupant reports of space-suited ufonauts began to phase out in favor of Gray aliens who seemingly needed no life support in Earth's environment. Thus, the paradigm of alien life-forms evolved from the beneficent "space brother" human types reported by the contactees, to the space-suited "scientist/astronauts" who were conducting a dispassionate survey of Earth's biosphere, to mysterious humanoids who kidnapped hapless people in lonely places in the dead of night and subjected them to enigmatic medical and psychological experiments.

In the ensuing decades, abduction research would come to dominate other aspects of UFO investigation, but the path ahead would prove to be fraught with many difficulties.

Chapter Three

Abduction Research Begins

The ufological community did not rush to embrace abduction research. The subject was met with resistance from many quarters for a variety of reasons. For starters, there was the "giggle factor" involved in researching the pop science fiction notion of "little green men," a term designed to render the subject absurd and even comical. There was, however, a much deeper reason for dismissing abduction reports. It was one thing to analyze the various properties of the UFOs; it was much more psychologically threatening to contemplate the beings that were operating the celestial machines.

For instance, when researcher David Jacobs queried Dr. J. Allen Hynek about wanting to pursue abduction research, "Hynek warned me to stay away from the abduction cases because they were eccentric and led us off the main path of sighting analysis…. Abduction reports were too bizarre for him; he could not subject them to the kind of scientific analysis that he could use for sighting reports."[1] Similarly, NICAP, the most prominent and respected research organization during the 1960s and '70s, shied away from investigating abduction reports in favor of continuing to analyze more mundane UFO sightings. In fairness, this was partly due to the outlandish antics of the contactees during the 1950s.

It was left to the other prominent American research group, APRO, to fully embrace the subject. The organization's founders, Jim and Coral Lorenzen, would author two seminal volumes on the subject. *Encounters with UFO Occupants* (1976) offered a comprehensive catalog of Occupant and abduction cases, including the first accounts of the Villas-Boas case in English, the Betty and Barney Hill and Pascagoula incidents. They followed this up with *Abducted! Confrontations with Beings from Outer Space* in 1977 that provided material about the

Pat Roach, Sergeant Moody, Travis Walton and Kentucky abductions, among others. These were cases that the Lorenzens and APRO had personally investigated. In *Abducted!* they were the first to recognize the importance of the missing time aspect of the phenomenon in a chapter entitled "Memory Loss and UFOs—A New Development."

Other print sources for information about abduction reports included John Fuller's best-selling book on the Hill abduction *The Interrupted Journey*, published in 1966, and articles in the British quarterly publication *Flying Saucer Review*. While mainstream newspapers and magazines for the most part ignored or ridiculed the subject, the weekly tabloid *The National Enquirer* published stories on the phenomenon and provided funding for APRO to investigate cases such as the Travis Walton and Kentucky abductions. Unfortunately, the *Enquirer* was not the ideal venue for a serious study of these incidents, as these accounts would appear in the same issues as stories about Elvis sightings, Bigfoot encounters and other lurid and dubious subjects. Additionally, men's magazines *Argosy* and *Saga* also carried accounts of abductions.

Eventually even Hynek came to have a grudging acceptance of humanoid sightings and abductions. The 1964 sighting of Occupants by a respected police witness and the presence of ground traces of a landed UFO served to convert Hynek from being a skeptic to an agnostic about the subject. Later in the decade, Hynek would be present during a session in which Dr. Benjamin Simon placed the Hills under hypnosis so that the scientist could question the couple in person about their experiences. He would eventually coin the phrase "close encounters of the third kind" to describe human interactions with UFO occupants.

Hynek's fellow scientist Dr. Jacques Vallee would emerge as a prominent theorist of the UFO phenomenon during this period. In his 1969 book *Passport to Magonia: From Folklore to Flying Saucers*, Vallee presented his thesis that equated modern-day Occupant sightings and abductions with legends of gods, fairies and other fanciful creatures of yore. This is accomplished by juxtaposing narratives drawn from folklore of the past with 20th century accounts of aliens and drawing ambiguous comparisons between the two phenomena. He also cites a number of 19th century reports of "airships" culled from unreliable contemporaneous newspaper articles. Vallee followed this up with his book *Messengers of Deception: UFO Contacts and Cults* in 1979, in which he claimed that UFOs were not extraterrestrial spacecraft but were illusions generated by covert human groups using either Hollywood special effects technology or an esoteric system of magic as part of a "control system" designed to manipulate and deceive society for their own obscure motives.

Vallee felt that there were too many sightings and landings than could be accounted for by alien expeditions to Earth from trillions of miles away. He also cited the UFOs ability to change shape and dematerialize as evidence against the extraterrestrial hypothesis, which he claimed was not strange enough to encompass the phenomenon. Vallee's theories would incorporate concepts culled from occult literature that would inspire mystical and transcendental thinking about the nature of the UFO conundrum. He was the template for "Lacombe," the French UFO investigator portrayed by François Truffaut in the popular movie *Close Encounters of the Third Kind* (1977).

It soon became evident that the study of abductions might provide the key to the UFO mystery, but the examination of this aspect of the phenomenon would require a different skill set than a mere statistical analysis of UFO flight characteristics, sighting locations, lighting and structural details, etc. New research paradigms would be required to investigate this novel avenue of inquiry, which would ultimately prove to be profoundly disturbing.

The individual who would initiate this paradigm shift was Budd Hopkins. An artist by profession, Hopkins initially became interested in UFOs in 1964, when he observed a disc-shaped craft along with two other witnesses while driving from Truro to Provincetown on Cape Cod. For years he continued to have a casual interest in UFOs until November 1975, when an acquaintance, local merchant George O'Barski, told him about his Occupant sighting in North Hudson Park (as related in Chapter One). Hopkins was so impressed that he wrote an article for the New York weekly newspaper *The Village Voice* that received a great deal of media coverage. As a result, Hopkins began receiving correspondence from people who had experienced contacts and abductions. His curiosity piqued, Hopkins began to study the phenomenon in earnest, and after investigating several compelling cases he authored his seminal study, *Missing Time: A Documented Study of UFO Abductions*, in 1981.

Working with psychotherapists Dr. Aphrodite Clamar and Dr.

Girard Franklin, who were professionally trained in the use of hypnosis, Hopkins explored the experiences of several abductees, who recovered their memories through the use of hypnotic regression. While the Lorenzens and APRO had done a comprehensive job of investigating and collating abduction reports, Hopkins took a more analytical approach that would reveal hitherto unknown features of the phenomenon.

One of the cases Hopkins explored in *Missing Time* was that of Steven Kilburn (a pseudonym for abductee Michael Bershad), who experienced a vehicular abduction while driving down a deserted stretch of Route 40 from Frederick, Maryland, to Baltimore one night in 1973. Bershad had no memory of having a close encounter, but had an irrational fear of a certain stretch of the highway. Under hypnosis Bershad revealed that he observed a pair of anomalous lights in the sky just before he lost control of his car, which was violently pulled onto the shoulder of the road by an outside force. While he stood beside his car in a paralyzed state, he was approached by a group of dwarfish humanoids with frail physiques, large black eyes and whitish-gray skin who placed a metal clamp-like device on his shoulder that further immobilized him.

Bershad was led up a ramp onto a landed saucer-shaped craft and down a passageway into a large, brightly-lit room, where his clothes were removed and he was placed on a table. An intricate machine descended from the ceiling that was used to probe the vertebrae on his back that produced reflex reactions in his nervous system. He also recalled that a heavy, cylindrical object was placed on his chest. The entities used mental telepathy to communicate with Bershad and to control his actions. During hypnotic recall he insisted that he was not supposed to remember the abduction and that he might even die if he remembered what had happened.[2]

An eerily similar account of an abduction would emerge years later that would also come to Hopkins' attention. In 1988 a sympathetic article by reporter Gary Smith appeared in the *Washington Post* detailing the experience of a D.C.-area attorney named Michael Shea. One night in 1973 or 1974 (Shea couldn't remember the exact date), he was driving down Route 40, the same highway where the Bershad abduction had taken place, from Baltimore to the small town of Olney to meet a friend about a summer job. While he was driving, he observed a UFO approaching his car and felt something like a mild current of electricity flowing down his back. The next thing he knew he was arriving at his destination only to find that it was two hours later than it should have been.

The incident haunted him for years until one day in 1985 when he was in a bookstore and happened upon a copy of *Missing Time*. Reading about the Bershad abduction he was overcome with anxiety and resolved to pierce the veil of amnesia and find out what had happened to him that night. He was eventually able to contact Hopkins and undergo hypnotic regression that revealed a close encounter with aliens that looked like "grasshoppers" wearing what looked like black, plastic armor. The entities placed him under mental control and led him onto a landed craft where they took samples from his body. Recalling the event would eventually aid Shea in integrating his unusual and terrifying experience into his normal life.[3]

Another abductee, who Hopkins refers to as "Virginia Horton" in *Missing Time*, underwent hypnotic regression to explore two enigmatic memories from her past. Her first experience took place in 1950, when she was six years old, on her grandfather's farm in Manitoba, Canada. She was abducted from the farmyard, although her memory of how she was taken into a craft was vague. Once onboard, she had a long conversation with an entity she described as being kindly and grandfatherly about space travel and the different varieties of earthly fauna. The alien insisted on taking a tissue sample, and after the abduction she found she had a bleeding wound on the back of her calf that left a permanent scar.

Her next encounter took place in 1960, when she was 16 and her family was on vacation in France. They had gone on a family picnic and Virginia wandered off into the woods where she recalled coming face to face with a beautiful deer that fascinated her. She had been gone for about an hour, and when she emerged from the forest, her blouse was covered in blood. Under hypnosis she recalled hearing a voice in her head calling her name that guided her to a landed craft. Once onboard, she met a friendly being she perceived as female, with whom she had a long discussion about various aspects of life on the alien's home world. The entity insisted on taking a blood sample, which was accomplished by inserting a small object inside one of her nostrils, a procedure that was responsible for the bloodstains on her blouse. The next thing she knew she was saying goodbye to the "deer," which was an illusion masking the appearance of her alien friend.

The Virginia Horton case revealed several hitherto unknown aspects of the abduction phenomenon. She was first abducted when she was six years old, one of the first cases of this type to be reported (the abduction of Pat Roach's four children was another). Then she was taken a second time at 16, which indicated that a person could be abducted several times during their lifetime. A tissue sample was reportedly collected, leaving a permanent scar, a procedure that would become a common feature of subsequent cases. Virginia's viewing of a beautiful deer was an illusion that her alien friend employed to mask its identity. This phenomenon would come to be referred to as "screen memory," a term borrowed from psychiatry that referred to a process whereby the mind superimposes a less threatening memory to overlay a traumatic event. Abductees report that the aliens frequently disguise themselves as nocturnal animals with prominent eyes such as owls, cats, raccoons, and in Virginia's case a deer. It is not known whether screen memories or perceptions are illusions generated by the being's mental powers, a perceptual overlay that conceals the alien's true appearance in the abductee's mind, or a mixture of both.

Another seminal aspect of her experience involved the object that was placed inside her nose that caused a nosebleed. Virginia claimed that this procedure was performed in order to obtain a sample of her blood, but other abductees have described having a small object the size of a BB inserted inside their nasal cavity. For instance, Betty Andreasson mentioned such an implantation, and a similar operation would later be noted in connection with the Allagash abductions. Abductees frequently describe waking up with nosebleeds that are thought to be a result of this procedure. These alleged implants are thought to be "tracking devices" similar to devices used by biologists to trace the movements of animals in the wild. Researchers speculate that the implants can be used to locate abductees, control their behavior or even eavesdrop on their thoughts.[4]

Missing Time also contained a picture section with illustrations of alien Grays drawn by Betty Andreasson, Travis Walton and Sergeant Moody, which exhibited remarkable similarities. There was also a representation of the beings seen by Michael Bershad painted by artist Ted Seth Jacobs, who would later design the iconic image of the Gray alien that would appear on the cover of Whitley Streiber's 1987 abduction account *Communion*.

Hopkins' next book was *Intruders: The Incredible Visitations at Copley Woods* (1987), which begins with Hopkins receiving a letter from an abductee who he refers to as "Kathie Davis," whose real name was Debbie Jordan. In July of 1983 Debbie had experienced an enigmatic event that had taken place at her home in a suburb of Indianapolis. She remembered having observed anomalous lights on the property one evening, and had experienced a period of missing time in connection with the incident. Debbie also included some photos of a circular area that appeared to have been subjected to intense heat, presumably from the landing of a UFO. Debbie also claimed that her sister "Laura Davis" (a pseudonym for Kathy Mitchell) had experienced an incident involving a UFO and an episode of amnesia in 1965 that suggested an abduction experience. Hopkins was intrigued by the letter and the photos and contacted Debbie, which would lead to a thorough examination of the alleged close encounters over the next three years.

Debbie traveled to New York to meet Hopkins in October 1983 and was hypnotized by Dr. Aphrodite Clamar, which led to the disclosure that she had experienced a number of abduction events going back to her childhood. She recalled having implants placed in her ear and in her nasal cavity, but the most stunning revelation came in a chapter entitled "the Presentation." During an abduction that reportedly took place in the first week of July 1983, Debbie was taken aboard a UFO where she was shown a hybrid girl that her abductors told her telepathically had been derived from her DNA and therefore was her daughter. She described the child as having the stature of a four-year-old girl, with pale skin, a high forehead, thin, wispy white hair, large blue eyes and facial features that she described as being like those of an elf or an angel. Debbie felt an intense rush of maternal emotion for the hybrid girl and was dismayed when the aliens told her that the child, whom she later named "Emily," had to remain with them because it could not survive in an earthly environment. The beings also insisted that she physically hold the child, a practice that would continue to be reported in many subsequent abduction accounts.

The Jordan abduction and other cases cited by Hopkins in *Intruders* pointed to a human/alien hybridization program as being the primary focus of the aliens' abduction program. "A central goal of UFO abductions," he states, "I now believe, is the apparent interbreeding of an alien species with our own. And that process, it would seem, is both covert and very widespread."[5] Further evidence of this breeding program emerged during his investigations that would prove to be controversial, namely "Wise Babies" and "missing fetus syndrome."

Several of the female abductees Hopkins worked with reported having dreams in which they were presented with what appeared to be human/alien hybrid babies. The abductees are often told that the babies are their offspring. These babies were always described as being pale and sickly, as if they had been born prematurely, but appeared to possess wisdom and knowledge well beyond their years. Debbie described one of these Wise Babies thus: "He looked like an old man," she related, "and he looked so wise. I looked in his eyes ... he was so smart ... more wise than anybody in the world."[6] The abductees were frequently manipulated or even coerced into holding the babies in order to nurture them.

This odd practice may actually have a basis in science. When skin to skin contact is made between humans a hormone called oxytocin is released. Called the "love hormone," it is produced in the hypothalamus and is known to have a positive impact on relaxation, trust and psychological well-being. Babies that are not held or cuddled can suffer from health or developmental problems. It may be that the act of holding the hybrid babies can provide a vital function that can only be provided by a human being to enable the ailing infant to survive. Although Hopkins makes no mention of the oxytocin connection, he does grasp the importance of touching during these baby presentations. He writes, "Unlikely though it may seem, it is possible that the very survival of these extraterrestrials depends upon their success in absorbing chemical and psychological properties received from abductees."[7]

Female abductees frequently report that their ova are harvested or that they become pregnant after a close encounter, but when they visit their OB/GYN they find they are no longer pregnant and there is no trace of the fetus. This alleged phenomenon, dubbed "missing embryo/fetus syndrome" (ME/FS) by researchers, is one of the most controversial features of the abduction experience. These women reported being between six and 12 weeks pregnant when the embryo or fetus mysteriously vanished, presumably due to intervention by the aliens. This procedure seems to make sense if the abductors are interested in harvesting egg cells (oocytes). By the fifth month of pregnancy the ovaries of a female fetus have about seven million oocytes, the most the organism will have during its entire lifetime. Over time, the number of egg cells gradually declines.

While ME/FS is widely reported by female abductees, it has become extremely difficult to document. During the 1990s, California physician Dr. Richard Neal studied these cases for three years and was unable to document a single verified instance of an alien intervention in an abductee's pregnancy. Dr. Neal acknowledged that many women were unwilling to release private information about their medical conditions to researchers, including lab, X-ray, ultrasound and pathology reports. He attributed these ME/FS cases to hysteria associated with the abduction experience, or to medical conditions that can mimic pregnancy. Dr. Neal died in 1995, and little further research on this aspect of the phenomenon has been undertaken since the early '90s.

Another aspect of abduction explored by Hopkins concerned members of the same family being taken. During his investigation of Debbie Jordan, Hopkins also explored a 1965 abduction experienced by her sister Kathy Mitchell, who would reveal her encounter with a six foot tall insectoid creature aboard a UFO. Kathy's son "Stevie" was also reportedly abducted. This series of events indicates that abductions manifest as an inter-family and an inter-generational process. Hopkins also noted that Debbie had experienced a series of abductions over the years, unlike the cases previously reported which were one-off events aimed at targets of opportunity. In 1995 Debbie and Kathy would author the book *Abducted: The Story of the Intruders Continues*, which would provide additional details about their unusual experiences.

By the time Hopkins wrote *Intruders,* he claimed he had investigated about 100 abduction cases and was conducting the hypnosis sessions himself rather than utilizing the services of psychiatrists trained in hypnotic regression. Critics have pointed out that Hopkins was not a trained therapist and may have misapplied these techniques, causing his subjects to fantasize and confabulate about their experiences and may have even harmed them in the process. Hopkins claimed that he acquired this "routine skill" from sitting through hundreds of hours of hypnosis sessions conducted by trained psychologists and psychiatrists. The controversies surrounding the use of hypnosis will be considered in more detail in a later chapter.

Budd Hopkins would attain the status of a minor celebrity, appearing on national television shows and attracting the attentions of the press. One of his alleged abductees, however, would rise to even greater prominence. Successful horror novelist Whitley Strieber, author of works such as *The Hunger* and *The Wolfen*, contacted Hopkins about a series of strange events he had experienced at his cabin in upstate New York in 1985. Strieber underwent a number of hypnosis sessions conducted by Dr. Donald Klein of Columbia Presbyterian Hospital, with Hopkins in attendance, to explore what he claimed were incidents of alien abduction. He would write about these revelations in his 1987 best-seller titled *Communion: A True Story*.

Under hypnosis, Strieber explored an enigmatic event that had occurred on the evening of December 26, 1985. He recalled experiencing an unusual feeling of dread before going to sleep that night, then waking up sometime later to observe a diminutive figure entering his bedroom. Strieber described the entity as wearing what appeared to be body armor and a metal hat or helmet. The creature rushed into the room toward him, causing him to lose consciousness and his next memory was of being transported through the woods to a room inside a landed craft. Paralyzed, he was taken to a circular chamber he described as being filthy and confining, with soiled clothing strewn about the floor. His abductors were described as short, stocky beings with blue-gray skin, wide faces, pug noses and deep-set glittering eyes. Also present was a five foot, slender being with black, slanted eyes that fits the general description of a Gray alien. Strieber perceived that this personage was feminine, although no secondary sex characteristics were evident.

The short gnome-like creatures, who seemed to be in charge of conducting the procedures, inserted a thin needle into Strieber's brain, which caused him to experience a brief flash-bang reaction inside his head. Then two of the beings spread his legs apart and inserted a gray, scaly, triangular object with a wire cage on its tip into his rectum. Its purpose was presumably to obtain a sample of his fecal matter, but Strieber felt like he was being raped. Another one of the creatures made an incision of the forefinger of his right hand, and his next recollection was awakening in his bed on the morning of the following day with only the memory of a barn owl staring at him through his bedroom window.

Strieber reportedly suffered from bouts of depression and physical exhaustion in the aftermath of his encounter. Returning to his New York apartment, he came across the name of Budd Hopkins while reading a book about UFOs and decided to contact him. Hopkins lived nearby, in the Greenwich Village neighborhood of lower Manhattan, and an initial consultation was arranged. On the basis of this meeting Hopkins arranged for a series of hypnotic sessions to recover his memories of the events that took place on December 26 and an earlier possible abduction that had taken place in October 1985. Strieber recalled that during the October event a small Gray had entered his bedroom and used a wand-like device to generate mental images of a nuclear conflagration in which he saw his son perish. Further hypnosis sessions revealed a number of abductions that had taken place when Strieber was a boy in San Antonio.

Abductions that take place over an individual's lifetime are widely reported, as are alien-induced visions of apocalyptic scenes, but otherwise details of Strieber's experiences are not typical abduction experiences. For instance, his description of the filthy interior of the UFO with dirty clothing strewn around has never been a feature of abduction reports, nor has the insertion of a needle in an abductee's brain. The squat, blue-gray, pug-nosed creatures, which Strieber identifies with "kobolds," subterranean gnomes that appear in Northern European mythology, are likewise atypical. He was reportedly comforted in the arms of his abductors, something that is unusual behavior for the usually cold, clinical aliens.

In spite of these apparent discrepancies, Strieber's account became a number one *New York Times* bestseller. The portrait of an alien being that graced the cover of *Communion*, painted by artist Ted Seth Jacobs, would serve as a visual catalyst that enabled other abductees to spontaneously recall their own missing time experiences. Strieber's polished prose incorporated equal portions of wonder and terror that wove a vivid narrative of alien visitation. On the other hand a fiction writer, who makes up stories for a living, is arguably the least reliable witness to document encounters with such an otherworldly phenomenon, especially if there's a profit to be made by exploiting the topic in a seemingly endless series of fiction and nonfiction books.

Being a horror novelist, Strieber imbues his experiences with a heavy dose of apprehension and terror. He writes, "Who had come to see me during the night? Did they really drop down from the sky, or have they come from some other cosmos, a place where dreams are real and reality a dream, where shadows and those who cast them are one in the same?"[8] Yet he also views abductions as a process of spiritual transformation in which the "Visitors" (as he refers to the aliens) are raising human consciousness to a higher level. He cites a number of sacred writings from various sources to bolster this notion derived from Hinduism, Buddhism, and the Bible, as well as mystics such as Meister Eckhart, G.I. Gurdijeff and P.D. Ouspensky. This mindset is reminiscent of that of the contactees, albeit much more intellectually sophisticated.

Both *Communion* and *Intruders* made the *New York Times* best-seller list, although *Communion* would prove to be the more popular title. These books would enhance the profile of the abduction phenomenon to new levels in the public mind, and for a while the alliance of Strieber and Hopkins would provide new vistas of respectability to an otherwise esoteric subject. Alas, their association would prove to be short-lived due to some erratic behavior on the part of Strieber. Without informing Hopkins, Strieber contacted Hopkins' publisher and attempted to delay the publication of *Intruders* so that it would not be in direct competition with *Communion*, which understandably caused a rift between the two men. Additionally, Hopkins would express the opinion that Strieber was mentally unstable and possibly even suicidal, making their further association problematical, although he would also insist that Strieber's abduction experiences were genuine. After his rift with Hopkins, Strieber retreated from the mainstream of UFO research but continued to be an influential figure in the field by authoring a number of follow-ups to *Communion* as well as several UFO-themed novels. He also established a website called *The Unknown Country* which served as a kind of clearinghouse for discussions of various paranormal phenomena.

David Jacobs, who was an associate professor of history at Temple University in Pennsylvania, also began an association with Hopkins. Jacobs had a fascination with UFOs and had written his Ph.D. thesis on the subject, which was published in book form as *The UFO Controversy in America* in 1975. He met Hopkins in 1982 and was impressed with his research, which inspired him to conduct his own inquiries into the abduction phenomenon. Learning techniques of hypnosis from Hopkins, he began to perform his own sessions with abductees, and by the early 1990s claimed to have had more than 325 regressions with over 60 abductees. The results of his research would be published in 1992 as *Secret Life: Firsthand Accounts of UFO Abductions.*

Jacobs presented a much more elaborate schematic of the abduction experience and explored novel aspects of the phenomenon that had not previously been touched upon. He formulated a three tiered pattern of activities performed by the abductors that included *Primary Experiences* such as the physical exam and reproductive procedures, *Secondary Experiences* that involved machine examinations, visualization and staging events, including Wise Baby presentations, and *Ancillary Procedures* that included induced sexual activities, pain experiments and other bizarre and enigmatic practices. He reported on a process he dubbed "Mindscan," in which a Tall Gray being will bring its eyes very close to the eyes of the abductee in order to facilitate an intense telepathic exchange. The alien compels the abductee to gaze deeply into its huge, black eyes, which causes the abductee to completely lose their will and be subjugated to the overwhelming consciousness of the being. Some abductees sense that the being is stealing their thoughts or memories; others find the procedure calming and develop a positive emotional bond with the alien. Another experience involves the abductee being ushered into a special room called the "Incubatorium" which contains as many as fifty to a hundred fetuses gestating inside containers filled with fluid and attached to a life support apparatus. Some female abductees report having a fetus removed and placed in an incubation tank during a medical procedure.

A new and controversial type of abduction experience was described in *Secret Life* that would come to be known as the "bedroom visitation." Prior to the revelations in the book, the majority of abductions reportedly occurred to individuals who were fully conscious, and the experience took place outside the home. Abductees were now reporting being awakened, taken from their bedrooms by the ufonauts, transported through the solid matter of walls and windows and floated up into a hovering craft. Skeptics would relate this type of experience to a fairly common sleep disorder known as sleep paralysis, a condition that takes place in a twilight zone between sleep and wakefulness, during which the sleeper may experience what they perceive as encounters with fantastical beings.

As provocative as this book was, Jacobs followed it up with *The Threat: The Secret Agenda: What the Aliens Really Want and How They Plan to Get It* (1998). In this work Jacobs explored the concept of the infiltration of human society by hybrid beings as part of an alien master plan to wrest hegemony of the planet from humankind and ultimately to supplant us. He cited abductee reports of these human-like beings interacting with people in everyday settings in which they are being trained by abductees to live among us in secret. The hybrids are reportedly able to employ their superior mental powers to manipulate abductees and "brainwash" them into becoming willing participants in the aliens' designs. He documents abductee observations about the hybrid's lack of compassion for their human subordinates that inclines toward cruelty and sadistic psychosexual behavior.

The scenario outlined in *The Threat* is profoundly disturbing, even more so than Strieber's dark ramblings, as the aliens are supposedly orchestrating the end of human-centric society, which is to be replaced by a world dominated by the aliens and their hybrid progeny. The alien presence on our world is depicted as a covert invasion which has been going on for decades and may take further decades to come to fruition. He cites a number of cases in which these hybrids are already interacting with abductees in the human world and are able to walk among us unnoticed. According to Jacobs, abductees speak of an event they refer to as "the Change," a future in which the aliens will reveal their presence on Earth that will be a time of tribulation and upheaval when life as we know it will cease to exist. This scenario is a far cry from the science fiction concept of "contact," in which humankind and the aliens will meet on more or less equal terms.

Like Hopkins, Jacobs has been criticized for employing hypnotic regression techniques without being a trained therapist or psychiatrist. Skeptics have also pointed out that Jacobs claims to be able to distinguish fact from fantasy in his analysis of his abductee's narratives, which critics believe constitutes highly subjective reasoning.

The most prominent abduction researcher, however, was Dr. John Mack, a Harvard professor, physician, psychiatrist and Pulitzer Prize winner for his biography of T.E. Lawrence (a.k.a. Lawrence of Arabia) entitled *A Prince of Our Disorder*. Mack heard about the work Hopkins was doing with abductees and met with him during a trip to New York on January 10, 1990. Impressed with Hopkins and his examination of the phenomenon, Hopkins suggested that he refer cases in the Boston area to Mack, and he agreed. In the spring of 1990 Mack began to conduct interviews and hypnosis sessions with abductees in his home and hospital offices, and after three and a half years, he had referred and treated over a hundred individuals who claimed to have been abducted or had other anomalous experiences and had formulated a therapeutic approach to the treatment of these witnesses. The result of his investigations was published in book form as *Abduction: Human Encounters with Aliens* in 1994.

His book analyzes the experiences of 13 abductees that he obtained using hypnosis. Unlike other investigators, however, Mack stressed that his primary responsibility was toward the emotional health and well-being of the abductee rather than to establish the reality of their experience. His therapeutic approach was to consider himself and his patient as "co-investigators" who would explore the abductee's trauma together. Unfortunately, this method would lead to much apparent confabulation and fantasy on the part of his hypnotic subjects.

Mack brought a distinctly New Age sensibility to his study of the phenomenon which would be reflected in the narratives he obtained from his group of abductees. One of them would claim he could "sense the earth" and talk to nature spirits; another viewed abductions as having something to do with Tibetan Buddhism. An individual claimed they were shown a vision of a past life in ancient Egypt, while another embraced Native American spiritual traditions as being tied in with their abductions. Others reported having out of body episodes while being abducted. One abductee even claimed that he had impregnated a woman by breathing into her uterus during one of these out of body sojourns.

This interpretation of abductions as transformational and spiritual phenomena would draw the ire not only of skeptics, but of his fellow researchers as well, who embraced a "nuts and bolts" viewpoint about the alien presence. Mack felt that his exploration of abductions would also lead to his own spiritual enlightenment as part of a planetary evolution of human consciousness. His "co-creative" approach to the study of the phenomenon was criticized because it supposedly imposed his own belief system on the abductees he analyzed. Some felt that his most egregious heresy was the inclusion of "past life" narratives into the fabric of these abduction narratives. These tales of hypnotically retrieved reincarnation experiences had been a fad since the 1950s and had been debunked as pseudoscience for decades. Past lives and other fantastical notions expressed by his patients would indicate that Mack had abandoned the scientific method in favor of a philosophical approach that emphasized mystical and non-rational ways of knowing.

Due to his investigation of the abduction phenomenon, Mack was subjected to a review regarding the clinical care of the abductees he was treating by a Harvard Medical School review board in 1994. This was the first time that a tenured Harvard professor had ever been subjected to such a review process, and Mack stood to not only lose his tenure but his license to practice medicine as well. The investigation lasted 14 months and resulted in Mack's receiving a censure from the board, but he remained a member in good standing with the Harvard faculty. This investigation illustrates the utter intolerance and contempt that the academic establishment holds for the study of UFOs and abductions.

In 1999 Mack published his second book on the subject, *Passport to the Cosmos: Human Transformation and Alien Encounters* in which he attempted to link abductions to the practice of shamanism in various world cultures. By this time he had been studying the phenomenon for ten years and had interviewed another hundred abductees. Shamanism is an ancient spiritual tradition in non–Western cultures in which selected individuals (shamans) seek wisdom, knowledge and supernatural power by employing techniques such as fasting, drumming and the ingestion of psychedelic plants to achieve a visionary state. Mack perceived a confluence between shamanic journeys to spirit realms and the abduction experience, and sought out spiritual practitioners from diverse non–Western cultures to corroborate a link between the two otherworldly phenomena. In their insistence that abductions represented a positive spiritual transformation that would affect all of humankind, Mack and Whitley Strieber were more or less on the same page.

The late 1980s and early 1990s were a heady time for abduction research and depictions of the phenomenon in popular culture. Strieber's *Communion* was released as a feature film in 1989, *Intruders* became a 1992 two part CBS-TV miniseries and a film based on Travis Walton's biographical account of his abduction, *The Walton Experience*, was filmed in 1993 as *Fire in the Sky*. On television, the popular science fiction TV series *The X-Files*, which would run for 11 non-consecutive seasons from 1993 to 2002, had a story arc that revolved around the phenomenon. The most prestigious event, however, was the 1992 Abduction Study Conference held at the Massachusetts Institute of Technology (M.I.T.) in Cambridge, although it was not conducted under the official auspices of the Institute.

The five-day conference was organized by co-chairs Dr. John Mack and M.I.T. physicist David E. Pritchard. The conference assembled a group of scientists, academics, researchers and abductees in an effort to unravel the mysteries of the phenomenon. In addition to John Mack, David Jacobs and Budd Hopkins, a number of prominent researchers would present papers and provide their insights, including John Carpenter, Eddie Bullard, Jenny Randles, Dr. John M. Miller, Richard Haines, Joe Nyman, Don Donderi, Richard Boylan and others. A detailed account of the conference was written up by journalist C.D.B. Bryan and published in 1995 as *Close Encounters of the Fourth Kind: Alien Abduction, UFOs and the Conference at M.I.T.* A series of lively debates on various aspects of the phenomenon were conducted at the conference, along with panel discussions during which a number of abductees offered firsthand accounts of their experiences.

Arguably the most influential presentation at the conference was folklorist David Hufford's paper entitled "Sleep Paralysis and Bedroom Abductions." Hufford had authored the seminal study of this little understood phenomenon, *The Terror That Comes in the Night* in 1982, which examined folklore regarding the perception of nocturnal visitations by entities that assail sleepers while they are in a state between dreaming and full wakefulness and experience a feeling of being paralyzed. The sleeper typically perceives that a shadowy, usually malevolent being enters the bedroom and crawls into the bed, causing sensations of suffocation in the subject. Vivid psychopompic hallucinations can also occur while the sleeper is in this paralyzed state. Sleep paralysis is a fairly common sleep disorder, and in the wake of Hufford's revelations skeptics would use sleep paralysis and its attendant psychopompic hallucinations as a handy explanation for all abduction experiences.

This phenomenon would also affect the results of a poll formulated by Hopkins and Jacobs that was designed to estimate the number of abductees among the general population. The survey was conducted by the Roper Organization, who polled nearly 6,000 adults using 11 questions designed to ascertain if they had experienced an abduction. The question that received the most positive responses was "Waking up paralyzed with a sense of a strange person or presence or something in your room," to which 18 percent of respondents answered in the affirmative. This was extrapolated to indicate that 34.2 million people in the United States had experienced an abduction, but these results could just as well be attributed to an incident of sleep paralysis and therefore this question in all probability compromised the accuracy of the poll results.

The M.I.T. conference would prove to be the high water mark for the scientific study of the abduction phenomenon. Never again would such a prestigious assemblage of scientists, researchers and experiencers be convened to analyze this enigmatic phenomenon. Revelations about the relationship between abductions and sleep paralysis would provide a ready explanation of the phenomenon for skeptics. In addition, a new UFO mythos that focused on the alleged crash/retrieval of a craft and alien bodies at Roswell, New Mexico, was evolving that would engage the public imagination more intensely.

The book *The Roswell Incident* by William Moore and Charles Berlitz, which had appeared as early as 1980, recounted the story of the recovery of a crashed saucer and its dead crewmembers in the New Mexico desert in 1947 and the cover-up of the event by the U.S. government that followed. *The UFO Crash at Roswell* by Kevin Randle and Donald Schmitt was published in 1991 and inspired the 1994 Showtime television network feature-length telefilm entitled *Roswell: The UFO Cover-Up* that dramatized the events in the book and proved to be highly successful. Former Army intelligence officer Colonel William Corso authored *The Day after Roswell* in 1997, which claimed that Corso was in charge of a secret Pentagon program to reverse engineer alien technology salvaged from the crash.

The alien beings allegedly retrieved from the Roswell wreckage resembled the Grays familiar from abduction accounts in most respects. The UFO crash/retrieval narrative shifted focus away from the frightening stories about enigmatic aliens abducting people in the dead of night to a much less threatening and more appealing narrative about government conspiracies and cover-ups, along with the acquisition of alien technology. In this sense, the crash/retrieval tales offered a reassuring mythos to counteract the fears and anxieties that were part and parcel of the majority of abduction accounts.

During the M.I.T. conference, Budd Hopkins had given a presentation entitled "A Double Witnessed Abduction" that he later expanded into his 1996 book *Witnessed: The True Story of the Brooklyn Bridge UFO Abductions*. The book put forth an incredible story about a New

York City housewife named Linda Cortile (whose real name is Linda Napolitano), who was allegedly abducted from the 12th floor of a hi-rise building in lower Manhattan at 3 a.m. on November 30, 1989. Ms. Cortile was reportedly floated out of her apartment window, along with three Gray alien escorts, and beamed up into a hovering UFO in a column of light. In February of 1991 Hopkins received a letter from "Police Officers Dan and Richard," two individuals who claimed to have independently witnessed the abduction while they were on duty guarding the then–Secretary General of the United Nations, Javier Perez de Cuellar, while parked in a limo on the FDR Drive. They reported that once Linda and the aliens had entered the craft, it submerged itself in the East River in the vicinity of the Brooklyn Bridge. During the ensuing months Hopkins would receive a series of follow-up letters and audio tapes from Richard and Dan that provided further details about the event and their subsequent kidnapping of Linda, with whom they had become obsessed.

Hopkins promoted the Napolitano case as the most important event in the history of abduction research, but under closer scrutiny, the case began to fall apart. Several alleged independent witnesses to the abduction either recanted or made themselves unavailable for further comment. Hopkins would never actually meet Richard and Dan, and there was no way to even verify their existence. When confronted by Hopkins and news reporters, Pérez de Cuellar firmly denied having any knowledge concerning the incident. Elements of the tale strained credulity, such as a dramatic abduction taking place in plain sight in lower Manhattan that was supposedly seen by only a handful of witnesses. Oddly, neither Ms. Napolitano nor her husband saw fit to report that Linda had been kidnapped to the police.

The *Witnessed* abduction was touted by Hopkins as being the case of the century, but it wound up being vigorously debunked by UFO proponents and skeptics alike, causing Hopkins to lose some of his credibility as an investigator. A number of indicators suggest that the case may have been a hoax, although if so, it's unlikely that it was perpetrated by Hopkins himself. He may even have been the victim of a plot orchestrated by government intelligence agents "Dan" and "Richard" in an attempt to discredit him. A precedent for this scenario took place in 1987, when researchers William Moore and Jaime Shandera were anonymously sent a series of documents that supposedly related the formation of a group of government officials and scientists, referred to as MJ-12, who were tasked with investigating a crashed saucer and its occupants in Roswell, New Mexico, in 1947. After much scrutiny the "MJ-12 papers" were deemed to be a hoax perpetrated by unknown government entities in an apparent attempt to spoof the UFO community.

In any event, Hopkins did not write another book until 2003, when *Sight Unseen: Science, UFO Invisibility and Transgenic Beings*, co-authored with his wife, Carol Rainey, was published. In the chapters written by Ms. Rainey, the book explored 21st century scientific developments in the fields of invisibility, genetic engineering and quantum theory in relation to reported alien technological abilities. In his chapters, Hopkins expanded on ideas initially posed by his colleague David Jacobs regarding alien hybrids infiltrating our world. "Do these people live here among us, renting rooms and apartments, holding down jobs, driving cars, eating in restaurants and having romantic and even sexual relationships with unwary human beings?" he asked, rhetorically.[9]

Sight Unseen contains a number of unnerving narratives about these hybrids, or "transgenic" beings interacting with abductees in our everyday world. They are depicted performing all manner of quotidian tasks, but perhaps their most disturbing activities involve the conducting of bogus job interviews with unsuspecting applicants that are usually a prelude to abduction events. The abductees describe providing information to the hybrids about ordinary procedures such as operating office machines and protocols for interacting with fellow workers. In some ways these stories of this subtle infiltration of human society are more discomfiting than the notion of aliens abducting people in lonely places and flying back to wherever it is they come from.

Abduction research suffered an enormous setback in 2004 when Dr. John Mack was killed in a traffic accident while visiting London and Budd Hopkins died a few years later in 2010. The deaths of these two luminaries deprived the field of two of its most distinguished advocates. As the new millennium progressed, the notion of alien abductions became mostly passé in popular culture and was largely relegated to the realms of adult cartoon shows, television commercials and low-budget horror films.

Then in 2015 David Jacobs authored what was arguably the most disturbing book about the phenomenon, entitled *Walking Among Us: The Alien Plan to Control Humanity*. Expanding on the work of

Hopkins in *Sight Unseen*, and his previous book *The Threat*, Jacobs presented a chilling scenario in which hybrids are secretly integrating themselves into human society as part of the aliens' master plan to wrest hegemony of the planet from us. Toward this end they must be instructed in the complexities of living in human society, and Jacobs cites numerous instances of abductees cooperating with the aliens and instructing the human-like hybrids about the myriad intricacies of day to day life so that they can live among us in secret.

Jacobs delineates a typology of five basic alien types: Short Grays, Tall Grays, Hybrids, Reptilians and Insectoids along with their place within the aliens' hierarchy and the specific roles they perform within the program. He asserts that the UFOs reported by abductees are facilities that are purpose-built to conduct their reproductive and mind-altering procedures on their human subjects. Speculation is offered regarding the ultimate fate of humanity after the aliens implement their plans to acquire dominion over us after The Change. Jacobs hopes that if he can raise awareness of this profoundly disturbing and frightening scenario, some means may be devised to counter the aliens' program to subjugate humankind.

Are these dire predictions an accurate depiction of the alien presence on Earth, or are they tinged by the paranoid mindset of individual researchers and abductees? Or is it possible that these beings have more noble motives and are here to offer their assistance in solving the problems such as war and environmental devastation and usher in a new utopian age of spiritual enlightenment? There are proponents that argue on behalf of both possibilities.

CHAPTER FOUR

The Alien Intent

What are the aliens and where do they come from? What is the nature of their intentions toward humanity? There are basically two opposing viewpoints regarding these questions. Sometimes referred to as the "East Coast" versus the "West Coast" perspectives, they can also be called the "Positivist" and (for want of a better term) "Realist" interpretations of the alien presence and their motivations.

The most prominent advocate of the Positivist belief system was the late Dr. John Mack, who embraced a New Age spiritual perspective regarding the abduction phenomenon. According to Mack, the aliens had come to Earth on a mission to transform our consciousness in order to free humankind from its destructive ways and save us from the consequences of our world-destroying weaponry, overpopulation and the ecological collapse of the planet. For Mack, the alien presence constitutes a "passport to the cosmos," an influence that will enable us to transcend reality and expand our consciousness to a new level of spirituality. In this scenario, the hybridization program is designed to aid us in this transformation of the human spirit. The Positivists assert that the aliens are benign beings hailing from an advanced civilization who have humanity's best interests in mind.

Mack and other Positive researchers tend to downplay the negative aspects of the abduction experience such as gynecological and reproductive procedures, painful mental and physical probes and forced sexual episodes. The unsavory aspects of abductions are chalked up to media influence and researcher bias. Additionally, Mack embraced the quasi-mystical concept of "past lives" in connection with abductions. He writes, "Past life experiences provide abductees ... with a different perspective about time and the nature of human identity. Cycles of birth and death over long stretches of time can thus be relived, providing a different, less ego derived sense of the continuity of life and the smallness of an individual lifetime from a cosmic perspective."[1] The notion of hypnosis as a means to retrieve memories of past lives was a popular fad during the 1950s, typified by the 1956 nonfiction book *The Search for Bridey Murphy*, in which a Pueblo, Colorado, housewife named Virginia Tighe was placed in a trance by an amateur hypnotist and allegedly regressed back to a previous life as a 19th century Irishwoman named Bridey Murphy. The book caused a popular sensation and provided the basis for a Hollywood film, but when the story was subjected to scrutiny, numerous inconsistencies became evident, leading to the conclusion that Ms. Tighe confabulated her narrative from memories derived from an Irish neighbor of her acquaintance.

Author and self-proclaimed abductee Whitley Strieber also embraces a transcendental view of the phenomenon. In his 1988 follow-up to *Communion*, entitled *Transformation*, Strieber claimed to have had an out of body experience, which led him to speculate that the Visitors (as he refers to the aliens) were involved in a process of "recycling souls" during abductions. He further stated that the abductors can manipulate the soul and, "even draw it out of the body, with technology that may possibly involve the use of high-intensity magnetic fields."[2] In his later writings he would suggest that the Visitors had the ability to recycle souls into the bodies of newborns. He likens the abduction experience to the religious visions of historical seers such as Christ, Mohammad and Buddha. "I feel that it is up to each one of us to seek our own contact," he writes in *Transformation*, "develop it if it occurs, and to challenge ourselves to use it for intellectual, emotional, and spiritual growth instead of letting our fears overwhelm us."[3] Strieber, like Mack, views the abduction experience as a vehicle for personal spiritual enlightenment while decrying the negative views of the phenomenon espoused by Hopkins and Jacobs.

The most impressive proponent of the Positivist viewpoint is arguably John Hunter Gray, a sociology professor of Native American Studies at the University of North Dakota and winner of the Martin Luther King Award for his work in the field of civil rights. On March 20 of 1988, Hunter Gray and his adult son John III were traveling down Route 61 to an out of state speaking engagement when they experienced two periods of missing time amnesia, but consciously remembered having a UFO sighting.

About three months later Hunter Gray spontaneously recalled an abduction event experienced by him and his son on March 21. Their car had been diverted onto a dirt road, and as they exited their vehicle they were greeted by a human-like hybrid being and a group of Grays, who escorted them onto the craft. Once onboard they were immobilized and examined in the usual fashion. Hunter Gray described having implants placed in one of his nostrils, in the side of his neck and at the top of his chest. In the aftermath of the abduction, he reported an overall improvement in his general health. A scar on his body disappeared, wrinkles and blemishes vanished, his hair and fingernails grew faster and thicker, his circulation improved and he was able to quit smoking. He also attributes having surviving bouts of Systemic Lupus (SLE), a fatal, incurable disease, to the ministrations of the ufonauts.

Hunter Gray described his dealings with the UFO beings as being a cordial, life-affirming experience, and subsequently recollected several abductions occurring both before and after the 1988 event. He speculated that alien society resembled that of tribal cultures he was familiar with, in which the needs of individuals and the group are balanced harmoniously. In his view the beings are benign and are in the process of sensitizing humanity to the reality of their presence with the goal of eventual benevolent contact. Hunter Gray would go on to teach classes about extraterrestrial phenomena at the University of North Dakota. He died in 2019 at the age of 84 years.

Positive emotions experienced by abductees may be at least partially attributable to the aliens' psychological and psychic mind manipulation procedures. Abductees are nearly always forced to watch disturbing images of global catastrophes such as thermonuclear war, ecological disaster or other apocalyptic events. The aliens then intimate that the abductees must cooperate with them in order to forestall these cataclysms and rescue humanity from its worst destructive instincts. Abductees are told that they are special individuals who have been selected to assist the aliens in ushering in a new utopian age of cooperation between the races. Some are even led to believe that they themselves have a double human/alien identity, a belief system referred to by the term "dual referencing."

In many ways the Positivist paradigm harks back to the Contactee movement of the 1950s. Their view is that the aliens are spiritually advanced beings who are the benefactors of humankind. Like the Space Brothers of old, they have come to our world to rescue us from the problems we have created for ourselves due to our ignorance and hatred. One feature from the Contactee movement that has resurfaced is the practice of "channeling," in which aliens allegedly deliver messages verbally through an abductee who has entered a trance state. The entranced person, who is supposedly in direct communication with an alien mind, answers questions and imparts wisdom derived from this otherworldly source. This process bears a striking resemblance to practices associated with Spiritualism, a quasi-religion that originated in the 19th century, in which psychic "mediums" conducted séances during which they were thought to communicate with the dead or other entities. During the early 20th century, stage magician Harry Houdini was instrumental in exposing the fakery perpetrated by these bogus mediums. The foremost proponent of channeling in the UFO community is researcher Leo Sprinkle, a psychologist from the University of Wyoming, who claims to be a Contactee.

As to the abductees who claim to have positive experiences with the aliens, these are individuals who may have been led to participate in the abductor's program of planetary transformation via the aliens' mental conditioning procedures, which can involve direct neural engagement using mental telepathy. Alternately, the abductees may be attempting to cope with the physical and psychological stresses they have undergone by grafting a comforting New Age belief system onto their often terrifying ordeals. They have adopted alternative, less threatening terms to define their experiences; they refer to their abductors as "visitors" (a term popularized by Whitley Strieber) and call themselves "experiencers" rather than abductees.

Regarding accounts of healings associated with abductions, David Jacobs has written, "In extremely rare cases, the aliens will undertake a cure of some ailment troubling the abductee. This is not in any way related to the contactee/Space Brother concepts of benevolent aliens coming to Earth to cure cancer. Rather, in special circumstances, it appears that the aliens feel obliged to preserve the specimen for their own purposes. As one abductee said, 'It's equipment maintenance.'"[4] Budd Hopkins adds that "[i]t's kind of a sad thing because I have some abductees who have serious medical problems who wish they were being healed themselves, but are not."[5]

Some examples of abductees being healed in connection with their experiences include Pat Roach's daughter Debbie, who was reportedly healed of a serious childhood sickness during the family's abduction in October 1973. A well-known British case involved rural UK policeman Alan Godfrey, who had sustained an injury that rendered him infertile, but whose condition was reversed after being abducted in November 1980. Jacobs cites a 1962 incident in which six-year-old Alice Haggerty was cured of a life-threatening bout of diphtheria after being abducted. He also reports that two abductees were cured of severe cases of pneumonia by the abductors. Abductee Sgt. Charles Moody claimed that he was healed of injuries sustained during his capture in August 1975 by aliens who passed a rod-like device over the afflicted areas of his body.

Despite the aliens' attempts to condition abductees using neural engagement to make them cooperate with their program, seemingly miraculous cures of their physical afflictions and their exposure to feel-good notions derived from popular culture such as first contact between civilizations, many abductees remain deeply traumatized by their experiences. Many suffer from psychological problems such as post-traumatic stress disorder, phobias, hypervigilance and chronic insomnia. Commenting on a case in which a woman who had been abducted suffered a life-altering mental breakdown in the aftermath, Budd Hopkins remarks that "[c]ases like this—and this is only an extreme version of hundreds of other similar cases I have explored—leave me with barely concealed fury at those who would paint the aliens as benign saviors here to help us by spreading higher truth and demonstrating 'unconditional love.'"[6] By examining various facets of the phenomenon as documented by Hopkins and Jacobs, a more accurate paradigm of the alien intent than that promulgated by the Positives can be evaluated.

To begin with, the aliens consistently operate in secrecy, in lonely places under the cover of darkness or when the abductee is alone. Control of their human subjects is a universal constant during these events, which often begin with the mentally-induced travel urge that serves as a means to lure the abductee to the deserted locale where the abduction is to take place. Once the capture is underway the subject is placed in a paralyzed state and forced to undergo humiliating, painful and often terrifying medical, sexual and psychological procedures. Afterward, the abductee is induced to suffer amnesia about the entire experience or have their recollection distorted by mirage-like "screen memories."

Instead of being exploratory spaceships used as transportation for alien tourists or scientists, the craft seem to be purpose-built for the task of conducting the physical examinations of humans. These ships come pre-equipped with examination tables and various apparatuses that are utilized to perform these procedures. Although the comparison is flawed, the closest earthly analog would be hospital ships like the *Hope*, mobile facilities that are furnished with laboratories, operating rooms and other medical equipment. The alien craft are described as being strictly functional, having no wasted space, no adornments or recreational areas. Everything about them suggests they are an integral part of a highly efficient industrial process.

One enduring puzzle regarding the study of the phenomenon concerns the nature of the "medical" procedures that are performed during nearly every abduction. It has become evident through research that, unlike terrestrial medicine, these practices are not related to the health and well-being of the abductees. At the M.I.T. conference Dr. John G. Miller, an emergency room physician, noted that "[t]he alien physical exam seems to consistently focus on certain systems and omit or skimp on other systems.... The cardiac and pulmonary exam, a mainstay of human physical examinations and an item of great concern to the human patient and physician, seems absent or at least not clearly definable in most reports."[7] Furthermore, they also appear to have no interest in human respiratory and lymphomatic systems, or vital internal organs such as the liver, spleen, stomach and pancreas. These omissions would indicate that the aliens have no concerns about the primary life sustaining systems of the human body and that their procedures are not intended to be therapeutic.

Instead, the abductors concentrate on taking samples of skin, hair and fingernails, which might indicate they are studying levels of pollution in the Earth's environment, which can be measured by analyzing these biological samples. They also exhibit interest in the brain and the human neurological system, perhaps as a means to explore the manipulation of the mind and our consciousness. Their primary interest is the reproductive system; many abductees report having sperm and ova samples extracted as part of the hybridization program. Another procedure involves the insertion of small implants in the nose, ears and various parts of the body. These are thought to be tracking devices designed to locate abductees. Samples of skin tissue similar to biopsy "punch marks" are also collected. Female abductees report having embryos implanted and the fetuses removed once they are developed.

These practices indicate that the abductors are not practicing medicine, which is defined as the science of dealing with the maintenance of health and the prevention and treatment of disease. Instead, despite a few cases featuring seemingly miraculous cures, the aliens are using human bodies for their own purposes. Skin, hair and fingernail samples can be used to measure pollution levels in the Earth's environment on the planet they one day hope to co-inhabit. Collected skin cells might also be utilized to create what are called induced pluripotent stem cells (iPSCs) that could be used in a process called cellular reprogramming to regenerate various tissues in the body by differentiating into many different cell types in a manner similar to embryonic stem cells. These pluripotent cells may have some utility as part of the hybrid breeding program.

It seems evident that instead of using their high technology to improve the health and well-being of their human subjects, the aliens are instead extracting information about our environment from our bodies and harvesting sperm, ova, fetuses, tissue samples and possibly iPSCs from the abductees. These processes are similar to the extraction of useful biological substances from lower species as practiced in earthly laboratories. For instance, the blue blood of a primitive crustacean called the horseshoe crab has a unique protein that is used by drug companies and medical device manufacturers to test for toxins and harmful bacteria in their products. The crabs are bled of about 30 percent of their blood in labs before returning them to the ocean, although a significant number of the creatures do not survive the bleeding process. Humans have no qualms about this vampire-like exploitation of another species.

And if the abductors occasionally perform miraculous feats of healing, they are also capable of behavior that appears to be clinically detached at best and sadistic at worst. Consider the ordeal of the three ladies abducted in Liberty, Kentucky, who were subjected to painful and terrifying psychological procedures that are indistinguishable from torture. Swedish abductee Harald Andersson was forced to endure a frightening experience during which he fought against entities who forcefully placed a device against his temple that burned him and left a wound on his head. Abductees are routinely forced to undergo disturbing and humiliating psychosexual experiences at the hands of their captors, including forcible sexual intercourse with other humans. These activities, among others, are hardly indicative of the actions of beneficent entities who wish to aid humankind.

The origin and nature of the abductors is a hotly debated topic among researchers. The most popular and arguably the most plausible theory is referred to as the "Extraterrestrial Hypothesis," (abbreviated as the ETH), which posits that the ufonauts hail from an advanced civilization in another star system. Astronomers have pointed out that there are possibly millions of habitable worlds in our galaxy alone, and that intelligent life must surely have arisen on some of them. On the other hand, the distances between stars is, as pop scientist Carl Sagan was wont to point out, *extremely* far, a factor that might preclude the notion of interstellar travel. Additionally, the nearby stars in our immediate stellar neighborhood are relatively dim red dwarfs or multiple star systems that are not considered viable candidates for the development of life, intelligent or otherwise.

That having been said, it is within the realm of possibility that a civilization hundreds or even thousands of years older than our own could devise a means of traveling to Earth from another star system. Science fiction offers a number of exotic modes of transportation that might enable interstellar travel, including traversing space/time via "worm holes," "black holes," "warp drives" or even instantaneous conveyance anywhere in the Universe by means of "folding space." Skeptics, however, cite the vast distances between the stars as "proof" that extraterrestrial visitation from other worlds is impossible.

These objections are countered by the testimony of abductees concerning the aliens' point of origin. David Jacobs points out that when abductees ask the ufonauts where they are from, they indicate that they come from outer space. The best-known example is the "star map" displayed to Betty Hill by her abductors that presented a matrix of stars being visited by the aliens from their home world, which is thought to be in the constellation of Reticulum, about 40 light years from Earth. Other abductees have also been told that their abductors come from other planets. Others report that they are transported into outer space in a UFO. In the Buff Ledge encounter the abductees described being taken aboard a craft that docked with a much larger vessel parked in near-Earth space. Similarly, in his book *Devil's Den: The Reckoning,* abductee Terry Lovelace revealed details about his trip in a saucer shaped craft that rendezvoused with a city-sized "mothership" in orbit around the Moon, from which he was able to observe breathtaking views of outer space.

Other researchers, however, consider the ETH too simplistic an explanation for the aliens' origin. Jacques Vallee put forth the theory that the ufonauts originated from a parallel dimension in the space/time continuum, citing reports of UFOs that appeared to materialize, dematerialize and change shape. A case in point is provided by a series of Polaroid photos taken by highway worker Rex Heflin in 1965 that appear to show a hat-shaped UFO vanishing in a puff of smoke. The existence of these parallel realms, however, is highly speculative, and there is no actual evidence of them, yet the ability of these craft to appear and disappear in this manner remains unexplained, but may be an aspect of the aliens' high technology.

Another theory speculates that the aliens are time travelers from our future. This theory would explain how the ufonauts are able to breathe Earth's atmosphere and tolerate our environment without using protective gear. The macrocephalic appearance of the aliens comports with the notion of how humans might evolve with larger brains and frail bodies, which is a well-worn science fiction trope going back to the work of 19th century writer H.G. Wells. However, a number of UFO and abduction cases feature mysterious time anomalies. For instance, Betty and Barney Hill found that both their watches had inexplicably stopped after their abduction experience. One of the best documented cases involved Minnesota Deputy Sheriff Val Johnson, who had a close encounter late one night in 1979 with a glowing UFO that damaged his police cruiser. Johnson's mechanical wristwatch and the car's electric dashboard clock were both found to be inexplicably running exactly 14 minutes slow after the incident. Abductee Pat Roach reported that her abductors "limited time," but offered no explanation for this enigmatic phrase.

British researcher Jenny Randles theorizes that UFOs are actually "timeships" from our future rather than spaceships from other worlds. She documents the case of "Renard," a French naval technician who was driving near the city of Toulon in 1971 when he came upon a glowing object that levitated his car off the roadway and then placed it back down. While no missing time amnesia was experienced, when Renard arrived home he found he had unaccountably jumped three hours forward in time.[8] David Jacobs relates an even more bizarre incident that took place on an evening in October 1986 involving abductee "Allison Reed" and her husband "Jerry," who experienced a time anomaly lasting five days from Sunday to the following Friday after watching an anomalous light in the sky that approached their Florida apartment. During the five day period that had elapsed, neither of them had gone to the bathroom, and their baby's diaper was dry and unsoiled. They were not hungry or thirsty, none of the food in the house had been eaten, and everything was the same as it had been on Sunday evening.[9]

Some researchers speculate that abduction narratives originate in humankind's collective unconscious, which is able to materialize UFOs and aliens as a projection of mass thought. This manifestation of psychic "thought forms" has been referred to as "Supermind," a complex intelligence that exists as a projection of humanity's collective unconscious independent from individual human minds. According to this theory, the Supermind is able to convert mass thought patterns into material reality to produce UFO sightings and alien abductions. This theory is highly speculative and derives its basic concepts from science fiction. In the movie *Forbidden Planet* (1956), for instance, an alien machine, the product of an extinct race, is able to convert human thoughts and desires into material reality. Similarly, in *Five Million Years to Earth* (1968), a derelict Martian spaceship is accidentally reactivated and produces projections of psychic force that materialize a gigantic Martian apparition.

Perhaps the most bizarre theory regarding abductions involves the psychedelic substance Dimethyltryptamine (DMT). Sometimes called the "spirit molecule," DMT is a potent hallucinogen that is a component of the visionary drink ayahuasca and psychedelic snuffs used by South American shamans in their rituals. A DMT analog is also present in the venom of the Sonoran Desert Toad, which was used by the ancient Maya cultures in Pre-Colombian times. In its pure form, DMT may be administered in a laboratory setting via inhalation or intravenously. It also exists in trace amounts within the human body and is thought to be produced by the pineal gland.

DMT produces powerful visionary experiences that sometimes involve reported contacts with diminutive beings that have been described as "machine elves," which proponents of this theory equate with alien abductors. They speculate that, perhaps due to some environmental stimulus, the body begins producing quantities of DMT that produce hallucinations of alien contact. The spontaneous production of DMT by the pineal gland, however, has never been demonstrated by medical science, and provides a dubious explanation for abductions. Drug-induced visions can be categorized as "false hallucinations," that is, hallucinations that the percipient knows are not actually real. The nature of the DMT elves may be more akin to spirit entities encountered in shamanic journeys than physically real alien beings.

If the abductors are not the product of materializations produced by a Supermind, or are hallucinated machine elves as witnessed by psychonauts, what is their true nature and the nature of their intentions toward humankind? Researchers have identified five basic types of alien beings from the testimony of abductees. The most commonly encountered variety is the Small Gray, a creature that stands about 3- to 3½-feet tall; has a large, hairless head; and has a frail body with no apparent musculature or secondary sexual characteristics. They have pointed chins and their heads have rudimentary nose and ear holes. The most prominent features are the eyes, which are enormous and black and extend around the sides of the head.

The Small Grays have been likened to worker drones in a society of social insects like ants or bees. During abductions they perform the basic tasks of mentally subduing abductees and bringing them aboard the craft. Once onboard, they escort the abductees to various facilities on the ship and assist them in removing their clothing and preparing them for various procedures. When the abductees have been processed, they escort them out of the craft and replace them in their everyday surroundings. They

Generic picture of a Gray alien (Dreamstime).

communicate solely through telepathy and are capable of controlling human minds with their mental abilities.

Tall Grays are about 4 to 4½ feet in stature and in most respects resemble their smaller brethren, sporting oversized heads, diminutive facial features and huge, black eyes. Unlike the Small Grays, they are perceived as being "male" or "female" by abductees, although no physical gender differences are apparent. They are usually perceived as being "doctors" who conduct more complex reproductive procedures such as egg and sperm harvesting, the implantation of embryos and the extraction of fetuses. Their telepathic abilities are more potent and allow for greater intimacy with their human subjects. They conduct neural engagement procedures during which they can access an abductee's consciousness and memories, and can project images or complex scenarios into their minds.

Human/alien hybrids constitute a third type of alien being. Several intermediate types between individuals that appear more like the Grays and those that are indistinguishable from ordinary humans have been described. All types are over five feet tall with features that vary from appearing more alien-like, with pointed chins, small noses, ears and mouths and odd-looking eyes to "late stage" hybrids that have the appearance of normal people. They communicate using telepathy, although some are also capable of using verbal speech. Like the Grays, they participate in performing various procedures on abductees. "Early stage" hybrids are described as having wispy, white hair and are reportedly tasked with caring for hybrid children in nursery areas onboard UFOs. Early abduction reports, especially in the U.K., described human-like aliens that were termed "Nordics." These were thought to constitute a separate race of entities from the Grays, but were most likely late stage hybrids conducting abductions on their own.

The last two alien types are encountered less frequently and are more frightening in appearance. There are accounts of Reptilian aliens who are described as being about five or six feet tall, having a muscular build, scaly or mottled skin and lizard-like or snake-like features with cat-like eyes. They only communicate telepathically and usually perform some of the same tasks as the Tall Grays during abductions such as egg harvesting and fetal extraction. Their appearance is more frightening to abductees, possibly due to associations with dangerous or poisonous reptiles such as snakes or crocodiles, or even with the Biblical serpent in the Garden of Eden that symbolizes primordial evil. In some of the more paranoid accounts, the Reptilians are said to dine on the flesh of abductees. The presence of the Reptilians among the other alien types is not clearly understood, but David Jacobs speculates that they are the remnants of a previous planetary acquisition program that were brought into the Earth project as a readily available workforce.

Another possible origin for the Reptilians involves the concept of the "dinosauroid." In his 1977 book *The Dragons of Eden*, astronomer Carl Sagan theorized how dinosaurs might have evolved had they not gone extinct due to an asteroid collision 66 million years ago. He postulated that one of the smaller species with a relatively large brain size could have developed into a sapient, humanoid form. Then in 1982 Canadian paleontologist Dale A. Russell also speculated that dinosaur evolution over millions of years could have produced human-like creatures with high intelligence which he termed "dinosauroids" or humanoid dinosaurs. Russell commissioned an artist to create a sculpture of one of these creatures, which he called "*Troodon*," that bears more than a passing resemblance to a Reptilian alien. Is it possible that these Reptilians originated in an alternative time stream in which dinosaurs did not go extinct but evolved into human-like creatures?

The fifth type of aliens that are reported by abductees are termed the Insectoids. They are described as being six feet tall or taller, with features that resemble those of praying mantises. Kathy Mitchell, who was one of the abductees featured in the Budd Hopkins book *Intruders*, describes their appearance thus: "Its ... skin is dark and brownish, leathery in appearance. The body is rigid. The head is like nothing I have seen on earth ... except maybe the head of a praying mantis if you'd enlarge it beyond the size of a human head. Wide on top, it slopes at an angle downward and in to a pointed chin. The head simply sits on the body—no neck is visible—and moves with quick, jerky, insect-like movements. The eyes, huge and luminous and liquid and black, are trained solely on me."[10]

Insectoids are thought to be the ultimate intelligence behind the alien presence on Earth. They are said to wear brightly colored robes with high collars and appear to have more individuality than other alien types. Their mental engagement powers are reported to be superior to those of all the other alien types. They do not perform the more routine tasks during abductions, but are the most communicative about the aliens' planetary acquisition program.

Alien society appears to mirror that of earthly social insects like ants or bees. They co-exist within a telepathic hive mind that does not allow for individuality. It is a strictly hierarchical society in which the various types all perform their assigned tasks with maximum efficiency. Little empathy is shown toward the abductees, who are treated like experimental or domestic animals of a lower species. The aliens do not seem to exhibit emotions except for occasional outbursts of anger or peevishness when abductees fail to comply with their commands. They do not eat or excrete the way earthly organisms do, but seem to derive nourishment by absorbing nutrients directly through their skin. No food preparation areas or toilet facilities have been observed by abductees on their craft.

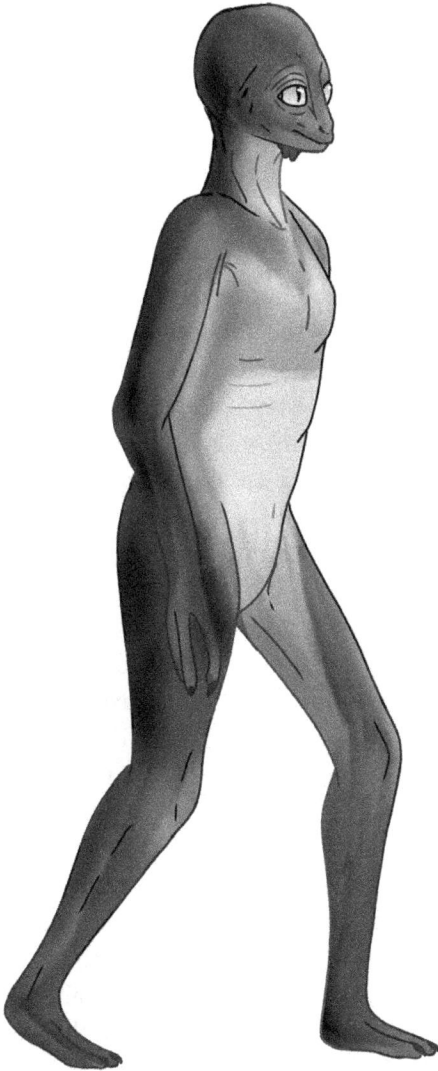

Drawing of a "dinosauroid" being by Hannah Moss as proposed by Canadian paleontologists Dale A. Russell and Ron Seguin (https://creativecommons.org/compatible licenses).

The creation of hybrid beings is the sole purpose for the alien presence on Earth. To facilitate this breeding program they harvest genetic material, fetuses and embryos that they will alter to produce the desired result. The abductees are also subjected to mind-altering techniques designed to indoctrinate them into collaborating with the hybrid program. The aliens' ultimate goal, according to some researchers, is to secretly integrate the hybrids into human society. Toward this end, some abductees are trained to develop their own psychic abilities to control other humans. These select individuals are trained in various tasks such as piloting UFOs, crowd control and techniques for locating people. David Jacobs cites one chilling case in which an abductee was coached by a hybrid in how to compel a second abductee to commit suicide by jumping off an imaginary cliff.[11]

All of this is to prepare the abductees for roles they are to play in the Change, an event in the future when the aliens will manifest their presence on Earth to usher in a new age in which they will be in total control of the planet. Jacobs and others have collected reports about abductees being involved in schooling hybrids about the myriad facets of everyday life so as to enable them to live among us surreptitiously. There are indications that the hybrids have already infiltrated human society and are interacting with us, a subject that will be explored in later chapters.

Aliens are able to use their mental abilities to completely dominate abductees before, during and after abductions. Prior to an event the abductee will often feel uneasy for no particular reason, which is often a prelude to the onset of the so-called travel urge. They will then be directed to a secluded place where the capture will take place. If they are riding in a vehicle, it is also placed under control; sometimes it is even levitated inside a hovering craft. Once onboard, if there are multiple passengers, some may be "switched off," or rendered into a state of suspended animation. The abductee will then be placed under the aliens' telepathic control and rendered compliant during the various procedures that follow. Once their work is completed, the abductors will induce amnesia in the abductee and place them back in their environs, sometimes in a different location than they had been prior to the experience.

There is some evidence to suggest that abductees are being selected because they possess latent psychic abilities. Jacobs observes that abductees seem to retain a measure of telepathic capability in the wake of an encounter experience. Some of them reportedly become disconcerted by this newfound ability and are disturbed by being exposed to other people's thoughts. Abductees report being exposed to other psychic phenomena as well. They are reportedly trained to manipulate physical objects with their minds while onboard UFOs, a phenomenon known as psychokinesis. This training may produce uncanny, poltergeist-like effects in the abductee's normal environment.

A poltergeist, a German word meaning "noisy ghost," is an outbreak of psychic force that is capable of moving large objects, causing electrical disturbances, fires and other anomalous events. It usually occurs in the vicinity of adolescents or young adults, who are referred to as the "focus" of the phenomenon. Paranormal researchers attribute these occurrences to a concept termed "recurring spontaneous psychokinesis," or RSPK, in which it is theorized that repressed sexual energy from these individuals is somehow converted into the psychic energies that cause these disturbances.

Poltergeist manifestations were experienced going back to the abduction of Betty and Barney Hill. In their book *Captured: The Betty and Barney Hill UFO Experience* by Stanton Friedman and Kathleen Marden (Betty Hill's niece), the authors reveal that the Hills were inundated with paranormal activities in their home and in the homes of others. For instance, the Hills had invested in acquiring several apartments near their home to be rented out to servicemen in the area, but all of these apartments were empty at the time. Betty Hill wrote in a letter, "As I sit here and write this, I can hear the sliding door on a closet in one apartment going back and forth; in another apartment we can hear the water running in one of the bathrooms. Also, on three occasions we found a light turned on in one of the apartments."[12] Another odd event that confounded them was finding a strange chunk of ice on their kitchen table one day when they returned home from work. The ice looked like it had been formed in a bowl, had leaves, twigs and dirt imbedded in it and was peculiarly flexible. Without a second thought Betty placed it in the kitchen sink and dissolved it in hot water.

Another well-known abduction was that of the Day family in Aveley, England in 1975, as related in Chapter Three. According to British researcher Jenny Randles, in the aftermath of their close encounter they began to experience paranormal activity in their home. She writes, "They were also having numerous psychic experiences, such as objects moving about the house on their own and apparitions being seen."[13] The family reportedly experienced mysterious clicking noises resembling Morse code in the middle of the night, while the oldest son, Kevin said he observed a clown-like figure at his bedside one night.

Debbie Jordan and Kathy Mitchell, the subjects of Budd Hopkins' seminal abduction study *Intruders*, were also subjected to poltergeist manifestations. In their book *Abducted: The Story of the Intruders Continues*, the authors relate how objects moved by themselves and disappeared and reappeared in unlikely places, appliances turned on and off by unseen means and strange calls originated from their telephone and answering machine. In one bizarre incident, Debbie found that the television had turned on by itself and a number of thumbtacks had been carefully placed point up around the set. Then she noticed that a videotape had been placed in the VCR in the wrong way. When the tape was pulled out of the machine, it turned out to be the UFO opus *Close Encounters of the Third Kind*. Debbie writes, "I don't know what all this poltergeist activity means, but I believe with all my heart that it is somehow connected to the UFO activity. It seemed to me that just before something UFO-ish happened, something paranormal would happen, and they both seemed to come in cycles."[14]

A much more obscure case was reported to abductee Terry Lovelace in a letter printed in his book *Devil's Den: The Reckoning*. The letter was from a girl named Mary, who related a series of strange events she experienced when she was 13 years old and living in a rural area of Nebraska. One warm summer night she went to her window and saw a light in the distance, which she remembered watching for a while before going back to sleep. Her mother woke her up the next morning complaining that Mary had gone outside that night without wearing shoes and had tracked mud and grass through the house and into her bed. (Note that this scenario is practically identical to the abduction experience of Shane Kurz, as recounted in Chapter Two.) The household was a strict religious one, and her mother suspected she had gone outside to meet a boy, but Mary remembered nothing about what may have transpired that night.

After this occurrence the family began to experience poltergeist manifestations in their home. Objects were observed moving around by themselves or would go missing and turn up in unlikely places. For instance, her father's wallet got lost and was found two weeks later on top of the hot water heater in the basement. The most dramatic event occurred when the family was gathered around the kitchen table and a heavy glass bowl filled with apples moved by itself and fell onto the floor. Mary's religious family believed that these occurrences were the work of demons and sent her away to live with an aunt in Omaha, whereupon the phenomenon apparently ceased. Subsequently, Mary had nightmares about meeting "little people" who subjected her to medical examinations, and experienced further abductions years later.[15]

One abductee attempted to enhance the psychic powers he claimed to have obtained after his close encounter. Harald Andersson (a pseudonym) reportedly experienced an abduction in March 1974 (see Chapter Two) and afterward consulted parapsychologist Arne Groth to explore his newly acquired paranormal abilities. Under Groth's direction, Andersson was reportedly able to manipulate a compass needle with his hands and move iron filings by psychokinetic means. He also claimed he could see people's auras, experience premonitions and mental telepathy, and could disable electrical equipment merely by going near it.[16]

A correlation between these types of electromagnetic effects and abductions has long been noted by researchers and is sometimes referred to as "electrical sensitivity syndrome." The effect is almost as if electrical and electronic equipment develop an "allergy" to the individual and malfunctions in their presence. This anomaly has also been observed in those who have had a near death experience (NDE) and individuals who are afflicted with Dissociative Identity Disorder (a.k.a. Multiple Personality Disorder).

In their book *Connections: Solving the Alien Abduction Mystery*, abductees Beth Collings and Anna Jamerson relate an anecdote that illustrates this peculiar electromagnetic effect. As the authors were driving down the Massachusetts Turnpike one evening, they observed this anomaly: "Mass Pike was nearly deserted as we sped west away from the city, bathed in the yellowish glow of the arc-sodium lights which lined both sides of the turnpike. Suddenly the row of lights on both sides of the thruway blinked out in unison as we drove past, flashing on again behind us as if the car had tripped invisible power lines as it rolled by."[17] The relationship between these electromagnetic effects and alien encounters is unclear, but some researchers speculate that the abduction phenomenon is a result of hallucinations caused by fluxes in the Earth's magnetic field or proximity to power lines or electrical equipment affecting the human nervous system.

Perhaps the most baffling instances of UFO/poltergeist activity involve the apparent pilfering and subsequent return of items of women's jewelry. For instance, after Betty and Barney Hill's encounter, they returned home one day to find a pile of dried brown leaves on their kitchen table. All of the doors and windows were locked and secure, but somehow an intruder had entered their home. When they cleared the leaves away, they were shocked to discover the pair of Betty's earrings she had been wearing during the night they were abducted that had been missing. Betty burst into tears upon finding the lost items and placed them in her jewelry box but never wore them again. The Hills were distressed that their home had been entered by someone (or something) unknown and felt vulnerable and violated. They later placed new deadbolt locks on their doors, and wondered if the discovery was connected to their strange experience.[18]

Abductee Debbie Jordan of *Intruders* fame reported a similar incident. Her boyfriend and future husband had given her a ring that she greatly cherished. One morning she woke up to find that the ring was missing and looked everywhere for it, to no avail. Three days later she was sweeping up in her son's room when she was struck by the notion that the ring was somewhere underneath her child's bed. She moved the bed away from the wall and noticed a slight bulge under the carpet. Moving the bed into the middle of the room, she ripped up the carpeting and the padding to expose the floorboards, where she found her lost ring. She was puzzled about how she had found out where the ring was hidden, but was ecstatic to have it back. How the ring came to be under the carpet was a mystery, but a possible explanation was a phenomenon associated with poltergeist activity called *apports*, in which objects are somehow capable of being transported through solid materials in a manner that seems to defy science.[19]

A third case involved Louise Smith, one of the three women abducted during the Liberty, Kentucky, case (see Chapter Two). Several months after the incident, Ms. Smith awakened from a sound sleep and heard a voice in her head telling her to return to the abduction site. At 3 a.m. she got dressed and returned to the spot where the women had been kidnapped. Upon getting out of her car she felt a tugging motion at her fingers and three rings she habitually wore were removed from her fingers and disappeared into the night. Sometime later, when she was returning to her trailer home, she found one of the rings on her doorstep. Without thinking, she picked it up and threw it into a nearby stream.[20]

In all three of these cases the items of jewelry mysteriously vanished and were subsequently returned in just as mysterious a fashion. The motivations of the abductors in these cases are obscure and seemingly senseless, but one possibility is that the aliens may have been involved in *psychometry*, a practice in which information about a person can be clairvoyantly obtained from handling an object that is intimately associated with that individual. Or perhaps these antics were a psychological experiment that was just another one of the abductor's mind games?

Researchers have long noted that abductees tend to be more psychically gifted than the general population. Are their psychic abilities a cause or a result of their close encounters? Are the aliens selecting for psychically sensitive individuals to abduct, or are their latent abilities deliberately enhanced in order to facilitate the abductor's mental domination? The answers to these questions remain a mystery.

CHAPTER FIVE

Some Skeptical Objections and Alternative Explanations

The fantastic scenario of alien abduction has drawn the ire of skeptics, most of whom subscribe to the dictum expressed by J. Allen Hynek as, "it can't be, therefore it isn't." In truth, the phenomenon is seemingly completely at odds with our everyday, commonsense notion of reality and defies our current scientific worldview. Additionally, hard evidence for abductions is practically nonexistent and overwhelmingly circumstantial and anecdotal. Attempts to extract and analyze alleged alien implants have currently yielded nothing of unambiguous alien origin. The preponderance of biopsy-like "scoop marks" on the bodies of abductees likewise does not provide proof of the phenomenon. Skeptics dismiss all abduction accounts as having mundane explanations.

Skeptical objections to the reality of abductions fall into four basic categories. The most prominent are psychological explanations that involve documented mental phenomena, including hallucinations, sleep paralysis, lucid dreams, the vagaries of hypnosis and other recognized psychological states. Next are psychosocial explanations that seek to trace the origins of the abduction narratives to the influence of science fiction popular culture. Then there are attempts to explain the effects as being created by natural phenomena such as earthlights caused by seismic activity. Finally there are theories that dismiss abductions as being sham events orchestrated by intelligence agencies for nefarious purposes.

Skeptics routinely rail against abduction narratives that are obtained using hypnosis, a process that they rightly point out is highly flawed and capable of being misused. They point to the use of hypnosis to elicit fantasies about past lives, Satanic Ritual Abuse (SRA) and

Multiple Personality Disorder (MPD). They also object to the use of hypnosis by researchers like Budd Hopkins and David Jacobs who are not medical professionals trained in these techniques. Researcher Jerome Clark points out that, "Contrary to popular misunderstanding, hypnosis is no royal road to the truth. Subjects of hypnotism are in a highly suggestible state and may seek to please the hypnotist. Thus if the hypnotist asks leading questions, the subject may provide the desired answers. Moreover, purely imaginary events can seem real under hypnosis; this is called confabulation."[1]

In order to prevent confabulation and the creation of false memories, researchers are urged to employ what are called forensic hypnosis techniques which are used by police departments to recover forgotten details of crimes. Forensic procedures seek to minimize confabulation by avoiding the asking of leading questions, which can sometimes uncover vital information about a crime scene from a witnesses' repressed memories. For instance, in 1976 a California bus driver and 27 students were kidnapped and buried alive by criminals. The driver managed to escape and enabled the police to rescue the children. He subsequently underwent forensic hypnosis and was able to remember the license plate number of the kidnapper's van, leading to the arrest and prosecution of the perpetrators. Hypnotic recall was also used to provide leads from witnesses that were instrumental in the convictions of serial killers Ted Bundy and the "Boston Strangler" Mario de Savio, and was used to obtain evidence that exonerated Sam Shepard in the murder case that inspired the movie and TV series *The Fugitive.*

The type of amnesia experienced by abductees is referred to as "traumatic amnesia" or "dissociative amnesia" in psychological parlance and is caused by the subject experiencing an event that is so disturbing that it is suppressed in conscious memory. Treatment typically consists of psychotherapy combined with hypnosis or the use of barbiturate "truth serums" such as sodium amytal or sodium pentothal that are utilized to unlock repressed memories. An interesting fictional example is the 1958 Tennessee Williams play, *Suddenly Last Summer,* in which a wealthy New Orleans socialite is struggling with an amnesiac episode that is threatening her sanity. The attending psychiatrist treats her with truth serum, which reveals the horrific memory of her cousin's brutal murder by a gang of youths when they were on vacation in Spain. The retrieved memory is the initial step in her process of healing.

In the seminal abduction case of Betty and Barney Hill, psychiatrist Benjamin Simon prescribed the standard treatment for traumatic amnesia that he had used to successfully treat World War II veterans suffering from Post-Traumatic Stress Disorder (PTSD) as a result of their experiences on the battlefield. In this case Dr. Simon uncovered a terrifying encounter with alien beings, and stated that the Hill's reaction was more emotionally intense than that of soldiers he had treated for severe stress associated with combat. Even though Dr. Simon did not believe the Hills had experienced contact with aliens, and attempted to convince them that their incident was a dream or fantasy, he failed to persuade them of this scenario.

Folklorist and UFO researcher Thomas Bullard conducted a survey of abduction narratives in cases dating up to the mid–1980s. He discovered that about one third of the witnesses had total conscious recall of their experiences without undergoing regression hypnosis, and that their encounter narratives were virtually identical to accounts obtained using hypnosis. Furthermore, descriptions of abduction details were consistent regardless of the individual hypnotist. Bullard's conclusion was that the abduction phenomenon was not a product of hypnosis. While regression hypnosis is admittedly a flawed process, it remains the only viable technique presently used to uncover repressed memories that are due to traumatic amnesia. The hypnotist must be careful not to lead the subject so as to instill false memories of events that never happened. Skeptics have criticized researchers whom they feel were guilty of leading abductees during hypnosis sessions or even unconsciously using subliminal cues to unknowingly influence the outcome of regression sessions. There is even a theory that a telepathic link exists between hypnotist and subject that can impart false memories.

Hallucinations are another psychological phenomenon employed by skeptics to debunk abductions. There are a number of serious physiological disorders that are capable of generating hallucinations, including Parkinson's Disease, Alzheimer's, epilepsy, schizophrenia and brain tumors. They can even be caused by more mundane issues such as sleep deprivation and vision problems like glaucoma and macular degeneration. Psychedelic drugs such as LSD, psilocybin, mescaline and PCP can also cause users to experience visions. None of the above conditions, however, are typically involved in people who report abduction incidents. Hallucinations in normal people can be associated with a fairly common disorder known as sleep paralysis.

Although the 22 cases cited in Chapter Two all occurred when the percipients were fully awake, another type of abduction experience began to be reported in 1973 that was termed "bedroom visitation." These occurrences supposedly took place when the abductee was in their bedroom, which was invaded by abductors who roused the witness from sleep, transported them through the building's walls or windows and floated them up into a waiting UFO.

Sleep paralysis (abbreviated as SP) is a fairly common sleep disorder that affects as much as 15 percent of the general population. It occurs during the twilight consciousness between sleep and wakefulness, when the sleeper is either waking up or falling asleep. The sleeper seems to be fully awake, although the body feels paralyzed except for the eyes. Unusual light phenomena may be perceived, along with tingling bodily sensations and sexual arousal. Then a mysterious, usually threatening entity approaches the sleeper, sometimes speaking to them and pressing down upon their chest and preventing them from

Abductees sometimes report being abducted from their bedrooms (Dreamstime).

breathing. The SP disorder may segue into an out of body experience (OBE) in which the percipient has the subjective experience of leaving their body and being transported to some fantastic locale. In rare cases, SP may be experienced by more than one individual at the same time. Also, SP can be accompanied by what are termed hypnagogic and hypnopompic hallucinations that take place when the sleeper is waking or going back to sleep.

This sleep phenomenon has been known since ancient times, when they were believed to be engendered by ghosts, evil spirits, witches or vampires. For instance, the French writer Guy de Maupassant suffered from this affliction and wrote the macabre short story entitled "The Horla" about an invisible supernatural being that was based on his firsthand experiences of sleep paralysis. It's easy to see how an episode of SP could be interpreted as an alien abduction. After folklorist David Hufford presented a paper on SP at the 1992 M.I.T. Abduction Conference, Hufford's paper made it glaringly obvious that many bedroom encounters were in reality episodes of SP, but in the wake of these revelations, skeptics like Carl Sagan and others in the media seized upon SP as an explanation for all abductions. Reviewing the UFO literature on the subject, the cases involving SP/OBE become glaringly obvious. There is an initial period when the witness believes they are awake and experiences paralysis, followed by a sensation that there is an entity in the room. When the percipient becomes fully awake, they are alone in the bedroom.

In his book *Missing Time*, Budd Hopkins recounts a nighttime visitation experienced by one of his informants referred to by the pseudonym Philip Osborne. Hopkins writes, "He awakened one night and found himself totally paralyzed. He had not been dreaming; there was nothing to prepare him for this total usurpation of control. He could not call for help. Worst of all, he sensed someone or something—a presence—in the room with him. His fear lessened as the paralysis ebbed away."[2]

Researcher Ann Druffel relates a similar narrative that was experienced by two women, Emily Cronin and her roommate, Jan Whitley. They had been on vacation and were returning home at night driving down a curvy road in Southern California when they thought it prudent to pull off to the side of the road due to the heavy truck traffic and sleep for a while. "At some point after going to sleep, both women abruptly awakened, unable to move. It was as though they were para-lyzed.... Emily remembers seeing a bright light nearby ... as well as an irritating, high-pitched sound that accompanied the paralysis."[3] Emily managed to break the paralysis by concentrating on moving one finger, whereupon both the light and the high-pitched sound abruptly ceased.

Similarly, one of John Mack's patients named Shelia described experiencing a series of what she described as "spiritual" dreams. According to Mack, "She also began to have recurring dreams in which she would experience terror, be unable to move, and her body would feel as if it were vibrating or 'full of electricity' ... they made her feel like someone or something else were controlling her body, as if she were 'possessed' by demons. Later she thought of the dreams as seizures."[4]

Another patient, Paul, reported a frightening incident that had transpired late one night. "Going in and out of sleep, he felt sure that there was 'something in the room.' But when he felt 'something on top of me' and found he could not move at all, he became terrified.... He 'dozed off again' ... and then upon awakening was able to 'break out of it' and look, but there was 'nothing' there."[5] It's possible that Whitley Strieber's alleged encounters may have originated in a similar episode of sleep paralysis.

It's easy to see how an episode of sleep paralysis could be misin-terpreted as an alien encounter. Some researchers proclaim that SP is responsible for perhaps one quarter to one third of all abductions, and others claim that all abductions can be ascribed to this common sleep disorder. It does not explain, however, every aspect of these bedroom visitations. For one thing, SP hallucinations tend to be short-lived, on the order of minutes in duration as opposed to much longer episodes that reportedly take place during bedroom abductions. During SP the subject frequently perceives that the invading entity gets on top of the dreamer and begins to choke them or otherwise interferes with their breathing, something that is not typical of alien encounters. Finally, when the paralysis is broken, the invader vanishes, unlike the beings encountered during abduction events.

Further complicating matters, it appears that abductees can suf-fer from episodes of SP after having undergone non–bedroom-type close encounters as part of what researchers call "Post-Abduction Syn-drome." Abductee "Steven Kilburn," who had first experienced an automobile abduction, later underwent bedroom visitations that were

This poster for the film *The Night Walker* (1957) illustrates the common perception of an inhuman being squatting on the sleeper's chest during an episode of sleep paralysis.

probably inspired by his initial incident. Jim Weiner, one of the "Allagash Four," also seems to have developed SP as a result of his alien encounter; SP alien visitations and non-bedroom abductions do not appear to be mutually exclusive.

Another hallucinatory state related to SP is known as the "Isakower Phenomenon," named after 19th century psychologist Otto Isakower who first observed the condition. It comprises a complex set of auditory, tactile and visual sensations that occur during hypnagogic sleep states as the dreamer is in the process of falling asleep. The subject may experience hearing rustling sounds, feeling odd abrasions of the skin and mouth, and sensations of floating. They may also have the perception of seeing a large, round, shadowy object that approaches and threatens to crush the percipient before it retreats and shrinks back into nothingness. While such an experience may superficially resemble a UFO encounter, a big difference is that the person undergoing the phenomenon is aware that it is an illusion, which puts the perception into the category of what are called "false hallucinations."

In this type of hallucinatory episode the percipient experiences visual or auditory illusions but knows that these perceptions are not real. An example would be hearing the voice of a loved one that has recently passed away, but is known by the hearer to be impossible. False hallucinations are capable of being generated via hypnosis. For instance, in preparation for Barney Hill's hypnotherapy sessions, Dr. Benjamin Simon demonstrated how this type of hallucination could be induced by placing Barney in a trance and making him experience the illusion of a small white dog coming into the room, jumping on his lap, licking his face and then leaving. All the while, however, Barney was aware that the dog was imaginary and not real.

Another sleep related phenomenon that skeptics believe is responsible for bogus accounts of alien abduction is called lucid dreaming. These are especially vivid dreams in which the sleeper is fully aware that they are dreaming and dwelling in an illusory reality. Lucid dreams are relatively rare occurrences that may be related to sleep disorders such as narcolepsy (sleepwalking). They are generally perceived as positive, even fascinating experiences rather than frightening nightmares. Like false hallucinations, lucid dreaming is a poor candidate for simulating abductions as real-world events due to the fact that the sleeper is fully aware that they are dreaming and not in a state of ordinary reality.

A common experience that is cited by skeptics as producing hallucinations of close encounters is known as "highway hypnosis." Also called "white line fever," this altered state occurs while motorists are driving down a monotonous stretch of roadway and fall into a dissociative condition in which they continue driving normally but have no recollection of where they had traveled when they arrive at their destination. It is believed to be associated with a psychological state called *automacity*, during which low-level tasks like driving can be carried out while the percipient's consciousness is unfocused. While highway hypnosis can be responsible for producing episodes of amnesia, it does not generate hallucinations of alien abductions.

The psychological condition known as Fantasy Proneness is thought to be responsible for alleged episodes of alien abduction. A Fantasy Prone Personality (FPP) has difficulty distinguishing between their internal fantasy world and external reality, which is summed up by the common phrase, "living in a dream world." Examples from literature include the novel *Don Quixote* by Cervantes, in which the protagonist believes himself to be a medieval knight who thinks windmills are giants, and James Thurber's short story "The Secret Life of Walter Mitty," a humorous tale about a man with a rich fantasy life.

Fantasy Prone individuals were encouraged to read fairy tales and had imaginary friends as children. As adults, they tend to daydream a lot, sometimes spending up to half of their waking consciousness in a fantasy world. They frequently claim to have psychic episodes such as out of body experiences, healings and contacts with supernatural beings. They also are alleged to have religious revelations and are often highly creative individuals. Psychologists theorize that the condition is used as a coping mechanism to deal with childhood abuse or severe loneliness and isolation early in life. It is not classified as a mental disorder except in an extreme form referred to as Maladaptive Daydreaming, in which the individual's fantasy life has a negative impact on their normative societal functioning.

Fantasy Proneness is relevant to the abduction scenario in a number of ways. These individuals tend to be highly hypnotizable, which is a factor in the use of hypnosis to recover memories in the majority of abduction cases. They are able to produce physical changes to their bodies, which could account for scars and markings that are reportedly the result of alien encounters. Additionally, they are prone to experience episodes of hypnagogic hallucinations. Perhaps the most compelling correlation with abductions is that about 60 percent of women with Fantasy Proneness report having undergone false pregnancies, including physical symptoms such as the swelling of breasts and the cessation of menstruation.

While it's certain that some abduction reports are submitted by individuals with FPP (this would probably include some of John Mack's subjects, for instance), people with this mental configuration comprise a very small percentage of the general population and therefore FPP probably is not a factor in the majority of these accounts. Minimal screening has been done to differentiate between abductees who are afflicted with FPP and those who are not. A 1991 study titled "Psychosocial Characteristics of Abductees" conducted by social scientists Mark Rodeghier, Jeff Goodpaster and Sandra Blatterbauer indicated that two different types of people report abduction experiences. One group was judged to be mentally stable while the second group showed evidence of psychological problems such as sexual abuse and Fantasy Proneness.[6] More research needs to be done in order to ascertain the degree that FPP may be a psychological aspect of the phenomenon.

Some researchers take Fantasy Proneness to a deeper level by theorizing that these individuals, like shamans in indigenous cultures, are uniquely able to enter an alternate reality called the "Imaginal Realm" where these alien encounters reportedly take place. They point to similarities between visionary journeys in which shamans are said to come into contact with spirit beings, and the uncanny experiences of abductees. According to this theory, abductions do not occur in ordinary reality, but only in this ethereal Imaginal Realm. This theory, however, cannot account for multiple witness abductions such as the Aveley, England, Liberty, Kentucky, or Allagash events. Moreover, the spirit entities encountered by shamans during altered states of consciousness induced by hallucinogenic substances or other means have only a tenuous resemblance to the alien beings in abduction narratives.

Another psychological phenomenon that skeptics link to abductions is called Hysterical Contagion. This is a type of mass delusion that occurs among a group of people who report illnesses or experiences that are deemed to be illusory yet create anxiety within the group. Outbreaks of Hysterical Contagion are usually confined to a relatively small geographical area and take place within a limited time frame. Some of these occurrences involve sightings of fantastic humanoid creatures that are said to wield preternatural powers.

One of the best known examples is that of an apparition known as "Spring-Heeled Jack," tales of whom first emerged in England in the 19th century. Spring-Heeled Jack was first reported in London in 1837, where he was supposedly responsible for attacking several women. The creature was described as wearing a dark cloak and having glowing red eyes and claw-like hands. Jack could reportedly breathe fire and had the ability to execute great leaps in defiance of gravity, hence the moniker. This strange being would eventually become an urban legend and was featured as a fantasy character in many "penny dreadfuls," publications that featured sensationalistic fictions during the Victorian Era. Sightings of Spring-Heeled Jack in London and other locales in England and Scotland ceased around 1904. Although pranksters were thought to be responsible for sightings of the apparition, no one was ever apprehended in connection with these encounters, and skeptics have pointed out that the kind of leaps attributed to Jack would break the ankles of a normal human.

Other apparitional figures were reported during the 20th century, beginning with the case of the so-called "Mad Gasser of Mattoon." In August of 1944 a mysterious figure was thought to be responsible for a series of gas attacks in the small town of Mattoon, Illinois. Victims of the Mad Gasser reported they were exposed to assaults with chemical vapors that left them sick or temporarily paralyzed. Some of the sufferers reportedly caught glimpses of their assailant, who was variously described by one witness as a tall man wearing dark clothing and a tight fitting cap, and by another as a woman dressed as a man. The local police chief launched an investigation and the FBI was even called in to assist, but no actual evidence of the Gasser was ever unearthed, and the case was ascribed to war nerves and noxious fumes wafting into the town from a nearby industrial plant.

Another, more well-known series of incidents that supposedly had some connection with UFOs was the urban legend known as the "Mothman." This flying creature was allegedly encountered by the citizens of the town of Point Pleasant, West Virginia, from November 1966 to December 1967. Witnesses reported seeing a man-sized winged creature with glowing red, hypnotic eyes soaring through the skies above the town. Around a hundred people in the Point Pleasant area alleged that they had observed the apparition over a period of nearly a year. Other phenomena such as anomalous aerial lights and visits from the enigmatic Men in Black were reported in connection with sightings of the Mothman, and the mysterious being was even blamed for the catastrophic collapse of the nearby Silver Bridge that killed 46 people on December 15, 1967. The creature eventually became a local legend and was the subject of author John Keel's sensationalistic account, *The Mothman Prophecies* in 1975, and a 2002 film adaptation of the book. No physical evidence of the Mothman was ever brought to light, and the collapse of the Silver Bridge was found to be due to a structural deficiency. Skeptics claimed that the sightings were due to observations of a large, red-eyed crane native to the area, while anomalists sought an extraterrestrial explanation, noting that there have been a number of cases in which floating, flying ufonauts were observed.

Regarding the hysterical contagion hypothesis, David Jacobs observes that "[a]bduction claims do not fit the model of mass hysteria events. Although some claimants know each other, most do not. They are usually not in close proximity to one another; they do not engage in mutual reinforcement; prior to 1987 they were not subject to ongoing publicity about others with similar claims; and the phenomenon is not restricted in time or in geographical area.... The abduction claims sometimes involve more than one witness, and the narratives that are related are greatly detailed. They have a beginning, a middle and an end.... They do not involve only a single event, like the classic mass-hysteria cases."[7]

Some skeptics claim that the abduction scenario is related to the erotic fantasies of what they consider sexual "deviants." In their book *The Abduction Enigma*, Kevin Randle, Russ Estes and William P. Cone take note of the preponderance of sexual motifs in abduction narratives and state that "[a] very high percentage of both the male and female abductees that we interviewed openly stated a sexual preference of homosexuality or bisexuality. An equally high number were hypersexual and highly promiscuous in their human sex lives. Of the remaining abductees at least half of them claimed that they had no sex drive whatsoever. That leaves us with a low number of abductees who claim to have what would be considered a normal sex life."[8] Of course, the authors are being judgmental in defining what constitutes a "normal sex life," and if some abductees suffer from various forms of sexual dysfunction, these conditions may be the result of traumas suffered during their experiences rather than being their cause.

Furthermore, David Jacobs points out that abductees are exposed to bizarre reproductive and sexual experiences at the hands of their abductors from childhood. They may witness their parents or other adults undergoing urological and gynecological procedures, which can cause them to experience profound feelings of guilt and shame that will impact their future psychosexual development. As adults, they may be subjected to further sexual depredations as the aliens perform sperm and ova gathering practices, while showing no regard for the psychological health of their helpless human subjects.

Other psychological explanations involve guilt feelings engendered by abortions, citing a resemblance between the imagery of aborted fetuses and the appearance of Gray aliens. Some skeptics also see a similarity between the iconography of the Grays and images of starving children in Third World countries. Another theory is that abductees are experiencing suppressed memories of surgical procedures nebulously recalled while under anesthesia.

Sometimes skeptics will be obliged to employ multiple psychological phenomena to explain away an abduction event. For instance, a Navy veteran named Jack Wilson and his son Peter were driving down a desolate stretch of highway near the New Mexico–Arizona border when they reportedly experienced a close encounter. They were floated into a UFO by stereotypical Gray aliens and taken to an "operating room" facility where Jack claimed that he was compelled to relive memories of his life that were projected into a recording device. After his thoughts had been taken, he and his son found themselves back in their vehicle after seven hours of missing time had elapsed.

After his experience, Wilson contacted Ronald K. Siegel, a psychology professor at UCLA who was an expert in hallucinations, seeking an explanation for his abduction experience. Siegel conducted a battery of physical and psychological tests and found no medical or mental abnormalities. In order to explain Wilson's close encounter, he had to string together hypnogogic hallucination, the Isakower Phenomenon and lucid dreaming, along with an optical illusion called a "glory" which produces a halo-like effect around a human figure, to explain away the sighting. This convoluted reasoning that invoked multiple psychological phenomena to debunk Wilson's abduction event, seems almost as unlikely as a genuine alien encounter.[9]

Psychosocial explanations for UFOs and abductions revolve around the influence of American science fiction culture as an explanation for the phenomena. The late 1920s and early '30s witnessed the inception of pulp magazines. The pulps, as they came to be known, were inexpensive, mass-market publications printed on cheap, wood pulp paper. They offered sensationalistic, sometimes exploitative fiction stories in a variety of genres. *Black Mask* and other detective pulps, for instance, featured the exploits of hard-boiled sleuths, while *Weird Tales* printed stories of horror and fantasy. Adventure pulps like *The Shadow* and *Doc Savage* chronicled the fantastic escapades of superhuman heroes.

Amazing Stories, founded by Hugo Gernsback in 1926, was the first of the science fiction pulps. The magazine printed works by sci-fi writers such as Ray Bradbury, Robert Heinlein and Richard Matheson who would later achieve prominence in the field. More importantly, it featured a series of fantastic cover illustrations painted by artist Frank R. Paul that depicted aliens and spaceships of every imagined variety. A second sci-fi pulp, *Astounding Stories*, appeared in 1930 that presented similar fantastic yarns and lurid cover art.

Pulp fiction magazine covers presented images of all manner of alien beings such as giant insects and crocodile-headed humanoids that were conjured from the literary imaginings of the sci-fi writers. Some of these featured bald-headed extraterrestrials that bore a vague resemblance to alien Grays and situations that were similar to images that would later appear in abduction narratives. There were also illustrations of disc-shaped flying machines that appeared prior to Kenneth Arnold's sighting of flying saucers in 1947. The problem with assigning influences from the pulps on the UFO phenomenon is that these magazines had a very limited circulation and appealed mostly to youngsters and science-minded adults. During the formative years of the phenomenon, *Amazing* had a circulation of between 15,000 and 25,000 readers, while *Astounding* fared a bit better, reaching a peak readership of around 50,000. The fantastic imagery that appeared on pulp magazine covers did not reach a large audience and therefore had a limited influence on popular culture.

During the 1930s and '40s extraterrestrial themes on movie screens were relegated to the realm of kiddie matinee serials featuring the exploits of interplanetary heroes like Flash Gordon and Buck Rogers that were derived from the pulp magazines and comic strips. Low-rent serial productions like *Flash Gordon* featured ludicrous aliens like rock men and hawk men who were inhabitants of the planet Mongo. The first screen alien to visit Earth appeared in the serial *The Purple Monster Strikes* in 1945, two years before the first appearance of flying saucers. The Purple Monster was an invader from Mars who arrived via rocket ship and was able to disguise himself as an ordinary earthling as he went about his preparations for an invasion from the Red Planet. Another Martian invader landed in a flying saucer in the serial *Flying Disc Man from Mars* in 1950 in the wake of Kenneth Arnold's famous sighting.

The science fiction film cycle of the 1950s, however, vaulted the SF genre into mass popularity. George Pal's seminal interplanetary adventure *Destination Moon* in 1950 kicked off a series of sci-fi movies that achieved mass popularity that lasted until the end of the decade. A number of these films featured alien visitors and themes that would later appear in abduction narratives. *The Man from Planet X* (1951) was the first feature film in which an extraterrestrial used mind control techniques to abduct humans. *Invaders from Mars* (1953) depicted Martians placing implants inside people's bodies, while *It Came from Outer Space* (1953) featured the first vehicular abductions in screen history. In *The 27th Day* (1957) five persons from different nations are kidnapped and taken aboard a flying saucer as part of an alien master plan to invade the Earth. The plot of *I Married a Monster from Outer Space* (1958) involved ETs seeking to mate with human females. Human/alien hybrid children appeared in *Village of the Damned* (1960).

The film most often cited by skeptics as a direct inspiration for abduction motifs is a low-budget gem called *Killers from Space* (1954). Directed by F. Lee Wilder (brother of famed writer/director Billy Wilder), the film stars Peter Graves who plays nuclear scientist Dr. Doug Martin who is observing a Nevada A-bomb test in an observation plane that crashes under mysterious circumstances. His body is missing from the wreckage, but he later wanders back to the base with a large scar on his chest and total amnesia about what may have happened to him.

Dr. Martin begins acting suspiciously and steals scientific documents, an action that brings him to the attention of security officers at the base. In order to break through his amnesia, he is subjected to interrogation while under the influence of sodium amatol truth serum. Under the influence of the drug, he is able to recall awakening on an operating table inside a cavern where a group of bug-eyed humanoids had performed a heart transplant operation in order to revive him. The alien leader Denab (John Merrick) explains that they have resuscitated him because they have need of his nuclear expertise to accomplish their invasion plans. They hail from the dying world of Astron Delta and are hoping to use atomic weapons and giant mutant creatures to destroy humanity and conquer the Earth. The scientist then has the memory of these revelations wiped from his mind and is dispatched back to the base to pilfer documents under the aliens' hypnotic influence. Once his memories have been restored, Dr. Martin manages to use his expertise to create a nuclear conflagration that destroys the invaders.

Killers from Space contains many abduction motifs in a film that appeared years before the Betty and Barney Hill case became known to the public during the early 1960s. These narrative elements include missing time amnesia, recovered memory, scenes depicting apocalyptic events on a vision screen, medical procedures performed by aliens on an operating table, extraterrestrials who hail from a dying planet, healings, anomalous scarring discovered after the abduction and aliens with large, haunting eyes that possess telepathic powers. Skeptics have seized upon these similarities as proof that all the abduction stories that followed are fantasies that derive their origin from this film.

While it's undeniable that these plot elements prefigure abduction themes (at least on paper), it would seem that few skeptics have actually watched *Killers from Space* before submitting their analysis. A typical example of low-rent, 1950s sci-fi cinema, the film is reasonably well-made but suffers from the limitations of a tight budget and minimal production values. Gray aliens are described in abduction reports as being dwarfish creatures possessing enormous black eyes that project their telepathic mind control powers, but the Astron Deltans in the film are normal sized actors sporting bulging eyes reportedly fashioned from cut-out egg cartons that give them a ludicrous appearance. The abduction scenes were filmed inside a cavern near Los Angeles rather than in the interior of a UFO for budgetary reasons, and the aliens' high

Did these goofy-looking aliens in the low-rent 1954 film *Killers from Space* inspire the ufonauts described by Betty and Barney Hill? You be the judge.

tech machines are obviously military surplus equipment used as props. To anyone who has heard the abject terror in the voices of the Hills on the taped transcripts of their hypnotic sessions, the notion that these emotions were generated by memories of watching this cheesy, low-budget film is especially laughable.

Abduction themes that appear in science fiction films made during the formative period of the 1950s may have an alternative explanation. These similarities may be due to an uncanny type of prescience that arises from the creative process. This theory is further explicated in detail in the author's previous study, *Alien Abduction in the Cinema* (McFarland, 2023).

To be sure, there have been instances in which a purported abduction experience can be shown to have been directly influenced by a media source. One abductee reported seeing creatures that were obviously derived from the aliens depicted in the 1956 sci-fi thriller *Earth vs. the Flying Saucers*. Jenny Randles cites a case she investigated in which the witness recounted details of her experience that had appeared in an abduction-themed episode of the nighttime soap opera *The Colbys*.

Skeptics have also noted a resemblance between the appearance of the ufonaut reported in the Herb Schirmer abduction case and the Martian portrayed in *Mars Needs Women* (1968), which had been released a few months earlier.

In their skeptical study, *The Abduction Enigma*, Randles, Estes and Cone state, "Small aliens, some with large heads, pointy chins and huge eyes are featured in many of the 1950s science fiction films,"[10] but this claim is erroneous. The only diminutive, macrocephalic screen aliens appeared in *The Man from Planet X* (1951) and *Invasion of the Saucer Men* (1957). The alien being in *Planet X* most closely resembled the space-suited creatures that populated the "Occupant" reports of the 1950s (see Chapter Two) while the *Saucer Men* are depicted as dwarves with bulging, venous heads and protruding eyes that have only a vague resemblance to the ufonauts of later decades. No movies released during the formative years of the 1950s or '60s featured the iconography of the Gray alien along with many specific facets of the phenomenon that would later be reported by abductees. In cinematic terms, big alien creatures are more threatening than little dwarves, so the overwhelming majority of alien invaders were at least human-sized.

Skeptic Martin Kottmeyer has claimed that the descriptions of the abductors in the Betty and Barney Hill case was derived from the appearance of an alien being featured in an episode of the science fiction TV series *The Outer Limits,* entitled "The Bellero Shield." The creature depicted in the episode was bald-headed and had "wraparound eyes" that communicated with earthlings via telepathy. Kottmeyer points out that the episode aired on February 10, 1964, just 12 days before Barney drew a picture of the alien Leader under hypnosis with wraparound eyes, implying that he had derived this description from watching the television show and that, by extension, all subsequent descriptors of Gray aliens are ultimately based on this seminal portrayal. This analysis ignores the fact that Barney had clearly observed the unusual eyes of the Leader through binoculars at a distance of 80 to 100 feet during the initial phase of the sighting in 1961, about three years before the broadcast of "The Bellero Shield." Barney's observation of the Leader's eyes was consciously remembered and not part of the material recalled under hypnosis.

Many adherents of the "psychosocial" explanation for abductions cite Steven Spielberg's 1977 saucer opus *Close Encounters of the Third*

Kind as providing the origin for the iconography of the Gray alien. While *Close Encounters* was the first theatrically released film to depict Gray aliens onscreen, this imagery was derived from descriptions of ufonauts culled from abduction reports and the files of Dr. J. Allen Hynek, who was a technical advisor on the movie. Spielberg instructed his production designer Joe Alves to conform the visual appearance of the film's extraterrestrials to that of the stereotypical Gray. The most clearly seen alien, which appeared at the very end of the film, was an elaborate puppet fashioned by creature designer Carlo Rambaldi that resembled a ghost or apparition.

From the 1970s to the 1990s, four adaptations of abduction narratives were produced for film and television audiences. *The UFO Incident* (1975) offered an accurate account of the Hill abduction as an NBC-TV movie of the week. Based on John Fuller's book, *The Interrupted Journey*, the telefilm featured riveting performances by James Earl Jones as Barney and Estelle Parsons as Betty, and depicted Gray aliens for the first time onscreen. Whitley Strieber's abduction memoir was filmed as *Communion* in 1989, which was the first theatrically released movie on the subject. This low-budget adaptation sported chintzy special effects

A troop of Grays escort actor Richard Dreyfuss inside a massive mother ship at the conclusion of *Close Encounters of the Third Kind* (1977).

and an often laughable performance by Christopher Walken as Strieber. It has since become a cult classic. The Budd Hopkins abduction study *Intruders* became a two part CBS-TV miniseries broadcast in 1992 that accurately reflected complex aspects of the phenomenon. Travis Walton's abduction experience was filmed as *Fire in the Sky* (1993), which offered a sincere but highly flawed account of Walton's ordeal. In addition, a number of popular films made during these decades featured aliens, but abductees do not describe creatures that resemble the creatures that appear in movies like *E.T., Alien* or *Predator*.

A basic problem with screen adaptations of abduction experiences is that they are open-ended, without clear resolution, and their narratives do not conform to the three act structure of dramatic construction. By the 2000s, abduction-themed movies had become firmly mired in a low-budget, horror movie venue in offerings such as *The Fourth Kind* (2009), *Dark Skies* (2013), *Extraterrestrial* (2014), *Alien Abduction* (2014), and was satirized in films like *Evil Aliens* (2005) and *Paul* (2011).

Yet another skeptical explanation for the abduction phenomenon concerns the alleged effects of what are called "earthlights" or atmospheric plasmas. Earthlights, which are sometimes called "spook lights," are a worldwide phenomenon in which anomalous lights are observed from a distance that appear at certain locations, frequently over long periods of time. Examples include the Brown Mountain Lights in North Carolina, the Marfa Lights in Texas and the lights observed in Hessdalen, Norway. While they have been studied for decades, scientific explanations for the earthlights phenomenon have remained elusive.

A theory propounded by Canadian neurologist Dr. Michael Persinger claims that energy from these earthlights can stimulate the human brain to hallucinate UFO sightings and abductions by directing electrical activity to the brain's temporal lobe. Persinger claims to have demonstrated this in the laboratory by placing experimental subjects inside a helmet that electrically stimulates the temporal lobe to produce hallucinations such as the subject perceiving a presence in the room. This theory is flawed in that earthlights are notorious for being elusive and maintaining a remote distance from observers. It is therefore highly problematical for energies from earthlights to affect the brain from so far away.

Arguably the most outlandish explanation for the abduction phenomenon could be dubbed the "Drugs and Mind Control" theory, as propounded by researcher Nick Redfern. He cites the work of another researcher, Rich Reynolds, who was approached by a retired spook named Bosco Nedelcovic, formerly of the CIA and the U.S. Agency for International Development (AID), with a wild tale. According to Nedelcovic, he was part of a covert AID operation conducted in Brazil during the 1950s that was designed to simulate an alien encounter. Nedelcovic related how he and a crew of technicians cruised in a helicopter through the night skies of the Francisco de Salles area seeking a subject for their experiment. Using heat seeking equipment, they managed to locate a farmer working on a tractor, who Nedelcovic claimed was the first acknowledged abductee, Antonio Villas-Boas (see Chapter Two).

According to this scenario, the helicopter began spraying a psychedelic gas down on Villas-Boas, which immobilized him and generated the illusion that the helicopter was a spacecraft. Then team members dragged the subject into the landed chopper where additional drugs were administered to make him believe he was inside a UFO. A prostitute was employed to simulate Villas-Boas' sexual encounter with the alien female. When they had finished their task, the team got back in the helicopter and flew off.[11]

Nedelcovic claimed that the motivation for the experiment was to ascertain how the public would react to contact with aliens by simulating a bogus close encounter and observing the results. While the above scenario is within the realm of possibility given the CIA's history of experimenting with LSD and other drugs during the 1960s, some elements of the Nedelcovic narrative are problematical. For instance, the notion that a helicopter crew flying around in a sparsely populated area in the early hours of the morning seeking an experimental subject, seems unlikely and illogical. Villas-Boas just happened to be doing farm work at 1 a.m. that night because it was too hot to work during the day, and encountering him under these circumstances would appear to be a suspiciously fortuitous circumstance. The technician/participants in this staged abduction must have been a group of circus midgets who were shorter in stature than Villas-Boas. The abductee recalled his experience in clear and exquisite detail which would not have been the case if he had been drugged. Contrary to popular belief, not everyone hallucinates under the influence of psychedelics, and many of those who do only see geometric shapes and spirals, not highly structured illusions. Lastly, revelations made by an ex-intelligence operative with no supporting documentation about an event more than twenty years after the fact should be viewed with extreme skepticism.

Redfern also makes a similar claim about the abduction of Charles Hickson and Calvin Parker in Pascagoula, Mississippi, in 1973 (see Chapter Two). According to his scenario, this was allegedly another bogus close encounter staged by the U.S. military in order to make aliens seem more dangerous and evil rather than benign during the 1973 UFO "flap." Once again a helicopter was supposedly used to simulate an alien craft, and military personnel in costumes played the parts of the robotic "claw men" reported by the two abductees. Hickson and Parker were allegedly dosed with a potent chemical agent called BZ that produced the illusion that they were being abducted and examined by non-human entities.[12]

In support of this theory, Redfern asserts that the two men were in proximity to a military facility on Horn Island, where he contends experiments into mind control, including the use of BZ were being conducted during the 1970s. In actuality, the U.S. Chemical Warfare Service operated a Quarantine Station on Horn Island during World War II between 1943 and 1945. Research was conducted on using flies and mosquitoes as biological weapons in connection with poisons like botulin and ricin. Aerosol application of anthrax germs was also tested on animals at the site. The Station was closed down when the war ended in 1945, and subsequently a hurricane destroyed all of the remaining structures on the island. No psychological warfare experiments using psychedelic drugs were ever conducted at the site. Yet Redfern cites rumors by unnamed locals in the Pascagoula area claiming that they had accidentally become dosed by vapors of BZ gas wafting inland from Horn Island, some ten miles off the Mississippi coast, where the military was secretly experimenting with hallucinogenic drugs during the 1970s. His scenario regarding a bogus abduction staged by the military using mind altering drugs is therefore highly specious in this instance, although later reports of so-called military abductions (or MILABS), will be explored in a later chapter.

Alternative explanations for alien abductions range from psychological phenomena, sleep disorders, hallucinations, mass hysteria, vagaries of hypnosis, sexual deviations, earthlights, psycho-social influences from pop culture and events staged by military or intelligence organizations. While these explanations surely are a factor in some abduction cases, they are insufficient to account for all of the complex aspects of the phenomenon.

CHAPTER SIX

The Creatures Walk Among Us

Do alien beings walk among us? Is human society being infiltrated by a race of human-alien hybrids genetically designed to resemble us outwardly in every way while inwardly possessing the telepathic and mind control abilities of the E.T.s? Are these quasi-human hybrids driving cars, visiting public places, renting apartments and quietly going about their business in our everyday world, under our very noses?

The notion of alien creatures in human form secretly intruding into our quotidian reality in order to further a hidden agenda invokes deep feelings of xenophobic paranoia. In the past, alien contacts usually took place in isolated locations and were of relatively brief duration, usually lasting only a few hours. When their obscure medical rituals were completed, the little Gray humanoids quickly returned to Planet X, Dimension X, Millennium X, or wherever it was they came from. Ever shy of direct contact with humankind, the ufonauts seemed to inhabit a sphere light years away from our little world and were only able to visit us in a temporary and limited way.

Over time, however, indications of the alien intent emerged from abduction research. The Grays were reportedly taking sperm and ova samples from the abductees in order to create a genetically engineered race of beings who outwardly resembled Homo sapiens but retained the aliens' powers of mind control. These "hybrids" or "Transgenics" were, according to some researchers, being designed to secretly infiltrate human society as part of an agenda to ultimately dominate and supplant humanity.

Although most abductees reported that their abductors were dwarfish, inhuman creatures, a number of reports, especially from the U.K., involved abductions that were conducted by what appeared to be ordinary-looking humans. Termed "Nordics" or "Aryans" by UFO researchers, these human-appearing aliens served to confuse investigators and were thought to be an entirely separate race of ufonauts. Their presence served to confuse investigators until details of the hybrid breeding program became apparent and revealed that these Nordics were simply late-stage hybrids conducting abductions without the Grays being present.

As abduction research progressed into the 2000s, investigators like Budd Hopkins and David Jacobs began to examine reports of the Transgenics conducting brief forays into human society as part of a long-term infiltration program. Recent reports seem to indicate, however, that their presence is becoming more permanent. Jacobs cites accounts in which abductees are involved in covertly training the hybrids in the many particulars of living among us. Knowing nothing about our world, they must be taught the particulars of everyday life and schooled about how to drive cars, how to shop at a store, how to operate a telephone, how to dress, how to decorate an apartment and the million and one little details that comprise human existence. This knowledge is vital to the Transgenic's aim of covertly living in our midst without being detected.

These individuals wield powers of mind that enable them to dominate ordinary humans, are able to disappear or become invisible at will and have other anomalous abilities. Yet they can appear somehow wrong or out of place in our reality, dressing in ill-fitting or anachronistic clothing and driving around in strange-looking automobiles. Their physical appearance can be subtly off kilter despite their efforts to blend in.

This shadowy invasion of our reality by genetically engineered Transgenic beings presents a profoundly disturbing scenario, if true. It's one thing to contemplate alien beings occasionally abducting unfortunate human subjects in lonely places and returning to their point of origin, it's quite another to think that the person riding next to you on the bus is actually an inhuman creature with superior powers of mind.

Throughout the years of abduction research, there have been certain related sub-phenomena that may be attributed to these hybrid beings. One of these consists of encounters with the enigmatic "Men in Black" or MIBs. These mysterious, dark-clad authoritarian figures who attempt to silence UFO witnesses have been reported since the beginning of the modern UFO era. While many reports of MIBs appear to describe entirely human military personnel tasked with suppressing information about sightings, other accounts seem to indicate that some of these apparitional figures may in fact be Transgenics who are conducting similar operations on behalf of the aliens' infiltration program.

In a similar vein are reports of what are termed "Phantom Social Workers," individuals claiming to represent government officials, social workers or corporate personnel interviewers. Like MIBs, these Bogus Social Workers (BSWs) show up at the witnesses' doorsteps and use their air of official authority to gain entrance to the household. Once inside, they begin to ask intimidating questions and issue outrageous demands in an attempt to gain custody of the home's children. Although BSWs don't generally target abductees, they have been involved in the attempted abduction of a number of children in the UK and elsewhere.

Bogus job interviewers use the promise of employment to lure unsuspecting victims into situations that lead to abductions or other inexplicable events. The non-interviews for these non-jobs are conducted in hastily assembled office environments that seem more like minimalist movie sets than real-world work spaces. These "offices" are usually located in out of the way places where the abduction procedures can be conducted. Needless to say, no employment is ever forthcoming from any of these interviews.

The MIBs, BSWs and Bogus Job Interviewers may all be aspects of the Transgenic infiltration program. In all of these scenarios, the hybrids present themselves as figures of power and authority who exercise control over their hapless human subjects. The emblems of our military, law enforcement, administrative and corporate power structures have been appropriated and subverted in order to further the aliens' agenda. These visitations and confrontations may constitute something in the nature of "field exercises," controlled scenarios designed to provide the hybrids with real-world experience interfacing with humans from a position of authority and learning how to exert control over them.

Oddly, the classic Contactees of the 1950s reportedly conducted liaisons with their extraterrestrial contacts in public places such as restaurants, bus terminals, hotel lobbies, trains and other venues, mostly in the environs of Southern California. Like the hybrids, these space brothers (and sisters) looked just like everyday people so as not to arouse suspicion as they conducted their clandestine rendezvous with their human counterparts. This is not to suggest that the Contactees' outlandish tales were based on real experiences, but the similarity with reported meetings between hybrids and abductees in public spaces is curious.

For instance, the first Contactee, George Adamski related how he was approached by two alien "contact men" in his 1955 book *Inside the Space Ships*. On this occasion in February of 1953, two unknown men reportedly approached Adamski in the lobby of a Los Angeles hotel, where one of them addressed him by name. According to his description one of the men was over six feet tall with wavy black hair who appeared to be in his early thirties. The other man was shorter and younger, with gray-blue eyes. Both of them wore dark-colored business suits.

The men, who he learned were named "Firkon" and "Ramu," invited Adamski to accompany them on a drive into the California desert. Along the way, the men revealed that one of them was from Mars and the other was from Saturn. They informed him that they were "contact men" who had lived and worked on Earth in secret for several years. The Martian and the Saturnian drove the Contactee to a secluded location where he boarded a saucer that flew him through outer space to an orbiting "mother ship," where he held further conversations with the Space Brothers.

According to the Contactees the aliens needed them to provide them with liaison services to assist them in their covert assimilation into human society, and they all became willing collaborators in this process. They were allegedly used to obtain food samples, clothing in contemporary styles, haircuts, bank accounts and false identification papers that enabled them to pass among us in secret. The contactees acted like secret agents, arranging covert meetings, using clandestine greetings and employing "drop zones" to exchange information in a manner similar to Soviet spies.

A prime example of this collaboration was provided by Contactee Howard Menger in his 1959 book *From Outer Space to You*. Menger was tasked by the aliens with obtaining terrestrial outfits for the space people in order for them to pass among us unnoticed, including women's attire for the females. Hilariously, he reported that the alien women balked at wearing fifties-era high heel shoes and brassieres! Menger also briefed them on human customs, slang and habits. He was even pressed into service as a barber and provided his alien friends with food and other items.

In contrast to the somewhat ludicrous accounts of the Contactees' secretive doings with the Space Brothers are two puzzling cases that have aspects of Contactee narratives but may possibly be associated with hybrid beings. One of these involved Air Marshall Sir Peter Horsely, a distinguished British aviator who served as Deputy Commander-in-Chief of RAF Strike Command and also served as Equerry to the British Royal Family. A mysterious incident had taken place in 1954, but was not made known until the publication of Sir Peter's 1997 memoir entitled *Sounds from Another Room: Memories of Planes, Princes and the Paranormal* that involved a meeting with an enigmatic individual known only as Mr. Janus.

As a senior aviation official, Horsely had been deeply involved in the investigation of UFO sightings for a number of years. One day Sir Peter received a phone call from an associate named General Martin, who was an advocate of the extraterrestrial hypothesis. General Martin suggested that he meet with an acquaintance of the General who was knowledgeable about the phenomenon. A meeting was arranged for Sir Peter to confer with this individual at a flat in London's Chelsea district, although the General would not be present.

Entering the flat, Sir Peter was greeted by a woman named Mrs. Markham, who ushered him into a dimly-lit drawing room where he was introduced to a man named Mr. Janus. Janus was perhaps 45 or 50 years old, with thinning, slightly gray hair and was neatly dressed in a suit and tie. Oddly, after the interview, Horsely could not recall any exact facial features. Over the next two hours the mysterious stranger would discuss UFOs along with a number of philosophical and spiritual concepts with Sir Peter.

Janus explained that the Earth was being monitored by an extraterrestrial race he called the "Observers," who had placed our planet under surveillance for a long time. The aliens hailed from another solar system and were far more technologically advanced than Earth, which was described as being a galactic backwater inhabited by a race of half civilized beings. Although they were not interested in directly interfering in our affairs, the ETs took an active interest in our moral, spiritual and technological development as we entered a new age of space travel. From time to time, Janus intimated, the Observers came among us and made covert contact with selected individuals. They had concentrated their infiltration efforts on the USA and Western democratic nations due to the difficulties of operating in dictator-ships and police states.

According to Janus, the Observers were able to surgically alter their bodies to enable them to survive in Earth's environment, obtain the right sort of clothing and find means to move about freely. The ETs relied on their psychic powers of telepathy and hypnosis and their abil-ity to manipulate different dimensions to protect themselves while carrying out their missions on our primitive world. Janus intimated, although he did not specifically state, that he was one of the alien Observers. During the interview, Sir Peter felt that Janus exhibited tele-pathic abilities that enhanced his aura of authority and left Horsely feeling shaken afterward.

Mr. Janus predicted that rocket travel to near–Earth space and orbiting satellites would become commonplace over the coming decades. This, in turn, would lead to great strides in the miniaturiza-tion of 1950s-era technology, advances in navigational guidance and communication over vast distances. Interestingly, unlike many bogus predictions made by the Contactees, the techno-prophecies of Mr. Janus actually came true, as today we live in a world of electronic min-iaturization, global positioning systems and worldwide satellite phone and television communications.

As the interview ended, Janus expressed a desire to meet person-ally with Prince Philip, and after the liaison Sir Peter submitted a full report to security officials, as the affair involved the Royal Family. In an odd postscript, Horsely made several phone calls to Mrs. Markham's flat to set up another meeting with Janus, but his calls were never returned. When he contacted General Martin, the General suddenly became distant and evasive about the matter. Finally, Sir Peter went down to Mrs. Markham's apartment only to find the place empty. He never saw Janus, Markham or General Martin again.

In the aftermath of the affair, Horsely wondered if Mr. Janus was an imaginative prophet of the future, a gifted psychic or one of the alien Observers. He also entertained the possibility that he had been the victim of an elaborate hoax. Janus' story contains many themes found in Contactee narratives, including the notion of the Earth as a primitive world being watched by a superior yet benevolent race, the need for a spiritual transformation of humankind, and the idea that human-like aliens had secretly infiltrated our planet and were carrying out clandestine missions on behalf of their race down here on Earth. The telepathic abilities reportedly exhibited by Mr. Janus may lend credence to the idea that he was one of the alien Observers, but alternately may only indicate that he was a psychically talented, but entirely human individual.

Decades later, a similar tale involving another famous aviator would unfold. Colonel Gordon "Gordo" Cooper was a jet fighter jock, a military test pilot and one of the original seven Mercury astronauts who flew in space during the Mercury and Gemini programs. He later served as head of NASA's flight crew operations during the Apollo and Skylab missions. Gordo was considered by his peers in the space program to be an especially "steely-eyed missile man" who possessed the proverbial "right stuff" in great abundance. Col. Cooper also had a life-long interest in the UFO phenomenon and had been involved in a number of UFO-related incidents during his Air Force career. In Cooper's 2000 autobiography entitled *Leap of Faith: An Astronaut's Journey into the Unknown*, the former astronaut related a curious story regarding his relationship with a mysterious, beautiful woman who possessed apparent psychic powers and claimed to be in contact with an intelligence of extraterrestrial origin.

After leaving NASA, Cooper went to work for Disney Imagineering, the research and development division of the Disney organization. His job was evaluating emerging technologies in the entertainment industry. In 1978 he began receiving telephone calls from a person he did not know who wanted to set up a business meeting. Cooper eventually consented and had lunch with the woman, whose name, he learned, was Valerie Ransone. Ms. Ransone, then in her late twenties, was described by Cooper as a striking beauty who bore a resemblance to the French actress Catherine Deneuve. She claimed to have worked for the White House during the Gerald Ford administration developing a national energy conservation program. Ransone had contacted Cooper because she was assembling a research and development team consisting of technical people with unusual backgrounds. This private group would be tasked with developing novel technologies that were developed from alien sources.

In subsequent meetings she explained that she had a missing time experience when she was 17 years old, during which she claimed that she had been contacted by a group of extraterrestrial beings calling themselves the Universal Intelligence Consortium. The ETs wanted to use Ransone as a telepathic conduit for communicating technological and cultural data that would assist in the spiritual and material transformation of humankind.

She further explained that she had been associated with Dr. Andrija Puharich, a psychic researcher conducting studies at the Institute of Noetic Sciences in Ossining, New York. The Institute was run by fellow ex-astronaut Edgar Mitchell, who, like Gordo, also had an interest in fringe phenomena. Puharich had been involved in experiments in clairvoyance and psychokinesis (mind over matter) with the controversial Israeli psychic and stage magician Uri Geller. Geller, like Ransone, claimed to have experienced Contactee-like close encounters with an alien intelligence via telepathy. Ransone claimed to be one of a number of "space kids" being studied by Puharich who were attempting to use their telepathic gifts to communicate with extraterrestrials. During one of their meetings at a restaurant, Valerie demonstrated her apparent psychokinetic powers by bending a fork, a feat frequently performed by Geller. On another occasion she reportedly provided Cooper with highly technical information about a possible failure of the Space Shuttle's cooling system that later proved to be accurate.

Beguiled by this heady brew of beauty, psychic mystery and charisma surrounding Valerie Ransone, Cooper agreed to join her consortium, a start-up known as the Advanced Technology Group that was headquartered in Washington, D.C., on a part-time basis. He was introduced to other scientists and techie types working for the Group, and was impressed by their credentials. One day in 1979 Valerie introduced him to a middle-aged former rocket scientist who turned out to be none other than '50s-era Contactee Daniel Fry (see Chapter One). As a former astronaut Cooper was impressed with Fry's scientific background, but suspended judgment about Fry's dubious claims of alien contact. During the meeting, Ransone proclaimed that she had received telepathic instructions that Fry was due for another ride in a flying saucer, only this time he would be accompanied by Gordo.

Cooper was understandably stunned by this revelation. Valerie instructed him to take various items along to the tryst, including a compass and a camera loaded with infrared film. She had been instructed to drive Cooper and Fry to a prearranged spot in the desert outside of Yuma, Arizona, a town near the U.S./Mexico border, where the UFO was scheduled to land. Unsurprisingly, but perhaps predictably, Ransone showed up at Cooper's office about two weeks before the landing was supposed to take place in a highly agitated state. She announced that the planned saucer ride had been abruptly canceled due to a strong disagreement between "certain parties." Terribly disappointed by this turn of events, Cooper lost faith in Ransone and began to drift out of her orbit. The Advanced Technology Group fizzled out soon thereafter due to lack of financial backing and became defunct by late 1980.

At the end of the day the Valerie Ransone affair proved to be just another ufological red herring. The predicted ET technology never materialized and the promised flying saucer ride was abruptly withdrawn. Ms. Ransone had been exposed to Contactee ideas through Pucharich and fellow psychic Geller, and she may have come to believe these clichéd notions implicitly and become self-deluded. She may also have been a gifted individual with natural telepathic, clairvoyant and charismatic abilities. Or she may have actually been in contact with an alien intelligence as she claimed, or perhaps was even a hybrid being, a "star kid" possessing advanced mental capabilities.

There is a similarity between the twin encounter narratives involving Mr. Janus and Valerie Ransone. In both cases a distinguished aviator with a deep interest in UFOs was contacted by a mysterious individual who claimed to have personal knowledge about the phenomenon. Both of these personages appeared to have telepathic abilities that served to convince the witnesses that their claims of alien contact were well founded. Barring further information, the jury is still out as to whether these two individuals were outright charlatans, people who possessed unusual psychic and charismatic abilities, or were hybrid beings with superior powers of mind intent on fulfilling an alien agenda.

The first report of a hybrid being harks back to the very first abduction narrative, that of the Brazilian farmer Antonio Villas-Boas in 1957, as recounted in Chapter Two. The witness was abducted by four small beings and taken aboard a landed craft, where he was stripped and placed in a room with a naked female. The woman was about four-and-a-half-feet-tall and had wispy blond hair, large slanted eyes, high cheekbones, a thin-lipped mouth and a pointed chin. Her body was well proportioned, with bright red pubic hair. Villas-Boas, who had likely been treated with an aphrodisiac by the ufonauts, had sexual intercourse with the woman twice. Mating incidents involving humans and hybrids would be a scenario that would be repeated in many subsequent abduction reports throughout the decades. This episode would also seem to indicate that the abductors had produced a hybrid being that greatly resembled a normal human being as far back as the late 1950s.

More alarming perhaps than meetings with hybrids on board alien craft are the cases in which these beings are encountered in our everyday world. One of the earliest examples was experienced by abductee Shane Kurz, whose 1968 abduction narrative was recounted in Chapter Two. The incident reportedly occurred in 1967, about a year prior to her close encounter. At the time Shane was attending high school and had decided to go to school early one morning. It was raining and she was using an umbrella as she approached the school entrance when she heard a male voice in back of her call her by name and ask if she could share her umbrella. This was odd because she had not seen anyone in the vicinity as she neared the entrance.

She turned around to see a man she did not know approaching her. This individual was described as being about five feet four inches tall with light brown hair. The most unusual things about his appearance were his ears, which she described as being sharply pointed, and his eyes, which were slightly slanted like those of an Asian person. The eyes were gray and seemed to have what was described as a "magnetic" quality. He was not wearing a coat, which was unusual because the weather was cold and rainy, and he was attired in corduroy pants and a plaid shirt that seemed somehow out of place. He wore no tie and his shirt was left open.

Shane asked the man how he knew her name, but he avoided the question. He then asked her what she did during her lunch hour and she replied that she usually played basketball or volleyball. Oddly, he didn't seem to know what these sports activities were, but instead asked her if she would like to take a ride during lunch. He pointed to a nearby field and told her he had a white car parked there, although it was not visible. Shane politely declined the offer and told him that it was nice meeting him, but after a few seconds she turned back around to find that he had disappeared, yet there was no way that he could have dropped out of sight so quickly. Out of curiosity, she asked some of her friends if they had seen the man, but instead they asked her about the identity of that "cute boy" she had been talking to.[1]

This case has all the earmarks of later encounters with what are apparently hybrid creatures trying to pass for ordinary humans in our everyday reality. The "man" in this occurrence was oddly dressed in a subtly off-kilter fashion that did not reflect the weather, and had distinctly peculiar facial features that included a pair of compelling, "magnetic" eyes. He apparently possessed telepathic abilities that enabled him to identify Shane and call her by name, yet professed ignorance about everyday sports activities. He seemed to have the ability to vanish in the wink of an eye, and to disguise his appearance to Shane's friends. An automobile may or may not have been involved in what could have been an abduction event had Shane not had the good sense to refuse the man's rather ominous offer to take a lunchtime ride.

An abduction event that featured contact with an unusual person took place during an evening in August of 1974 to a Florida housewife named Lydia Stalnaker, who remembered having been previously abducted as a child 19 years earlier. Stalnaker was driving on a road north of Jacksonville when she observed a bright light hovering over a wooded area nearby. At about 9 p.m. she pulled off the road into a parking area and got out of her car to take a closer look at the light, and was soon joined by a man who drove up and exited his vehicle to watch the light alongside her.

She described the man as being short, less than five feet five inches tall with a swarthy complexion, and she had a vague feeling that she knew him. When she asked if he could see the light, he replied cryptically, "Yes, and it's right on time." They watched as the mysterious light descended to the ground behind some trees, and thinking that a helicopter had crashed, the man convinced Stalnaker to accompany him in his car in order to investigate and perhaps render assistance to the victims of an accident if necessary.

As they drove to the wooded area where the "crash" had supposedly taken place, she began to experience an intensely unpleasant feeling of being suffocated while her companion apparently felt nothing. As they drew nearer, the light from the grounded object came into view, but the next thing she knew it was three hours later at midnight, and they were driving back toward Jacksonville on another road. She had no memory of what had transpired during the three hours of missing time, but her forehead hurt and her stomach was nauseated.

Stalnaker experienced severe headaches and nausea over the next several days until her symptoms gradually improved. She began to have nightmares about the incident, and in May of 1975 she decided to undergo therapy under the direction of hypnotist Dr. Art Winkler. Under hypnosis she recalled being placed on an operating table and subjected to an examination by several types of alien beings who took thoughts out of her mind. When she made inquiries about the man who had driven her to her rendezvous with the UFO, she discovered that he had quit his job and disappeared. Checking with his former employer, she was told that the man had shown up in town one day looking for work, but nobody knew who he was or where he had come from. Stalnaker came to believe that the man was sent by her abductors to lure her to the landing site.[2]

This scenario suggests two possible explanations: either her companion was a normal human being who was working in concert with the aliens to assist in Stalnaker's abduction, or he was a human/alien hybrid being. While ordinary people are sometimes observed working alongside the abductors, these individuals are usually fellow abductees who are only performing this assistance on board UFOs. It is more likely that he was a hybrid being who was living among the general populace and was assigned as a facilitator to assist in luring abductees to a site where the abduction could take place.

Debbie Jordan, who was the subject of Budd Hopkins' 1987 abduction study *Intruders*, may have also had an encounter with these enigmatic beings. In *Intruders* Ms. Jordan recalled an odd incident that had taken place during a July 4 camping trip to Kentucky's Rough River State Park in 1975 with her friend "Nan" (a pseudonym) and her family. They were staying at a cabin in a remote area of the park, where Debbie and Nan were listening to the CB radio late at night in the family truck when they received a communication from some young men who wanted to meet them and party. After a while Debbie observed lights from what appeared to be a car or small truck approaching.

Three young guys then approached the cabin and one of them did all the talking while the other two remained silent during the entire meeting. The talker was short, stocky and good-looking and had curly blond hair and blue eyes; the other two were taller and thinner, with nondescript but identical features and seemed to be guarding the blond guy. Oddly, none of the three ever stated their names. Likewise, their spokesman claimed that he and his companions were all members of a rock 'n' roll band but never revealed the combo's stage moniker. Debbie and Nan sat around the campfire and drank beer with the trio well into the night, and during this time Debbie felt a strong attraction to the blond lad from whom a special warmth seemed to emanate. When the hour became late, he kissed Debbie chastely on the cheek and departed along with his companions.

This supposedly chance meeting had several odd features. One was that the three boys never revealed their names. Another was that the blond youth, who seemed to have a certain charisma, did all the talking while his "bandmates" never spoke a word. The vehicle that the trio arrived in seemed to have unusual qualities in that it appeared to glide over the dirt road to the cabin, which was extremely bumpy and full of potholes. The lights on the conveyance also had an unusual configuration and seemingly lacked a headlight and tail lights. This event took place approximately eight years before Debbie's abduction experience in 1983.[3]

In abductee Terry Lovelace's 2020 book *Devil's Den: The Reckoning*, the author solicited letters from his readership regarding UFOs and abductions and printed a response from a woman named "Delores" (a pseudonym). In her account she recalls an incident that took place in 1968, when she was a teenager hitchhiking from her home to attend a party in Long Beach, California. She was picked up by a driver in an unusual silver car sporting fifties-era fins. Debbie was impressed by the car's gleaming silver finish and white leather upholstery. While the car's design appeared to date from a previous decade, it appeared to be brand new.

The driver was a small, slightly built middle-aged man wearing jeans, a white tee shirt and sunglasses, who wore his hair slicked back. He seemed to have a laid-back attitude and an unthreatening demeanor that enabled Debbie to accept the ride. She asked the driver what make of car it was, but he only replied, "It's foreign." Right after this conversation she began to feel sleepy, as if she had been drugged, although she hadn't had anything to eat or drink. Nodding out, she soon fell asleep on the sedan's spacious, comfortable seat.

It seemed like she had only dozed off for a moment when she awoke and the driver announced that they had arrived at her destination. This seemed odd because this drive was usually much shorter in duration.

After she said goodbye to the driver and exited the vehicle, Debbie still felt wobbly while walking to her friend's house where the party was to take place that evening. She was so tired that she had to sleep for several hours and had unusual dreams. After the party she got a ride home with friends but had a vague suspicion that something odd might have happened to her during the ride.

During the next week she missed a menstrual period and had her older sister take her to the doctor, who examined her and found no evidence of a sexual assault, and two subsequent pregnancy tests came up negative. In the aftermath of her strange experience, Debbie never hitchhiked again and would later make a career in law enforcement as a dispatcher. After many decades the incident remained very vivid in her recollection, and she always suspected that something had happened to her during the drive that had been wiped from her memory during a period of what may have been missing time amnesia.[4]

Another bizarre encounter involving a strange automobile and its unusual occupant was related in an account that appeared in Whitley Strieber's 1997 compendium of correspondence titled *The Communion Letters*. The unnamed letter writer related an incident that had taken place in a rural farm community one night in October of 1979. He had been parked with his girlfriend in a dead-end lover's lane for about an hour when he happened to look out the driver's side window, where he observed an unusual 1930s model black sedan that was parked nearby facing in their direction. They were both spooked because the car had somehow driven close to them without making a sound.

The couple became even more frightened when they observed what appeared to be a four-foot-tall child standing next to the car. The "child" was wearing a pajama suit complete with footies and was carrying a metallic object resembling a pail in its hand. The sight was so eerie that the couple thought they were seeing the ghost of a child that had been killed in a car accident. As they observed the being walking back and forth in front of the vehicle, they had a vague impression of perceiving a light in the sky above them. The next thing they knew, the strange car and its diminutive occupant were gone.

Although no further details about this incident were forthcoming, it seems possible that the couple may have experienced an abduction event, and that the child they had seen was an illusory screen memory of an alien or a hybrid. Like the vehicle in Debbie's enigmatic encounter, an anachronistic automobile was involved in the close encounter. Note that odd-looking, out of place cars are frequently reported being driven by the mysterious Men in Black.[5]

Researcher David Jacobs describes how abductees are pressed into service to school hybrids on how to dress so as not to attract undue attention in their daily sojourns among unsuspecting humans, but it would seem that their efforts are not completely effective. Abductees report encounters with individuals who are oddly dressed and seem out of place in our everyday world. In his book *The Uninvited: An Expose of the Alien Abduction Phenomenon*, British researcher Nick Pope cites an incident experienced by an abductee he refers to by the pseudonym "Mary." In the spring of 1992 Mary was working in the South Kensington neighborhood in London and was exiting the Underground station when she noticed an unusual looking individual standing nearby. It was a small man, about five feet tall, with a petite build and a large head who was wearing an oversized pair of glasses that gave him an owlish appearance. He was wearing an ill-fitting, light gray suit that was too large for him, and his overall appearance conveyed the impression that something about him was "not right." He seemed nervous and out of place in the busy urban environment.

Mary made eye contact with the man, which seemed to initiate a telepathic exchange. He was asking her directions to the Science Museum, which she communicated to him via a visual mental exchange. When she had finished, the man ran up the stairs and exited the station and Mary elected to follow him, but upon reaching the street she found he had vanished. Mary got the impression that he had become separated from a group of his fellow hybrids and that the Science Museum was a meeting point for the group. The unusual nature of the man's attire, combined with his ability to communicate telepathically and his mysterious disappearance led Mary to conclude that he was not a human being.[6]

Another strange encounter discussed by Pope in his book concerned an abductee he refers to as "Patsy." The incident took place on Saturday, September 23, 1995, when Patsy and her co-worker "Maggie" were working at a small art shop in central London. Saturday was usually a slow day because the store was located away from the main roads, but on this occasion a group of 13 people entered the shop. At first Patsy thought they were part of a tour party, but there was something about them that made Patsy uneasy. All of them were oddly dressed and seemed to be composed of a number of mismatched individuals speaking in different accents and dialects that the two women had trouble understanding.

Both Patsy and Maggie felt that an uncanny atmosphere had permeated the shop along with the strange visitors, and for some reason, Patsy felt herself unable to speak to them. As the group finally began to leave the shop, a woman who appeared to be of Scandinavian ethnicity purchased a pencil, which was the only sale made to any member of the group. Oddly, when Patsy handed the woman a receipt for the purchase, she seemed confused and handed it back, as if she did not understand the concept of what a receipt was. This incident may have been something in the nature of a "field trip" designed to familiarize a group of hybrids with earthly customs regarding buying items from a store.[7]

A controversial case involving alleged physical evidence from a hybrid being was examined by Australian researcher Bill Chalker in his 2005 book *Hair of the Alien: DNA and Other Forensic Evidence of Alien Abduction*. The book chronicles the abduction-related experiences of a Lebanese immigrant to Australia named Peter Khoury. Peter's mother related a strange incident that had taken place in May of 1964 when the family was living in the port city of Chekka, Lebanon. Peter was only 22 days old at the time, when at about four in the morning his mother was nursing Peter in her arms and looked up at her window to observe an odd-looking man watching her from the street outside. The stranger was very fair-skinned, with long, blond hair and handsome features that contrasted with the dark hair and complexion typical of Lebanese men. Peter's mother felt no sense of fear during the encounter but could not remember how it had ended.

Khoury reportedly had several close encounters as he was growing up, but the most significant of these took place on July 23, 1992. Peter was feeling ill as a result of having been injured after getting attacked at his job site by three men and decided not to go to work that day. After driving his wife Vivian to the train station to go to her job, he returned home and went to bed. Sometime later he awakened to find two strange naked women sitting on the bed facing him. One of them was a dark-haired woman about five feet, eight inches tall. Her features appeared to be those of an Asian person, except that her cheekbones seemed abnormal and her eyes were dark-colored, almost black, with no white visible. The other woman was blond-haired with Caucasian features, a long face with high cheekbones and a pointed chin, who was perhaps in her mid-thirties. Peter was struck by her hair, which was elaborately coiffed, and her eyes, which were two or three times the size of normal human eyes. Her naked body, however, was normal-looking and well-proportioned.

As the Asian woman looked on, the fair-haired one reached out and drew Peter to her chest. The woman exhibited unusual strength that intimidated Peter, and for some reason he reacted by biting the nipple of her breast. She did not scream or otherwise indicate she was in pain, nor was there any blood, but Khoury bit off a piece of her nipple. He swallowed a piece of it, which caused him to have a severe coughing fit and temporarily take his eyes off the women for a split second. When he looked back, both of them had vanished.

Peter had the impression that what he had bitten off was not real flesh, but was some elastic or rubbery substance, or possibly a prosthetic device. He described both women as having blank, expressionless stares, which he likened to the glass eyes of a mannequin. There was an impression that he was supposed to impregnate the blonde woman, but he had no recollection of actually performing sexual intercourse with her. However, after the women had disappeared, he felt the urge to go to the bathroom, but when he tried to urinate he found he was in severe pain and discovered that a hair had been tightly wrapped around his penis. He removed the hair and carefully placed it in a plastic bag. The fragment of the woman's nipple caused him to have coughing fits for days before subsiding.

Several years later Bill Chalker submitted the hair to a laboratory for DNA analysis. The hair was found to have some interesting qualities, which will be discussed in a later chapter. How the women were able to enter Khoury's locked apartment and then vanish hints at their otherworldly origin. There are resemblances with the case of Antonio Villas-Boas decades earlier, an abductee who was also compelled to have sex with a female being for the purpose of procreation. This case has provided the only physical evidence for the existence of hybrid beings, but remains highly controversial.[8]

Psychic and artist Ingo Swann is considered the father of the U.S. government's remote viewing program. Prompted by reports of psychic research being conducted in the Soviet Union, the United States sought to establish its own psi-spy program and enlisted Swann, a gifted psy-chic, to formulate protocols and theories for its implementation. Swann devised a system, in collaboration with UFO researcher Jacques Vallee, called "co-ordinate remote viewing," in which the program's clairvoy-ants were directed to view targets located at precise latitude and longi-tude geographical coordinates.

In his book *Penetration: The Question of Human and Alien Telepa-thy*, Swann told a complex and fantastic tale about his interactions with some mysterious individuals. In February of 1975 Swann was work-ing on developing remote viewing techniques at the Stanford Research Institute in Palo Alto, California, when he received a phone call from a highly-placed person in Washington, D.C., possibly a U.S. Congress-man, who informed him that Swann would be contacted by an indi-vidual named "Mr. Axelrod," and recommended that he render any assistance possible to him. Soon after the call Swann was contacted by Axelrod and arrangements were made to have the psychic perform some private remote viewing tasks, for which Swann would be paid $1,000 per day.

Swann was instructed to wait on a street corner outside a Wash-ington museum, where he was picked up by two men with military bearings who looked like twins. He was subjected to a melodramatic espionage-style procedure during which he was blindfolded and driven out of the city to a large, underground facility manned by what appeared to be military personnel wearing civilian clothes. He was domiciled in a windowless room where Axelrod tasked him with view-ing coordinates on the Moon. The psychic reportedly observed mon-umental alien structures on the Moon's far side and was well paid for services rendered.

The psychic kept up sporadic contacts over the next few months. Then, in 1976, Swann was grocery shopping in a Los Angeles supermar-ket when he encountered a strikingly beautiful, very well-endowed and scantily-clad young woman. While she paid no attention to him, Swann became terrified by the intuition that she was not a human being. Just then the Twins seemingly appeared out of nowhere and hustled him away. Subsequently, Alexrod told him in a phone call that the woman was very dangerous and might have harmed him if he had approached her. During their final meeting, Alexrod and the Twins transported Swann to Alaska, where he reportedly witnessed a large, triangular

UFO emerge from a lake. Afterward he was quizzed by Axelrod about his psychic impressions concerning the craft and its inhabitants.

In the aftermath of these strange experiences, Swann theorized that Axelrod, the Twins and the buxom woman in the supermarket were all hybrid beings, and that the situations he encountered were all staged to ascertain the extent of his psychic abilities. Oddly, decades later, abductee Terry Lovelace would describe alien structures similar to what Swann had remote viewed on the Moon's far side that he had observed during an alleged lunar excursion; however, space probes from the U.S., Russia and China have not detected any trace of this extraterrestrial moonbase. The narrative presented in *Penetration* contains a number of fantastic elements that seem to strain credulity, and it's notable that Swann has authored a number of novels on fictional psychic themes.

The Budd Hopkins book *Sight Unseen: Science, Invisibility and Transgenic Beings* (2003) contains a number of accounts in which abductees encounter what appear to be hybrid beings who inhabit our everyday reality. One of the most interesting of these is referred to in the book as the case of the "Phantom Support Group" that took place during the early 1990s. Hopkins relates how two abductees, "Dennis Johnson," a news reporter, and "Don Mehlman," a former law enforcement officer, had produced a videotape of their joint investigation into a local abduction event and had organized a public talk that had been attended by about 15 to 20 interested individuals. Dennis and Don had given a brief talk at the meeting, showed their video, and sold a few copies.

A week later Don got a phone call from a man who claimed to have attended the event. He was contacting Don to invite him to a meeting of an abductee support group he was conducting in the area. Don's curiosity was piqued by the notion that there was such a group in their sparsely populated area and immediately agreed to attend, whereupon a date, time and location for the event was agreed upon. After the call, Don invited Dennis to attend the meeting, and they agreed that their wives, "Janice" and "Betsy," would also be present.

On the night the meeting was to take place the foursome drove to an address that turned out to be in a newly constructed condominium complex which was only partially occupied. When they knocked on the door of an apartment on the second floor of the condo they were greeted by a short, "blank looking" man who initially seemed confused by their presence but ushered them inside the apartment. As the two couples entered they observed that the place was sparsely furnished and lacked the usual amenities of habitation.

They encountered the alleged support group in the living room, where four or five attendees sat stiffly on a sofa and chairs. Like the man who answered the door, these people appeared blank-faced and exhibited a total lack of emotional affect that made them seem "zombie-like." The most unusual member of the group was described as being an extremely attractive but severe-looking woman. There were no refreshments provided or small talk made as is usual at such gatherings. As soon as Dave, Don and their wives were seated, their host began to scold Don and Dave about having made the videotape of the abduction case and claimed it was wrong to make money from their investigations, which should cease immediately. The other members of the group sat in stony silence as the host berated the two abductees.

Dennis and Don had finally had enough of this rude treatment, causing Dennis to inquire if the group was connected with Budd Hopkins or David Jacobs, the two most prominent researchers in the abduction field, but their host professed ignorance about knowing both of them. Wondering about the motives of the "support group," the two abductees had finally had enough of this weird group of people and made ready to leave the meeting with their wives. As they were leaving, the stunning-looking woman suddenly stood up, whereupon her features changed into those of a hideous, inhuman being with sparse hair and oversized eyes. This horrific metamorphosis propelled the two couples out of the apartment and into their car in great haste.

Commenting on the strange appearance and behavior of this support group, Hopkins notes that "[t]he first thing that must be said about the 'spooky' attendees and their leader is that their affectless demeanor prevented their guests from easily accepting them as normal human beings, despite their somewhat unexceptional physical appearance … none of these vacant-seeming individuals 'looked right' and none behaved as normal humans would under such circumstances. Though members of this unusual group were obviously able to rent a condo, assemble furniture, use the telephone and sit for the so-called support group meeting, this was apparently the extent of their ability to mimic human behavior."[9]

The motivation behind the group's actions appears to be to intimidate Don and Dennis into abandoning their research into and their advocacy of the abduction phenomenon. They were obviously familiar with the concept of an abductee support group, and chose to exploit it for their own purposes. The sudden metamorphosis of the beautiful woman into an ugly hag may have been meant to frighten Don and Dennis into discontinuing their investigations into the phenomenon, and also illustrates the being's ability to disguise their appearance using mental manipulation. The motivations of these creatures in this instance are similar to those attributed to the dreaded Men in Black, which will be discussed in the following chapter.

The cases cited above illustrate how the hybrids are able to masquerade as ordinary people and move among us surreptitiously, although it would seem that their skills at human mimicry are far from perfect. Reports indicate that they are working behind the scenes, beyond the fringes of our perceptions, performing unseen actions that further the aliens' hidden agenda.

CHAPTER SEVEN

Night's Black Agents

Men in Black

If one performs a Google search on the phrase "Men in Black" the results will mostly reflect info about the 1997 hit sci-fi comedy *Men in Black* and the three sequels in the movie franchise. Based on the Marvel/Malibu comic book series of the same name, the films posit a secret, worldwide organization tasked with monitoring, concealing, policing and regulating extraterrestrial activity on Earth. One of its most important functions is to erase the memories of witnesses to UFO and alien encounters using a "neutralizer" device that induces amnesia. The organization supports itself with funds from patents on inventions derived from E.T. technology. Its agents transport themselves in black limousines that employ special, hi-tech gadgetry and wear black suits and sunglasses. The tag line for the films proclaims that the MIB's mission is "protecting the Earth from the scum of the universe," and the movies posit the notion that alien beings disguised as humans have infiltrated our planet and are living among us in secret.

While the films are funny and entertaining, they derive their inspiration from real-world accounts of dark-attired individuals who have reportedly been involved in suppressing UFO evidence and silencing witnesses to the phenomenon. Like their screen counterparts, these Men in Black reportedly wear dark suits and drive sleek, black automobiles. Although some of them, perhaps the majority, are most likely agents of earthly intelligence services whose job is to collect physical evidence from UFO encounters and silence witnesses, a certain residue of reports suggest that some of them are human-like alien beings and are likely hybrids with mind control abilities who perform similar functions.

Accounts of Men in Black go back to the beginnings of ufology. On June 21, 1947, for instance, a harbor worker named Harold Dahl collected samples of a slag-like material that had allegedly been ejected from a doughnut-shaped UFO and fallen into Dahl's salvage boat near Maury Island in Puget Sound. On the morning of June 22 a man, about 40 years old, who was dressed in black and drove a black sedan, arrived at Dahl's home and escorted him to a café, where they had breakfast together. During the meal the conversation turned to Dahl's sighting from the day before, and the MIB recounted details of the event that were so accurate that it was as if he had been there to witness the incident firsthand. He intimated that he knew more about the sighting than Dahl would ever want to believe. He then proclaimed that the encounter "should not have happened" before delivering veiled threats against Dahl and his family if the witness didn't keep his mouth shut about the sighting.

His message having been delivered, the mysterious Man in Black left the restaurant, leaving Dahl to wonder how the MIB knew all the details about his sighting. Dahl did not heed the stranger's admonitions and returned to his boat, where he talked openly to his co-workers about his UFO sighting and the physical evidence he had collected. After making these revelations he suffered a series of business misfortunes that seemed to substantiate the MIB's threats. Some researchers consider this case to be a hoax, but the appearance and modus operandi of the mysterious stranger would be repeated during the ensuing decades.

The concept of the Men in Black was popularized by a writer and researcher named Albert Bender, a quirky individual who operated an organization called the International Flying Saucer Bureau (IFSB) during the early 1950s. In 1953 Bender abruptly abandoned his position at the IFSB and appointed an associate, fellow writer and UFOlogist Gray Barker, to be chief U.S. investigator for the group. In 1956 Barker published a book entitled *They Knew Too Much about Flying Saucers*, in which he recounted a story about how Bender had been visited by three MIBs in 1953. Bender claimed that he had been confronted by three men who invaded his bedroom one night. They all wore black outfits that reminded him of those worn by clergymen, and black, Homburg-style hats that obscured their features. The eyes of the three men suddenly lit up and focused on Bender, who felt that their eyes burned into his soul.

The mysterious visitants revealed that they were alien beings who had assumed human form as a means of remaining undetected by humans, and referred to themselves as numbers "One," "Two" and "Three." They supposedly imparted the "truth" about flying saucers to Bender and warned him that he could "come to harm" if he continued to pursue his research into UFOs. This was the reason that he had abrogated his position at the IFSB. Bender was known to be a susceptible, perhaps even a fantasy-prone individual who was obsessed with horror and science fiction films, and his claims about his meeting with the three MIBs may be pure fiction.

In 1957 the prolific producer/director Roger Corman lensed a low budget sci-fi horror program entitled *Not of This Earth*, which featured actor Paul Birch as Mr. Johnson, an alien vampire from the planet Davana who dresses in black and wears dark glasses that conceal his eyes. Johnson lives in a mansion in Los Angeles, where he is tasked with abducting humans and teleporting them to his home world in order to ascertain if their blood is suitable in preparation for a full-blown invasion. One of Corman's more memorable efforts, the film may have provided the iconography for later reports of MIBs.

During the late 1960s a cluster of sightings of a flying humanoid entity dubbed the "Mothman" emanated from the town of Point Pleasant, Virginia, that were accompanied by reports of MIBs in the area. Paranormal researcher John Keel collated these reports, some of which were possibly of dubious veracity. Other researchers have speculated that Keel, along with UFO trickster Gray Barker, may have been responsible for some of the reported MIB activity in the community, while another school of thought attributes these sightings to "spoofing" events conducted by U.S. intelligence agencies as part of a psychological experiment. In any event, the iconography of men attired in black business suits driving black sedans had become a cultural image that was capable of being manipulated by hoaxers, government spooks—or aliens.

One of the first encounters with what would appear to be an alien MIB happened to Edward Christiansen and his family, who had witnessed a glowing, spherical object in the sky near Mayville, New Jersey, on November 22, 1967. Afterward the family reported the sighting to the Air Force and were interrogated about the event by an officer. Several weeks later, on January 9, 1968, there was a knock on the door of

Actor Paul Birch poses as a black-attired alien vampire in Roger Corman's *Not of This Earth* (1957). The film perfectly captures the iconography of an MIB and was remade in 1988 and 1995.

the Christiansen home in Wildwood, New Jersey. Upon answering the door, they were confronted by a weird-looking personage who claimed to be from the "Missing Heirs Bureau," who wished to question Edward in order to ascertain if he was the Mr. Christensen who may have inherited a large sum of money.

The caller was a large individual, who stood about six feet three inches tall and weighed perhaps 300 pounds. He was wearing a Russian-style fur hat with a black visor, a long black coat and dark shoes with extremely thick rubber soles. Upon removing his coat, the Christiansens caught a glimpse of what appeared to be a badge of some kind, which their visitor quickly covered up. His head was large and round and his features were angular and pointed, with bulging eyes similar to those of someone suffering from a thyroid disease. He had close-cropped black hair and his skin had an unnatural-looking pallor. When he sat down his trousers rode up his leg, where a green wire was observed running from his sock up his pant leg.

The visitor, who referred to himself by the nickname "Tiny," questioned Mr. Christiansen about various aspects of his background. He queried Edward about scars and birthmarks on his body, about automobiles he had owned and schools he had attended. He asked him if he would be willing to fly anywhere in the country to be present when the will was read in order to collect the inheritance. During the questioning, Tiny's face began to redden and he requested a glass of water, which he used to swallow a large, yellow capsule. The interview lasted about forty minutes, whereupon Tiny donned his coat and hat and left the home. Edward's wife Arline watched as their visitor walked into the early evening gloom where a black 1963 Cadillac with its headlights turned off drove up and he got inside. The next morning Edward received a phone call during which a woman's voice informed him that the Christiansen heir the bureau had been seeking had been located in California.[1]

One of the strange aspects of the visitation was that the family had only moved into a new home very recently and their phone number and address had yet to be listed in the local directory, which begs the question about how the "Missing Heirs Bureau" was able to locate them. Their large-proportioned, black-attired visitor with unusual physical attributes seems to indicate that he was a quasi-human, perhaps even an alien entity. On the other hand, there is an ostentatious theatricality about his appearance that might suggest he was an actor made up to look like a grotesque cast member of *The Addams Family*, perhaps as a spoofing exercise being conducted by an intelligence agency. Unlike other MIBs, Mr. Tiny did not ask the family any questions about their UFO sighting that had taken place just weeks earlier.

The wave of UFO sightings, landings and abductions that took place in the fall of 1973 produced some memorable MIB sightings. British researcher Jenny Randles has chronicled the bizarre abduction experience of a 37-year-old housewife she refers to with the pseudonym of "Mrs. Verona," as discussed in Chapter Two. About eight weeks after the abduction event, which had taken place on October 16, she began receiving odd phone calls and anonymous letters urging her not to discuss her close encounter even though her experience had not been made public. Then one day two men arrived at the Verona residence in Taunton, U.K., to speak with her. Mrs. Verona felt an odd sense of "otherness" about the men, even though they were both normal in appearance. One of them was in his forties, while the other was perhaps 25, and they seemed to resemble each other, as if they were father and son. They both wore dark glasses and clothing that was not dark-colored, but nonetheless seemed out of date.

The older of the men did almost all the talking as he described Mrs. Verona's abduction in more detail than she herself remembered. Then they strongly warned her not to report her experience to anyone if she valued her health, sanity and welfare. The men refused to answer any questions, disclose their identities, or reveal how they had so much intimate knowledge about her abduction experience. After delivering their message, the two men left but returned several more times conveying the same demands until Mrs. Verona decided to report her abduction to a UFO research organization, whereupon their visits abruptly ceased.[2]

It should be noted that Men in Black do not always wear dark attire or business suits. In this case Mrs. Verona's visitors wore more casual clothing, but like many reports of hybrids their clothes seemed out of current style. Her two visitors followed the standard MIB procedure in the use of their intimidation tactics, however. They also exhibited an uncanny knowledge about her abduction experience. Randles reports that the MIBs seemed to exert a level of mental control over her actions. There was also the matter of an ominous black limousine with dark tinted windows that would drive slowly back and forth past the Verona house at night as if it was deliberately making itself visible in a threatening manner. These menacing black cars constitute another intimidating tactic employed by MIBs ostensibly to frighten witnesses.

In early November of 1973 a cluster of anomalous events took place in and around the rural community of Goffstown, New Hampshire. At about 8:30 on the evening of November 1, a woman named Florence Dow heard a loud noise coming from outside her back door and looked out of her window to investigate. She saw the figure of a "man" standing motionless in the gloom who was dressed in an old-fashioned black coat and a wide-brimmed black hat that was pulled down low over the figure's face obscuring its features. No mouth, nose or eyes were visible, but the face was entirely covered by what appeared to be masking tape.

The figure raised a gloved hand and motioned to the witness, whereupon she yelled at the MIB to come around to the front door where she would be able to see it more clearly in the porch light. Then she went around to the front door and opened it slightly with the chain attached and looked outside, but her strange visitor was nowhere to be seen. She then called the police to report the intruder, but when they arrived no trace of the mysterious prowler could be found.[3]

This monstrous, mummy-like entity constitutes what is perhaps the most bizarre appearance of an MIB on record, but this was only a harbinger of a number of anomalous events that would ensue in the small rural community. On the following evening of November 2 a woman named Lyndia Morel was abducted from a highway in the Goffstown area, as recounted in Chapter Two. Then two nights later on November 4, Mr. Rex S. had an encounter with two glowing Occupants in his yard, as related in Chapter One. Why an MIB sighting, an abduction and an Occupant encounter should take place within days of each other within a limited geographical area remains a mystery.

On the evening of October 27, 1975, two young men, David Stephens (his real name) and his roommate "Glen" (a pseudonym) were out taking a drive in their van in the small town of Norway, Maine, when they encountered two brightly-lit UFOs. The craft emitted a blanket of thick smoke that engulfed the van, leaving the men with a period of missing time before it eventually dissipated. After going public with the story, Stephens was visited by a six foot man wearing a blue suit and sunglasses who warned him in no uncertain terms to keep his mouth shut about his experience.

Undaunted by the threat, Stephens contacted a local physician, Dr. Herbert Hopkins, who agreed to conduct a series of hypnosis sessions to unlock his hidden memories. Under hypnosis, David recalled his ordeal aboard a craft where he was subjected to medical procedures by a group of dwarfish humanoids with bald heads, large, teardrop-shaped eyes and pale, white skin. The case was subsequently popularized by the tabloid newspaper *The National Enquirer*.

Nearly a year later, on the night of September 11, 1976, Dr. Hopkins was visited by a strange individual who claimed to be affiliated with a UFO research organization who wished to interview him about the Stephens case. The man, who did not give his name, was extremely thin, and had chalk white skin and appeared to be wearing lipstick. He was dressed in an ill-fitting black suit and wore a black Homburg-style hat.

The MIB ordered Hopkins to destroy all records of his sessions with Stephens in a melodramatic manner. He told the physician to remove a penny from his pocket and place it in his palm, whereupon the visitor made the coin vanish. The MIB then intimated that abductee Barney Hill had died because his heart had been made to disappear in a similar fashion. After delivering this threat he departed, and in the aftermath Hopkins thought it prudent to destroy all of his research materials about the Stephens case.

Hopkins went public about his encounter, which was published in the *Star* tabloid and appeared in the *Time-Life Mysteries of the Unknown* book series. The story would then go on to become a classic narrative of MIB lore. Then, in 2008, the doctor's relatives revealed that Hopkins was a fantasy-prone personality who was suffering from severe alcoholism at the time, and like Albert Bender, also had a fascination with the occult. These revelations have cast doubts about Hopkins' eerie tale, and now it is widely regarded as probably being a hoax. Note that Barney Hill died of a cerebral hemorrhage in 1969 rather than having his heart removed, which Hopkins, as a physician, would surely be aware of. Hopkins may have been inspired by Stephens' account of his meeting with the "Man in Blue" and decided to elaborate on it for reasons of self-aggrandizement.[4]

Another British case documented by Jenny Randles involved a 17-year-old office worker referred to by the pseudonym "Shirley Greenfield." On January 23, 1976, Shirley was returning to her home in Bolton, Lancashire, from a bus stop at about 5:20 p.m. The suburban street was dark and quiet when Shirley observed a light in the sky that quickly approached until it was hovering directly above her head. The UFO exerted a force that caused the young woman to experience pain in her shoulders and mouth. At this point Shirley's recollection of the event becomes confused, and her next memory is of bursting into her home in a state of shock. She had inexplicably lost about 40 minutes of missing time.

Shirley and her family contacted the police to file a report. They, in turn, passed the story on to a local newspaper, whose reportage generated some unwanted publicity for the Greenfield family. In the aftermath of her close encounter Shirley experienced pain in her eyes, a rash on her neck and shoulders and found small burn marks on her arm and side. Most disconcertingly, when she visited a dentist after experiencing pains in her mouth, some of her dental fillings were discovered to have crumbled into powder and fallen out. Years later Shirley underwent hypnotic regression that revealed an abduction event during which she was physically examined by a tall female entity with sparse, white hair (probably a hybrid), who placed her on an examination table and inundated her mind with a montage of images.

Nine days after her UFO experience Shirley's mother received an anonymous phone call asking about her daughter's health, and inquiring if any marks had been left on her body in the wake of her encounter. Mrs. Greenfield refused to answer the caller's queries, but at 7 p.m. on the following evening on February 3, 1976, two men in black business suits appeared at the Greenfield residence demanding to talk to Shirley. Despite the family's reluctance to speak with the visitors, Mr. Greenfield was somehow compelled to let the duo enter their home.

Both of the men appeared to be about 40 years of age and projected a feeling of power and authority. The taller of the two, who seemed to be in charge, did all the talking and referred to himself only as the "Commander." The other member of the pair, who remained nameless, sat in a chair while operating what was said to be an audio recording device in the shape of a black box. Shirley was subjected to an aggressive interrogation by the Commander that lasted for three hours. She was grilled about every detail of her experience, and her interviewer kept asking if she had any physical symptoms or marks upon her body, which she denied in order to mislead her questioner. The Commander also wanted to know if Shirley had seen anyone while on board the UFO, but she answered in the negative, since she had no memory of encountering the alien being at that time. Oddly, she was also asked if she had ever had a paranormal experience or possessed psychic powers like clairvoyance or telepathy.

When the interrogation had been completed, the Commander insisted that she had seen an RAF experimental aircraft, but Shirley did not agree with this explanation. Before leaving the Greenfield home, Shirley was strongly admonished not to talk to anyone, especially to UFO investigators, about her experience. The two men then left the house and got into a large black car that was parked outside. After their departure the Greenfield family was baffled by the odd behavior of the men and their seeming power to control their actions. Mr. Greenfield had stood by helplessly while the Commander had rudely questioned his daughter for hours while the second man had sat in a chair while staring at Shirley intently during the entire time.[5]

There are a number of similarities between the experiences of the Greenfield family and those of the Veronas. In both instances a female abductee was subjected to an intensive interrogation about their close encounters by a team of two men. One appeared to be the senior member of the team who conducted the interview, while his cohort remained silent. The men in both cases refused to introduce themselves or reveal their names. Ominous black automobiles provided transportation for both teams.

The most telling similarity, however, was in the mental control that the MIBs were able to employ in order to dominate the witnesses and their families during their interrogations. Shirley sensed that the Commander was probing her mind telepathically at the same time as he was questioning her verbally. If the MIBs were government agents, how were they able to exert this level of psychic influence? Outwardly, the MIBs had the appearance of normal human beings, but the witnesses perceived an "otherness" about the men. Their motivation for wanting to suppress information about the abduction events remains unclear.

On the evening of October 2, 1981, a man named Grant Breiland observed a large white light outside his home in Victoria, British Colombia. The sight was so unusual that he raced inside to retrieve his camera in order to snap a picture of the UFO. His camera was equipped with a telephoto zoom lens, through which he could see the object that was radiating beams of energy. He managed to take one picture of the UFO before it turned and sped away into the night.

Three days later on October 5 Breiland visited a Kmart store at a local mall to pick up a part for his CB radio rig. A friend who was supposed to meet him there failed to show up, so he went to a pay phone at the store to call him. It turned out that his friend had suffered an injury and was not going to show up. When he finished the call, he noticed two odd things. First, there were no other people in this part of the store, which contained vending machines and was usually crowded with youngsters. The second thing was that there was a pair of strange-looking men who were staring at him intently.

The men wore dark blue business suits that were almost black. They had sun-tanned complexions, no visible eyebrows and dark, unblinking eyes, and their overall appearance had a stiff, mechanical quality. They stood unmoving with their arms at their sides like soldiers standing at attention and made no motion to use the pay phone as they continued to stare at Breiland fixedly. Then the men asked Breiland for his name and address, but he refused to give out this information. Finally he was asked, "What is your number?" The man did not say "phone number," which left Breiland confused and unwilling to answer.

Their weird interrogation having apparently been concluded, the men turned away and exited the store. Breiland watched as they walked down a disabled ramp into a muddy field across from the store in the pouring rain moving in a robotic fashion. Oddly, there were no people or cars in the area, which was unusual at this busy commercial location during this time of day. The witness saw the men continue walking across the field as if joined together at the hip like Siamese twins. They passed through an idle construction site toward a blank wall at the end of the field. At this point Breiland heard a voice inside his mind calling his name several times. Momentarily distracted, he turned to look around and when he looked back the pair had vanished. Spooked by the strange encounter, he decided not to make his UFO photo public.

Earlier that day a gas station attendant in the area who also happened to witness the October 2 sighting had an encounter with what were apparently the same two men. They approached the station and asked the attendant for a can of "petrol," which is a British term for gasoline. The witness described them as wearing dark suits and having whitish blond hair and he noted that they lacked fingernails on both hands. One of the men paid for the gasoline with a ten dollar bill, but appeared baffled when he was handed his change in coins. The duo marched off with the can of gas until they turned a corner and were lost from sight, but returned with the can about 15 minutes later. After they had left, the attendant went to secure the can and was shocked to find it was still completely full.[6]

Once again the MIBs are seen operating in pairs as they intimidate UFO witnesses and suppress information about sightings. Their behavior seems pointless, even absurd, such as purchasing a can of gas and returning it unused, or asking a witness for their "number." However, these seemingly illogical actions seem to have achieved the desired effect of censoring UFO information, which is the MIBs overall mission. The two men's bizarre, robotic mannerisms seem staged, as if they were deliberately advertising their unearthly origin. How the two men who interrogated Breiland vanished in the middle of an empty field is a mystery. Another uncanny aspect of his MIB encounter is their apparent control of other shoppers in the store by causing them to be absent during their interrogation of Breiland and their subsequent disappearance.

Another enigmatic encounter with an MIB took place in November of 1980 in the University of Pennsylvania Library, where folklorist Peter Rojcewicz was researching UFO lore for a Ph.D. thesis on the subject. Rojcewicz was sitting alone near a window when someone soundlessly approached him from behind. He turned to behold a tall, gaunt man with a very pale complexion regarding him intently. The individual was attired in a loose, rumpled black suit, and wore black shoes, a black string tie and a white shirt.

With one fluid motion the man sat down next to Rojcewicz, folded his hands atop a stack of books and asked Rojcewicz what he was reading about in a voice with a slight European accent. When he replied that he was reading about flying saucers, the man asked, "Have you seen a flying saucer?" When Rojcewicz replied that he hadn't, the man further queried, "Do you believe in the reality of flying saucers?" Rojcewicz answered that he wasn't sure he was interested in the topic. At this point the man became vociferous and shouted, "Flying saucers are the most important fact of the century and you are not interested?" After this outburst the man stood up and said, "Go well on your purpose."

With that the man rose from his seat with the same fluid movement. Rojcewicz did not watch him depart, but sat at the table in shock for a few moments, then got up and looked around. He was shocked to see that the place was deserted. There were no librarians at the reference or information desk, no guards and no students using the usually busy library, which struck Rojcewicz as being extremely odd. He sat back down at his desk feeling disoriented and apprehensive and tried to compose himself, and after about an hour he got up to leave the library and found to his amazement that the library staff had returned to their posts and everything had returned to normal.

The unusual experience left Rojcewicz psychologically shaken and feeling that he had encountered a paranormal being from another reality and that he had been in an altered state of consciousness during the encounter. Unlike most MIBs, who reportedly dress in clean, well-tailored business suits, this one was clothed in a slovenly outfit that looked like he had slept in it. Although Rojcewicz was not himself a UFO witness, the MIB was somehow able to zone in on the one person in the library that was researching the topic at the time. The MIB's parting remark to "go well on your purpose" sounds suspiciously like the "live long and prosper" aphorism frequently mouthed by *Star Trek*'s resident alien, Mr. Spock. As in the Breiland case previously cited, the MIB apparently had the ability to clear the area of any onlookers who may have witnessed the conversation. This "isolation effect" has been noted in other contexts and types of alien encounter incidents.[7]

An MIB encounter that has resemblances to both the Breiland and Rojcewicz cases took place in Stratford, Ontario, on April 25, 1978. The witness was Pat De La Franier, a researcher for the Canadian UFO Research Network (CUFORN). She was working in her office preparing notes on UFO reports for her appearance on a radio show when there was a knock on her office door. This was unusual because she had heard no noise of anyone entering the building's front door or footsteps in the hall leading to where her office was situated.

When De La Franier opened the door she was confronted by a strange looking man dressed entirely in black. Her caller was about five feet six inches tall and extremely thin. His head was slightly enlarged and his hair was sparse, as if his head had been shaved and the hair was starting to grow back. He had an olive-colored complexion, thin lips and severely sunken cheeks. His most striking feature, however, was his eyes, which were dark and extended around the side of his head. De La Franier was transfixed by the man's eyes, which seemed to intrude into her mind and held her spellbound. After about a minute spent just staring at her, the man spoke up in a low, hesitant voice that suggested he had trouble speaking. He asked her, "Would you like a photograph of your family?" When she answered in the negative the MIB turned around and vanished before the astonished eyes of the witness.[8]

As in the Rojcewicz incident, the MIB approached the witness while they were in the process of conducting UFO research, with the aim of intimidating them into abandoning their investigations into the subject. In a manner similar to the Breiland case, the MIB asked the witness a seemingly nonsensical question, and when the inquiry was finished, the mysterious individual turned away and just disappeared into thin air.

One of the most bizarre MIB cases on record was investigated by British researcher Derek James, a colleague of Jenny Randles. The strange events began in August of 1971, when "Jim Wilson" (a pseudonym) observed a white light slowly moving across the sky near his home in the East Midlands of England. His sighting, taken by itself, was unremarkable, but sometime afterward Wilson was visited at his home by two men dressed in business suits who arrived in a dark-colored car. They claimed to be from the Ministry of Defense (MoD) and produced ID cards to identify themselves, then proceeded to question Wilson about his sighting. Their message to the witness was that the light he had observed had been identified as the Russian satellite Cosmos 408, which happened to be passing overhead at the time, and that he might as well forget about the entire event.

Why two government agents from the MoD would be dispatched to interrogate a witness about what was nothing more than a mundane UFO sighting with an entirely credible explanation would remain an open question. However, Derek James was able to ascertain that the Russian satellite was actually passing over Canada at the time of Wilson's sighting, and therefore the explanation provided by the alleged MoD agents was bogus.

After the incident, however, things took a really bizarre turn. Wilson began seeing a black Jaguar car with two men inside that would park outside his home at night, as if he was under surveillance. Unnerved by these nocturnal visitations, Wilson sought help from Derek James, who happened to have a relative who was a high-ranking police official in Wilson's East Midlands town. Considering it unadvisable to have the local police force investigate the MIBs, they concocted a cover story that the two men were planning a robbery at a toy factory that happened to be located near Wilson's home and were "casing the joint" in preparation for the heist.

By October 19 a patrol car had been assigned to monitor the black Jaguar and would begin to gather information about the vehicle's license and registration, along with other details. When it was ascertained that the car's ID information was false, the police decided to take action. On the night of October 21, two policemen were ordered to bring the two men in for questioning. The two officers approached the Jaguar from opposite sides and peered into the car's windows, where they could barely make out two men in the driver's and passenger's seats who were dressed in dark suits in the dim illumination.

Before they could proceed any farther the Jaguar vanished into thin air before the eyes of the terrified policemen. When they had regained their composure, they searched the area, but no trace of the vehicle could be found. The incident was covered up on the police logs because it was too unbelievable to have happened, but at the very least the phantom black Jaguar and its two MIBs would trouble Wilson no more.[9]

This incident implies that the car and its MIBs were not of terrestrial origin. Like the Shirley Greenfield case, the MIBs attempted to convince the witness that the UFO that had been observed was just a conventional object, and both cases involved MIBs who claimed to be from British intelligence services. Note that, as in many MIB encounters, a sinister-looking black car was employed to intimidate the witness. While this account of a disappearing vehicle seems utterly fantastic, it is not the only instance of a vanishing automobile connected to the Men in Black.

An anonymous witness reported his strange experience to the UFO Society International, an anomaly research group. The incident took place on the night of July 29, 1977, as a Canadian Pacific Railroad worker was driving down Highway 95 from Glacier National Park in British Columbia to visit his mother in the town of Invermere, B.C. At about 10:45 p.m. he had reached an intersection where a pristine early model Cadillac came out of nowhere traveling perpendicular to his car. The witness quickly slammed on his brakes to avoid a collision, and his high beam headlights briefly illuminated the interior of the Cadillac and its passengers.

He observed three people inside the car, one person seated in the rear, another on the driver's side looking straight ahead and a third person sitting on the passenger's side, all of whom were dressed in identical black coats and hats. The Cadillac was riding roughly along the road, leaving a cloud of dust in its wake. The witness had a good look at the person on the passenger's side who was staring directly at him with an intense, but unfazed expression given that the two vehicles had nearly collided. The black Caddy and its black-clad passengers drove past the intersection and was quickly lost from sight.

The witness got out of his car to inspect the scene and was shocked to discover there was no trace of the Cadillac to be seen, nor was there any noise from the car's engine to be heard. The only evidence of its passing was a cloud of dust that was quickly dissipating in the gloom.

In addition, he observed that there wasn't any road intersecting the highway, only a steep grade leading down to the valley floor. Thinking that he may have been involved in a freak accident, he backed up his car and shined the headlights down the grade, but there were no skid marks, no evidence of a crash, and the mysterious Cadillac had simply vanished into thin air.[10]

The MIBs car was observed by the witness to be driving in jarring movements over the rough surface of the unpaved grade, which indicates that the Cadillac was a material object and not an illusion. The notion of vanishing automobiles may strain credulity, but this capability has long been observed in connection with the appearance and disappearance of UFO craft. Unlike the other encounters with MIBs cited, in this case the witness had not experienced a UFO sighting, and his near-collision with one of their ubiquitous black limousines on a lonely road in Canada seems to have been a random event.

Another disappearing car case was reported to J. Allen Hynek, although few details were provided about the incident. Sometime in late 1975 a man was driving down a highway near a small town in Minnesota when he began to be harassed by a big black Cadillac that forced his car off to the side of the road and nearly drove it into a ditch. The driver was irate, and quickly righted his vehicle and drove off after the Cadillac in hot pursuit, but as he watched in amazement the big Caddy lifted off the roadway into the air and simply vanished. No MIBs were reported in this encounter, but the big Cadillac limo resembles the standard issue automobile used by MIBs, and the ability of the vehicle to disappear into thin air is consistent with other reports cited.[11]

Perhaps the most unambiguous clue to the nature and identity of the MIBs may have been provided by abductee Terry Lovelace, who experienced a contact with a Woman in Black at his home in Dallas. As chronicled in his 2018 memoir *Incident at Devil's Den*, Lovelace, who reportedly had endured a number of abduction experiences dating back to his childhood, had taken up jogging as a form of exercise. In 2012, after being able to run two miles for the first time, he sustained a painful injury to his right knee that entailed a visit to a hospital emergency room. An X-ray of his knee revealed the presence of an anomalous metal object imbedded in his leg, although his discomfort was actually being caused by a mundane condition called a Baker cyst that cleared up by itself.

Lovelace had undergone a traumatic abduction during the summer of 1977 while camping in Devil's Den State Park in Arkansas and was subjected to an intrusive military investigation of his experience that left him with full recall of the event. Decades later, he was still obsessed with his memories of the abduction and other enigmatic occurrences in his past that were giving him nightmares, and had started to go public about his abductions. The object in the X-ray also mystified him until one evening in October of 2017, when he experienced a visitation by a mysterious individual.

He had been asleep in his bedroom when he suddenly found himself fully awake and sitting upright in the home's family room. Seated in a chair across from him was a female being dressed entirely in black, wearing a black blouse, black slacks and shoes and oversized dark glasses. She wore a disheveled black wig that sat awkwardly on her head. The woman was about four feet tall, with a frame that was scrawny and petite and skin that was a pale, ashen hue with a bluish tint. Her manner and posture, however, seem relaxed and unthreatening, and was designed to put Lovelace at ease, and in fact he did feel as if he was sedated and detected what he described as an unusual ionized scent in the room's atmosphere.

The female began speaking telepathically to Lovelace using plain English words that reassured him that he would not be subjected to an abduction that night. He began to recognize her as a personage he had met and conversed with during an abduction event he had experienced in 1987. The woman then removed her dark glasses to reveal a pair of large, black, almond shaped eyes. Her appearance made Lovelace apprehensive. "She impressed me as a hybrid being made up of one-half human and one-half alien," he recollected. "She was not a human being. She was something else and that was disturbing."

She informed Lovelace that she was visiting him because he had memories of past encounters that could not be erased or suppressed, and that this was a matter of grave concern to her "hosts" (a term she used to describe her alien masters) now that he had gone public with his experiences. Their greatest concern, she told him, was that he would have the implant in his leg, that he had accidentally discovered in his 2012 X-ray, analyzed. It was then divulged that he also had a second implant in his other leg. He was told that her hosts would not allow his implants to be removed and studied by scientists, and that the objects would be removed painlessly while he was sleeping.

After revealing the purpose of her visit, Lovelace experienced a flood of images from his past abductions that she telepathically projected into his mind. He believed that she had done this as a warning against publicly revealing any recollections of these alien visitations. Her message having been delivered, Lovelace lost consciousness and woke up in the family room chair at dawn. About a month later on November 16 he woke up experiencing pain and bruising in both legs. When he had his legs X-rayed he found that the implants had been removed from both his legs while he was sleeping.[12]

Unlike the entities in most other MIB encounters, Lovelace's Woman in Black revealed information about her true nature and origin. In his 2020 follow-up book *Devil's Den: The Reckoning*, he claims that she told him, "As a hybrid, I'm incapable of having children."[13] Following standard MIB operating procedure, her visit to the abductee was designed to warn him about disclosing info concerning his UFO experiences, and ultimately to retrieve material evidence of the aliens' existence. Unlike other MIBs, however, the woman had a past history of interacting with the witness, and possibly had an intimate emotional relationship with Lovelace as what David Jacobs refers to as a "personal project hybrid," that is, a hybrid that has a special, one-on-one bond with an abductee.

This case may provide a clue about the identity of some of the more extraordinary MIBs as human/alien hybrid beings. Writers like John Keel, who have theorized that they have a demonic, supernatural origin, and other researchers who have speculated that they are interdimensional beings or other exotic theories, have perhaps created confusion around their true origin and existence. Like the hybrid beings discussed in the previous chapter, the MIBs can mimic the appearance of ordinary people, yet there is often something subtly off-kilter about their aspect or appearance. Some MIBs adopt the look of normal-looking government bureaucrats wearing smart business suits, while others present themselves to the witnesses in grotesque, quasi-human forms. The entities such as the humongous Mr. Tiny in the Christiansen case, the mummy-like apparition in the Florence Dow case, the strange-looking man in the De La Franier encounter or the robotic duo in the Breiland case seem to have utilized guises that are designed to deliberately call attention to themselves.

Like the hybrids, the MIBs are reportedly able to exert mental control over the minds of humans. One example is the Greenfield case, where the "Commander" displayed the ability to manipulate the witness and her family into submitting to an intrusive interrogation that lasted for hours. In the Rojcewicz incident the MIB was able to induce a sensation of apprehension and disorientation in the witness. A vague feeling of unease can accompany the arrival of even normal-looking MIBs, such as was evident in the Mrs. Verona case. Lovelace's Woman in Black exhibited the telepathic ability to project imagery directly into his mind. Another of their uncanny abilities is to project what has been termed the "isolation effect," in which the immediate vicinity in which they appear is cleared of all bystanders, as was observed in the Breiland and Rojcewicz incidents.

UFOs were involved in some way in all of these occurrences. In the Verona, Greenfield, Wilson and Lovelace cases the MIBs attempted to coerce the witnesses into suppressing disseminating information about their UFO experiences. On the other hand, in the Christiansen, Dow, De La Franier, Breiland and Rojcewicz incidents the MIBs did not query their targets regarding any specific UFO sighting, but perhaps their outlandish appearance was meant to frighten the witnesses and deliver an implied threat to keep quiet about the subject. In most cases these phenomenal intimidators aggressively confronted the witnesses inside their homes, deliberately invading the privacy of their sanctum sanctorum. Then there's the matter of how the MIBs seemed to know every intimate detail of the abductee's experiences, in some cases even more than the abductees themselves remembered. This implies that either they were briefed by the ufonauts, or had been participants in the event.

Another common denominator concerns the ominous black automobiles favored by the MIBs. They are invariably described as being official-looking black limousines such as diplomats or VIPs are chauffeured around in, which lends them an aura of authority. Some witnesses have described the vehicles as being outdated models that are oddly well-preserved and even have that "new car smell." In three cases cited these black cars reportedly have the ability to dematerialize, leading to speculation that they are of alien manufacture or incorporate an element of otherworldly technology into an outwardly terrestrial design.

Some researchers claim that MIB incidents have declined in recent years, but perhaps they have merely changed their style and appearance. In his book *The Uninvited* Nick Pope discusses a British case that has the ambience of an MIB intrusion without the requisite dark attire. The witness was an abductee he refers to as "Mary," whose UFO experience was recounted in Chapter Six. On New Year's Day in 1996 she received a visit from an unusual individual who knocked on her front door. When she opened the door she was confronted by a man wearing an unusual beige-colored coat and a pair of oversized tinted glasses with wispy, disheveled hair. An identification card was thrust forcefully toward Mary's face as the man explained that he was conducting market research for a local supermarket franchise.

The intruder asked Mary if she patronized one of the supermarket chain's stores that had recently opened in the area. Mary lied and told him she didn't, hoping her answer would get rid of her unwelcome caller. The man seemed to cross her name off a list and abruptly turned away and left, but Mary felt uneasy about the encounter and suspected that her visitor had not revealed his true identity. The ID card he had presented displayed the word "research" at the top, but was also inscribed with columns of figures and had what appeared to be a picture of a city skyline instead of an identifying photo of the "researcher." Mary observed that the man's hand holding the card seemed to be wrapped in folds of cloth.

In the aftermath of the intrusion Mary contacted the supermarket chain that the man was supposedly working for and was told that they had been contemplating conducting market research in her area, but that the project would not be implemented for several weeks. It also strains credulity that Mary's researcher would be working on New Year's Day during the holiday season, when many potential respondents would be indisposed while nursing a hangover from the previous night's festivities. The "market research" ploy seems to echo the visit from a representative of the "missing heirs" bureau in the Christiansen MIB case.[14]

Another sub-phenomenon that might be related to MIBs are cases involving what have been termed "Bogus Social Workers," or BSWs. Reports of mysterious individuals claiming to be agents of various social welfare organizations began to appear from all across England during the 1990s. A typical case occurred on the morning of October 10, 1995, when Mark Dunn was alone in his home in Manchester, his wife and children were out of the house, and a visitor came to the door. It was a well-groomed, official looking woman of about 35, who claimed to be a social worker with the Manchester City Council investigating alleged mistreatment of his younger child. When Mr. Dunn demanded to see her identification, the woman told him she had to retrieve it from her car. Dunn observed her retreat to a parked car in which two men were waiting. The woman then got in and the car raced off.[15]

Another BSW case occurred in Leigh, Lancashire, when a well-dressed couple came to the door of one Mrs. Carter, a local nurse who had two daughters. The man, who had the air of a petty bureaucrat, produced a photo ID that identified him as a worker with the community's social services department, while the woman wore a scarf emblazoned with the words, "Child Protection." The "social workers" claimed they were there to investigate reports that Mrs. Carter was not feeding her children properly. The pair inspected the home's pantry area, but Mrs. Carter balked when the man requested to examine her children and the visitors were asked to leave. Mrs. Carter noticed that a large van was parked outside their home, and the man explained to her that the van was used to remove children that were deemed to be at risk. There were three women inside the van wearing similar "Child Protection" scarves, but the man informed her that it would not be necessary to take her children at this time and abruptly left with his female companion.[16]

As reports of the BSWs proliferated, 23 local police forces combined to form "Operation Childcare," a program dedicated to tracking down the enigmatic social workers. Hundreds of BSW incidents were reported, leading the police to believe that multiple pedophile rings were involved. Yet children were not abducted or harmed, and the police were unable to apprehend any of the perpetrators. As the decade of the 1990s progressed, visitations by the BSWs quietly faded into nothingness and are now considered just an urban legend.

Like the MIBs, the BSWs reportedly visited homes, presented themselves as authoritarian figures from governmental agencies, attempted to intimidate the witnesses, and made threats that were never carried out. Unlike the MIBs, however, the BSWs had no connection with UFOs or abductees and did not seem to be anything but normal human beings.

Urban legends, hoaxes, government agents or human/alien hybrid beings, the MIB enigma may incorporate all of these scenarios, but a few select cases would indicate that at least some of these eerie intimidators may be beings of unearthly origin.

CHAPTER EIGHT

Bogus Job Interviewers, Phantom Road Workers and Alien Clowns

In an obscure 1965 British sci-fi/horror film entitled *The Night Caller from Outer Space* (a.k.a. *The Blood Beast from Outer Space*), an alien from Ganymede (a moon of Jupiter) travels to England using a teleportation device and hides himself among the London population. Soon afterward 23 young women in the city are reported missing, and a team of scientists led by Dr. Jack Costain (John Saxon) are assigned to help Scotland Yard unravel the mystery, which is thought to be connected in some way to the alien.

Scotland Yard Superintendent Hartley (Alfred Burke) eventually discovers that all of the missing women have answered a magazine ad for models placed by an enigmatic individual named Mr. Medra. As the investigation continues, one of the job applicants, Joyce Malone (Barbara French), arrives at the office of Medra's company, Orion Enterprises, for a job interview. The bare office is sparsely furnished as Joyce is greeted by Medra (Robert Crewdson), a shadowy figure who sits in a darkened space behind his desk that obscures his features. During the "interview," Joyce is hypnotized by an eye-like device and given a post-hypnotic suggestion to drive to a certain location late at night. As the police and the scientific team close in on Medra, they find his office deserted. They follow Joyce to her rendezvous with Medra but cannot prevent him from teleporting her and the 23 other abducted women to Ganymede to be used for breeding purposes.

The premise of this offbeat, black-and-white, minor-key film may seem ridiculous, yet it mirrors the experiences of a number of individuals who report having undergone what have been termed "bogus job interviews" conducted by human/alien hybrid beings. Although the film was shown on television for years, the connection with the abduction phenomenon did not emerge until decades later, and it's unlikely (although not impossible), that it provided the inspiration for the bogus job interview narratives that follow. Interestingly, the source material for the movie's screenplay was a novel that had been published in 1960.

The first recorded instance of one of these unusual "interviews" appeared in David Jacobs' 1998 exposé *The Threat*. He recounts the experience of a 31-year-old abductee he refers to as "Deborah," who received a phone call from a stranger that summoned her to appear at a job interview. When she arrived at the specified location, she found an office that contained nothing but a few chairs and a desk. An odd-looking person conducted the interview by asking a series of peculiar questions which served to put her into a trance state, and when the interview was over, Deborah suspected that the questioner may have had some sort of sexual interaction with her. She left the interview feeling confused, with a hazy memory of what had transpired. A few days later she was able to locate the office building again, but found that it was deserted.[1]

At the time, Jacobs chalked Deborah's experience up to what he called "Independent Hybrid Activity," which encompassed actions taken by hybrids independent of the Grays that usually involved sexual or romantic liaisons with abductees that took place in an everyday human environment. Subsequent research, however, would reveal that these bogus job interviews were part of a pattern that would later be replicated in other, similar incidents. Some common narrative elements would include receiving a telephone call from a stranger summoning the interviewee to a deserted, sparsely-furnished office; an interviewer who places the job seeker into an altered state of consciousness leading to a possible sexual encounter; and an induced memory lapse in the aftermath of the meeting.

This pattern did not become evident until the publication of Budd Hopkins' 2003 book *Sight Unseen*, which recounted three unusual job interview events experienced by abductees. The first of these was recalled by a woman he refers to as "Terry Bradshaw," who in addition to relating several abductions in her past also told a story about a mysterious event that had taken place in 1971, when she was just 16 years old. Terry was sitting in a pizza parlor with some high school friends when she was approached out of the blue by a man who came to their table and asked her if she would like to be interviewed for a summer job at his company. When she agreed, the man told her he would pick her up and drive her to the interview on the following day. Oddly, the man addressed her using her first name, even though they had never met. Terry gave her prospective employer her address and he left. He was described as being in his late 50s or early 60s, with graying salt-and-pepper hair and was wearing a suit and tie. Strangely, he did not give his name or the name of his company and provided no details about the nature of the job.

The next day at around 2 o'clock the man drove up to Terry's home to transport her to the interview. Oddly, her mother expressed no concerns about her teenage daughter going off with a strange man for an interview at an unknown location. She got in the car on the front passenger seat beside him and immediately felt herself slipping into an uncanny mood. During the drive to the interview site, which was located near the town of Flemington, New Jersey, the man began talking about intimate events in Terry's life that he could not possibly have known about, including being abandoned by her father and sexually abused by her stepfather. He told her he knew about everything she did, and even proceeded to relate how she had lost her virginity with her boyfriend on the previous day.

Terry and the man (whose name she could not recall) arrived at an old office building and they went inside. He led her into a large, empty room that contained nothing except for a desk and a chair, then proceeded to tell her about the business that he described as being about "trucks and people," presumably a dispatcher's position. Her job would entail answering the phone, taking messages and keeping track of the locations of the truckers. He stressed that it was a wonderful opportunity, and that all she had to do to get the job was to have sex with him. Shocked at this revelation, Terry resisted the man's advances and told him she didn't want the job, whereupon he seemed resigned and didn't insist.

They left the building but on the ride back to Terry's house the man took a detour, saying that he had to stop at a friend's house for a minute. As they drove through a deserted area, Terry's apprehension began to mount. They finally pulled into a dirt driveway in front of what she at first perceived to be a strange-looking little house with what looked like a flat stone roof and glass windows along the bottom that was partially obscured from view by a field of tall grass. Telling her to wait in the car, he got out and went into the house. From this point on, Terry's memory becomes confused as the man returned in the company of a troop of Grays and she was led out of the car and entered the "house," which was obviously a screen memory for a landed UFO. An abduction event ensued, and afterward she was driven home by her prospective employer with only a hazy memory of everything that had transpired.[2]

Hopkins summarizes the many anomalous features of Terry's experience, beginning with the fact that her "employer" appeared to be a normal-looking person who was able to perform everyday functions in our world such as driving a car and renting office space. Beyond that, he was somehow able to access Terry's most intimate memories, and was able to exert a measure of control over her actions. His sexual behavior toward a 16-year-old girl is perverse and shows a lack of understanding about human mores. All of these attributes would seem to indicate that he was not an ordinary person, but a hybrid being.

The phony "job interview" was only a ruse designed to lure Terry into a secluded area where an abduction took place. A pattern begins to emerge from these cases. First, the participant is contacted about a job and agrees to attend a meeting. Second, the interviewee is told nothing about the nature of the employment, job hours or salary, nor is the prospective employer interested in the résumé, background or experience of the job candidate. Third, the interview takes place in a deserted office building with minimal office furniture, as if it was a hastily constructed movie set. Fourth, the interviewer is able to exercise a degree of mental control over the applicant. Fifth, there is a sexual component to the experience. Like visits from the Men in Black, a prospective employer in a job interview situation wields a position of power and authority over a subservient individual.

The next case Hopkins presents has similarities with the experience of Deborah cited by David Jacobs. A 20-year-old woman Hopkins refers to as "Lisa," who had undergone an abduction experience when she was seven, saw an ad for a security job in a local paper and decided to apply, as the pay was good and the working hours were convenient. She received driving instructions over the phone on how to reach the interview site, which was located near the town of Woodbridge, New Jersey.

She arrived at an unassuming office building that was between three and five stories tall. There was no sign on the door, and the office space was shabby and minimally furnished. There were no filing cabinets, typewriters or other office accoutrements, only a desk with a phone and a wastebasket with nothing in it. A woman sat at the desk who was seemingly the firm's receptionist, but when Lisa asked her about a restroom she did not reply, but seemed frightened and quickly exited the room.

Lisa's interview took place in an adjacent room that contained nothing except a desk, a chair and a water cooler. Her interviewer was described as being a neatly-dressed African American man who seemed to have a stiff, military bearing. The man had her fill out some information on a clipboard, then offered her a cup of water, which she drank without giving it any thought. The interviewer proceeded to tell her about the particulars of the job, which involved keeping watch over her fellow employees at a warehouse and reporting any thefts she observed to the management. His voice droned on and on, putting Lisa into an entranced state which may have been augmented by the drink of water she had taken.

Lulled by the interviewer's voice, Lisa fell asleep while he was delivering his spiel. When she awoke, he quickly ended the meeting and ushered her out of the room without even a handshake. He had done all the talking during the interview, but had asked her no questions about her background or employment experience. When she stood up to leave she found that her pantyhose were not on right, leading her to speculate that she may have been sexually assaulted during the encounter. Leaving the building, she found it was totally deserted. There wasn't even anyone in the lobby.[3]

This incident has a number of similarities with the case of Deborah that was previously cited by Jacobs. Both women heard about the "job opportunity" under cryptic circumstances. They were both directed to the meeting site by a caller on the telephone. Both interviews took place in deserted buildings that seemed to be hastily constructed simulacra of office environments. In both cases a male interviewer entranced the applicant with his voice and rendered her unconscious, and both women felt that they had been sexually assaulted without their knowledge during the event.

Hopkins discusses a third instance of a suspicious job interview, that of an abductee he calls "Sally." An Ohio resident, Sally received a telephone call from a strange woman one day who insisted that she go on a job interview for a position she had not applied for. She was given a set of complex driving instructions and arrived at the site that afternoon, where she noted the presence of a number of men who were dressed in identical suits without ties. Sally was met by a lady who conducted her inside the building into a bare office containing nothing but a desk and a chair where the interview was to take place.

As she sat in the chair she was greeted by her interviewer, who explained that the job involved selling a new line of perfume. He held a bottle of the stuff under her nose for her to sample, and the fragrance was so strong she felt her head swoon. The man seemed to take control of her actions and kept the perfume bottle under her nose while he made her keep breathing the scent in. Sally nearly fell over and the next thing she remembered he was thanking her for coming on the interview, and that the meeting had gone well. She was then escorted back to her car and drove home with a hazy recollection of the event, but subsequently recalled an abduction experience that had occurred in the deserted office building.[4]

In all four of these cases the promise of a job interview served to lure the candidates to empty, unfurnished office spaces that were bare of any furniture or office equipment. None of the applicants were told anything about the nature of the job, were given any specific information about salary or even provided with a business card. They were not asked about the applicant's employment history, education, training or job skills, nor were they required to provide basic contact information such as their addresses or telephone numbers. The process by which the job seekers were informed about the interview and given instructions about how to get to the meeting site are also unusual and sometimes not clearly recollected. All four of the cases involved a sexual assault component, and two of them seemed to be a pretext to attract the women into a situation where they were subjected to an abduction experience.

These bogus job interviews are not confined to the United States. The case of Shirley Greenfield, who was abducted near her home in Bolton, Lancashire, in 1976 and was later visited by two Men in Black who interrogated her at length about her experience, was recounted in the previous chapter. This event, however, had a curious postscript.

In 1984, about a week after Shirley had undergone regression hypno-sis about her abduction, she received a mysterious phone call from a stranger who invited her to a job interview at a hotel in Manchester city center. It was supposedly a well-paying position, but would involve her immediately relocating to the African nation of Zimbabwe. The caller insisted that Shirley had applied for the position, but as she had not done so she declined to attend the interview. This scenario is consistent with some of the other cases in which the applicant was contacted by a stranger on the telephone who directed them to come to an interview for a job they had not applied for.[5]

In addition to these published accounts, the author would like to recount his own firsthand experience concerning an enigmatic job offer which bears a number of similarities to the narratives related by abduction researchers:

"Let me state at the outset that, although there have been some curious events in my background, I have no conscious recollection of ever seeing a UFO or an alien, and I do not consider myself an abductee. Yet, when I read these accounts it brought to mind an enigmatic occur-rence that has always puzzled me.

"It was during the spring of 1982, several months after I had grad-uated from college, and I was in need of employment but had few pros-pects. I was living in New York City, in the borough of Queens at the time, and had decided to travel to 'the city' (a.k.a. Manhattan) that day. Note that I was not going for an interview about a job and was not dressed in a jacket and tie or carrying a résumé, but was dressed in casual attire for pleasure, not business.

"Arriving from Queens via subway, I left Grand Central Station and was about to reach 42nd Street through the Vanderbilt Avenue exit. This exit is an enclosed space that is part of the Grand Central com-plex. Out of nowhere, a strange man walked up to me and asked me if I was looking for a job. The man appeared to be completely normal, and was dressed in a white shirt without a necktie and appeared to be in his late 20s to early 30s. My impression was that he was a 'salesman' and his bearing was somewhat aggressive."

"After asking if I was looking for work he told me, 'I have a great job for you.'" He doesn't tell me what kind of job it is, nor does he give me any information about hours or salary. He doesn't ask me about my employment experience or background. Instead of presenting me with a flyer or business card listing the company's name, he takes a piece of scrap paper from somewhere and writes down an address, a date and a time and tells me, "Be there. It's a great job."

"In retrospect, I was surprised that I hadn't asked him for more information about the position, but I was too flabbergasted by his offer and was caught off guard. I merely walked out onto the street and continued on my way. At the time I didn't think it was unusual that he had somehow picked me out of the crowd coming out of Grand Central and knew that I was sorely in need of employment, nor did I think it was odd that the man was recruiting job seekers in such a casual way without giving out any printed material or other information about the position."

"When I returned home I shared my good news with my wife, who was immediately suspicious about the offer. For one thing, the address for the interview was located somewhere in the borough of Queens instead of an office in Manhattan, where these kinds of meetings were usually conducted. For another, the interview was scheduled for 8 o'clock in the evening, which was also unusual. Under the circumstances I was urged not to go to the meeting and was forced to agree with her."

"Nevertheless, I remained very curious about the job offer, which seemed to be a fortuitous circumstance that had just fallen into my lap. Without telling my wife, I conceived a plan to go to the job site secretly to scope out the location for myself during the daytime. For all I knew the offer was legit and might be a good opportunity. My first task was to identify the location and figure out how to get there using public transit. Queens is the largest of the five boroughs in New York City, and its street layout is confusing. There are multiple streets bearing the same number, such as 67th Road, 67th Drive, 67th Street, etc. The address I was given was something like '48–23 37th Drive.' Consulting a map, I found that this address was situated in a section of the Borough called Long Island City, which was an industrial district consisting mostly of factories."

"One afternoon I set out on my secret mission. It wasn't easy to get there, as I had to take a bus from my neighborhood to Queens Plaza, then take an elevated subway line to my destination. When I got off the train I found myself in a factory area as I sought out the exact address. It turned out to be a dark, dingy-looking two story building that looked like it might have been deserted. Looking around at the area, it was not a locale where I would care to work, and there was no way that I would come to this forbidding place for an interview at 8 o'clock at night. I wondered what kind of job I might have been offered in a place like that, perhaps a night shift at a shabby factory. Right then and there I decided that I didn't want the job."

"It wasn't until decades later when I read the bogus job interview accounts in Hopkins' *Sight Unseen* that I realized the similarity to my own strange experience. Was the brief encounter with the 'salesman' in Grand Central something more than it seemed? He looked completely normal, but seems to have exerted some force of will that made me want to accept the job offer without question. I also felt that I was placed under a compulsion to go to the interview site, as if I was being lured to this isolated location for some hidden purpose. In a manner similar to the preceding narratives, I was not given any information about the nature of the job, salary, work hours, or even the identity of the prospective employer. The site where the interview was supposed to take place was the same kind of decrepit building described in the other accounts. After reading about those bogus job interviews and their connection with abductions, I have been left to wonder about what might have happened had I gone to that meeting at the appointed date, place and time."

Another mysterious aspect of the abduction phenomenon that might possibly be related to hybrid activity that directly affects our environment could be termed "Phantom Highway Workers." Researchers have long puzzled over the way that roads and highways that are usually well traveled are devoid of all vehicular traffic during the times that automobile abductions take place. Consider, for instance, the experience of Michael Shea, as related in Chapter Two. Shea was driving down Route 40 in Maryland early one evening on his way to meet a friend and noticed that this busy stretch of highway, which was usually well traveled during the peak of rush hour, was entirely free of other cars. This oddity turned out to be a prelude to an abduction experience.

In his book *The Black Triangle Abduction*, author Bill Foster, his wife and another couple were driving on Highway 601 near Yadkinville, North Carolina, at about 10:50 p.m. on November 16, 1996, when they noticed a triangular pattern of lights in the sky that appeared to be approaching their car. Foster happened to notice that no other vehicles could be seen traveling anywhere on the highway. As the lights drew nearer they resolved themselves into an enormous black triangular UFO which transported the car and its passengers inside the craft on a tractor beam where they were abducted.[6]

A similar event took place in Church Stowe, Northamptonshire, in the U.K. on November 22, 1978, when Elsie Oakensen was driving home by herself from a teacher's center at around 5:30 in the evening. As she turned onto Highway A5, she observed a "dumbbell-shaped" UFO in the distance that began pacing her car. She noted that there were no other vehicles using this frequently traveled stretch of roadway during the early evening rush hour. She was eventually taken inside the UFO where a typical abduction took place.[7]

Mr. Foster's black triangle abduction had a curious postscript. The incident had taken place on the night of November 16–17, roughly between 11:00 p.m. and 2:00 a.m., when he and his wife arrived at their home after experiencing several hours of missing time amnesia. Foster decided to go public with his story, accounts of which appeared in several local papers. About six months after the abduction event, Foster received an envelope from an anonymous source that contained a handwritten page from the dispatcher's log of the Yadkinville Sheriff's Department for the night of 16–17 November. The log sheet revealed that there had been a total radio blackout between all of the sheriff's police vehicles between 10 p.m. and 2 a.m. that evening. Beginning at 10 p.m., roughly an hour before the abduction took place, no communications could be made between the county's patrol cars and the central dispatching office. Then, at 2 a.m., the time that the Fosters arrived home, all of the Sheriff's Department radios mysteriously began functioning again. It would appear that some unknown agency had caused the breakdown of the entire communication system at the same time that the abduction had taken place.[8]

A clue as to how busy stretches of roadway can be cleared of all traffic during highway abductions may have been provided in Philip J. Imbrogno and Marianne Horrigan's 1997 book entitled *Contact of the 5th Kind.* The authors recount the experience of a computer programmer referred to by the pseudonym Bill, who was returning from his job in Norwalk, Connecticut, to his home in Stormville, New York, on the night of July 19, 1984. This was during a wave of sightings of large, triangular-shaped UFOs in the Hudson Valley region of upstate

New York. While driving down Route 54 in Dutchess County at around 11:00 p.m. he encountered an enormous, black triangular craft and was stopped by a posse of Grays on the road ahead who floated him up into the UFO where he was subjected to the usual quasi-medical procedures during the abduction.

The authors were puzzled by the fact that no other cars were traveling on Route 54 that night, which is a major thoroughfare in that part of the state. They received a communication from a motorist who travels the route on a nightly basis who claimed that he had encountered a roadblock on the route that evening. The road was closed and the driver was directed onto a side road by two or three men wearing coveralls and yellow outfits with hard hats who waved him onto the detour with glowing rods. The authors contacted highway authorities, local utility and telephone companies in the Dutchess and Putnam County areas to ascertain the identity of this mysterious road crew, but were told that no one from any of these agencies had been working on Route 54 that night. They concluded, "Perhaps the road was blocked off by the intelligence in the UFO, the same beings that abducted Bill. Their purpose, without a doubt, was to get him on that road by himself. What bothered us was that the people who blocked off the road were reported to be quite human-looking." This incident implies that hybrids disguised as highway workers were instrumental in clearing this stretch of highway of all vehicular traffic so that an abduction could take place in total secrecy.[9]

A related case was reported from the British UFO journal *Flying Saucer Review* as having taken place in South Africa on the night of May 30–31, 1974. The witnesses were a couple referred to as "Peter" and his wife "Frances" were driving from Fort Victoria in Rhodesia to Durban, Natal, South Africa. Toward the beginning of their journey they observed what they assumed to be a policeman sitting on the side of the road. The figure was dressed in a strange-looking metallic suit and was holding a device they thought was a "walkie-talkie" in its hand. As the trip progressed the couple remembered seeing a UFO that paced their vehicle, and at one point Peter lost control of the car which accelerated to a speed of 200 kilometers per hour. The couple experienced being in an altered state of consciousness, a total lack of audible sound (the Oz Factor), and feeling unusually cold. During a hypnotic regression Peter underwent months later, he recalled having undergone an abduction.

The couple reflected that it was odd that they had encountered no other motorists during their road trip, even though they were traveling on a busy route during the night before a South African public holiday, National Day, when an increase in traffic would be expected. Then there is the matter of the oddly attired "policeman" they had glimpsed at the start of their trip who was holding a "walkie-talkie" device in his hand. Could this person be analogous to the phantom road workers who cleared the highway of traffic in the Dutchess County case cited above?[10]

An incident reported by British researcher Nick Pope described a bizarre abduction experience that took place on a Florida Turnpike during the night of January 3, 1991. Peter (another pseudonym), a British man vacationing in the States, was traveling with his girlfriend "Jenny" and a mutual friend "Sharon" from Orlando, Florida, to Boca Raton via the Florida turnpike, a toll road that passed through a desolate area of the state. Using the turnpike obliges motorists to pick up a ticket at the beginning of their journey that will determine the toll they will pay when they exit the road. The ticket must be presented at an exit booth when the driver reaches their destination.

Jenny was driving, while Peter was in the passenger seat and Sharon was asleep in the back seat during the trip. Peter and Jenny were stunned to find that their car had somehow passed by the exit booth and entered Boca Raton without having surrendered the ticket. There appeared to be a period of missing time during which their vehicle had been transported on the other side of the exit point. Peter remained fixated on the incident and underwent regression hypnosis in 1995 to unlock his hidden memories of that night.

Peter recalled the car being drawn off the road and transported up into the air. He was the only person in the car who remained conscious, as Jenny and Sharon had been "switched off" by whatever force was manipulating them. Peter exited the vehicle and found himself walking alone down a metallic corridor that reminded him of a passageway in a naval vessel. He followed a series of tubular yellow lights imbedded in the floor that appeared to be guiding him down the corridor until he reached the open door to what he described as a large storeroom.

Entering the room he was surprised to find it was stacked with cardboard boxes, some of which were old and held together with masking tape. Inside the boxes Peter found various items used in highway maintenance work such as yellow hazard lamps, detour and stop signs. Peter seemed amused by this puzzling discovery and laughed out loud while remembering this during his hypnosis session. He remembered leaving the storeroom and going back into the passageway, where the yellow floor lights led him back the way he had come and into the automobile. After he was back in the passenger seat the car was deposited back on the roadway on the outskirts of Boca Raton, and Peter and Jenny were restored to normal consciousness (albeit with a period of missing time amnesia), while Sharon had slept throughout the entire incident.[11]

Taken by itself, the discovery of boxes of road maintenance equipment on board a UFO seems incongruous and mystifying until being put into the context of phantom road crews who would presumably make use of these items to establish roadblocks and detour traffic away from specified stretches of highway where abductions can take place without witnesses.

Oddly, many UFO abductees suffer from "colurophobia," or fear of clowns. This may be due to childhood abduction experiences in which the abductors take on the appearance of child-friendly fantasy characters such as clowns. Clown imagery is thought to represent "screen memories" that mask the true faces of the aliens. In their 1997 book *The Truth About Alien Abductions*, British authors Peter Hough and Moyshe Kalman write that "[t]he clown is the happy, smiling face in the car that tries to entice children to take a ride by offering sweets. It has been used to great effect in horror films and books. Yet it also surfaces in the twilight zone of anomalous experience. It is a thread that runs through the UFO phenomenon."[12]

Alien clowns have appeared in a number of films and TV shows. The most memorable is Pennywise, the homicidal clown featured in Stephen King's novel *It*, which was adapted into a 1990 TV miniseries and a 2017 movie version. By the end of the narrative Pennywise's clown disguise is discarded and his true identity is revealed to be a monstrous, spider-like entity. *Killer Klowns from Outer Space* (1988) featured an invasion of extraterrestrial bozos that menace the town of Santa Cruz, California, with their murderous circus antics. The 2002 TV miniseries *Taken* had a subplot involving a strange "circus" and a fantasy animal being that are illusions used by aliens to lure children into a UFO to be abducted.

There are reports in which brightly-colored circus-themed imagery has been used to entice children into situations in which they can be abducted. The authors cite the experience of "Stephanie," who had an unusual encounter in 1960, when she was 10 years old and living in Merseyside, in northern England. Stephanie and another girl were playing in a row of abandoned buildings that were awaiting demolition when they saw something that attracted them inside one of the ruined homes. Hanging in an alcove inside the drab, dusty structure was a brightly-colored clown costume. Beguiled by the sight, the girls entered the house to get a better look, but when Stephanie attempted to touch the suit it rippled like a disturbed reflection on the surface of water, causing the girls to flee in panic. It's possible that the gaudy image of the clown suit was a hologram designed to lure children to a deserted location where they could be abducted.[13]

An abduction case involving circus imagery was reported in a letter to Terry Lovelace in his book *Devils Den: The Reckoning*. The event took place on a family farm in rural Oklahoma about 60 years ago (date unspecified), where two sisters, nine-year-old "Julia" and her seven-year-old sibling "Mollie" were spending a two week summer vacation at their grandparent's farm. The farm was divided into two sections, a front yard where the girls were allowed to play, and a rear area containing a small pond and outbuildings where the farm machinery was stored. The children were strictly forbidden to venture into the rear area because of the drowning hazard presented by the pond. The two parts of the farmstead were separated by a ten foot high earthen wall that was used as a pathway for the tractor and also served as a barrier that the sisters were prohibited from crossing.

One day as the girls were playing in the front yard they heard the sound of calliope music indicating that a circus was in the vicinity. They became excited at the thought of the carnival amusements offered by the circus, but the sounds were coming from somewhere on the other side of the earthen berm. While they were unwilling to break the rules by going into the farm's rear area, they decided to clamber up the barrier just to have a look. What they saw there amazed them.

An enormous merry-go-round ride was spinning madly next to the pond. It was decorated with a million multicolored lights and the ride's horses were not attached to poles, but were galloping freely as if they were alive. The merry-go-round was not sitting on the ground, but was hovering about three feet in the air with a shadow clearly visible underneath. As they took in this phantasmagoric sight, the calliope music swelled louder, and as the girls watched the object they began to fall into a hypnotic trance and soon lost consciousness.

The girl's grandparents soon found out that the children were missing and called the police. An extensive search for them was organized that lasted well into the afternoon with no results. Thinking that the girls may have both drowned in the pond, a team of boatmen was called in to drag the bottom with long poles in order to dislodge any bodies that may have been concealed in its murky depths, but nothing was found. Then one of the boatmen discovered the sisters lying on the other side of the berm, seemingly asleep. The two girls seemed to have just materialized out of nowhere in an instant. When they awakened, neither of them had any memory of anything that had happened during the time they had been missing.

Oddly, the family never talked about the incident during the years that followed, but both Julia and Mollie suffered from post-traumatic stress for the remainder of their lives. Mollie in particular had been psychologically devastated by the experience, and the sisters only discussed what had been an abduction decades later, when she was on her deathbed dying of cancer. Both women wept as they recalled the aliens performing gynecological procedures on them that had shattered their lives forever.[14]

The fantastic carousel ride they had witnessed was doubtless an illusion created by the abductors to mask the true appearance of a UFO. The calliope music seems to have had the effect of lulling the girls into losing consciousness. Unsurprisingly, none of the other family members on the farm saw the merry-go-round or heard the circus music. The sudden reappearance of the girls in an area that had been in plain sight of the searchers for hours is likewise inexplicable.

One of the strangest close encounters in the history of ufology was the case of what has been called "Sam the Sandown Clown," which was investigated by the British UFO Research Association (BUFORA). The incident took place near the village of Sandown on the Isle of Wight, a British resort area, and as in the preceding case, the only witnesses were two seven-year-old children, referred to with the pseudonyms "Fay" and "Henry." One afternoon in early May of 1973 the children were playing near a golf course when they heard a siren-like wailing sound that drew them across the links to an isolated swampy area, where they encountered a strange, apparitional figure.

The being was described as being almost seven feet tall with a head that seemed to be wedged onto his shoulders without a neck. He wore a yellow pointed hat with a round black knob on top and two antenna-like protruding wooden spikes on either side. The face was chalk white, with triangular markings for eyes, a square brown splotch at the nose and yellow lips that did not move when he talked. His clothes consisted of a shabby green tunic and a pair of worn, white trousers. He had four fingers on each hand and four toes on his feet, and was holding what appeared to be a microphone connected to a cord, which had been making the siren-like noise.

A notebook was produced by the creature who wrote a message to the children in big block letters that said, "Hello and I am all colors Sam." Entranced by this friendly greeting, the children began asking Sam questions and he then spoke to them without moving his lips. When asked if he was a man, he replied in the negative, but when they inquired if he was a ghost, he answered, "Well, not really, but I am in an odd sort of way," but the being never revealed his true identity, even insisting he had no name, although he had already identified himself as "Sam."

The clown-like entity calling itself "All Colors Sam" is pictured in this illustration from the British *BUFORA* periodical.

The clown-like entity invited the children into a nearby hut that he claimed was his home. It was a squat, metal structure lacking windows, but having a curved roof. As the hut had no door, Sam and the children entered through a small flap in the hut's side. On the inside the hut had a lower level with walls that were covered with blue-green wallpaper and a pattern of dials. The room contained some simple wooden furniture and an electric heater. The children conversed with Sam for about half an hour before taking their leave and returned home without further incident.

Fay did not mention the strange incident to her father, who is referred to in the report as "Mr. Y" until three weeks later on June 2. While he thought Fay's story was far-fetched, he was impressed by his daughter's sincerity and the wealth of detail in her story. He went looking for Sam's metal hut, but could not find it or any indication that it had been where the children said it had been located. Another strange detail was that the children claimed that while they were conversing with Sam there were two workmen nearby who were repairing a post who did not perceive the bizarre figure of the clown entity. Although no UFO was seen in connection with the appearance of the being, Mr. Y reported to researchers that he had witnessed anomalous objects in the vicinity several years earlier. It's also possible that Sam's "hut" was in reality a landed UFO disguised by the aliens' powers of illusion and that the children had been abducted and taken inside the craft.[15]

A more recent case involving a clown-like alien was described in Hopkins' book *Sight Unseen*. The chief witness was an abductee named "Edward" (a pseudonym), who had contacted him concerning his experience with an unusual individual inside an Outback restaurant in River Oaks, a suburb of Chicago in 1999. Edward, who was dining with his wife "Doris" and a friend, "Doug," had finished having dinner when he became aware of a man standing by another table who was staring at him intently. The man was dressed in an outlandish fashion, in Hopkins' words, "as if he were a clown from a circus or an actor of some sort."[16] Clad in a brightly-colored plaid jacket with a circular collar and leather elbow patches, he sported a distinctive beard and had dark, bronze-colored skin like a Native American, and was wearing a brown fedora. There was another person standing next to him who could not be seen clearly but who appeared to be a female with short, black hair. These two parties were the only patrons in the restaurant at that time, but the waiters ignored the strange man and his companion as if they were somehow invisible.

After Doug paid the bill the trio left the restaurant through the front door, leaving the two odd people behind them inside the restaurant. When they reached the parking lot, however, they were astounded to encounter the weird man and his companion standing near a red sports car about 200 feet in front of them. There was no way the two persons could have exited the restaurant's door and somehow taken up their position during the few moments it had taken Ed, Doris and Doug to reach the parking lot. The strange man and woman were still glaring at Ed fixedly.

Ed's next memory is clouded in confusion. He recalls being lifted up into the air and looking down to see Doris and Doug looking like they were asleep in the back seat of his car and had apparently been "switched off." He was taken aboard a hovering UFO where he underwent a number of procedures while lying on an examination table. Afterwards, he was returned to the parking lot to rejoin Doug and Doris and drive home, with only a sketchy remembrance of the abduction.[17]

Unlike most accounts of hybrids that describe them as wearing unobtrusive clothing and striving for a normal overall appearance, the entity in this case was attired in an outlandish, circus-like outfit that seemed designed to deliberately attract attention. Ed claimed that he saw the strange man on board the UFO while he was undergoing his abduction experience. Like the Sandown Clown, the figure could only be perceived by select individuals and was invisible to others. How did the man and his companion manage to exit the restaurant and take up position in the parking lot in front of Ed, Doris and Doug in such an anomalous manner? Note that another strange vehicle, in this case a red sports car (possibly a BMW model), was involved in the encounter.

Bogus job interviewers, phantom road workers and mysterious clowns are all facets of the hybrid presence in our everyday world. These uncanny entities exist on the boundaries of what we consider reality, intruding into our human sphere only to meddle in the lives of abductees before fading back into the shadows.

Chapter Nine

The Darkside Hypothesis

Black Helicopters and Military Abductions

In a scene from Steven Spielberg's classic 1977 saucer movie *Close Encounters of the Third Kind*, a group of small town folks have gathered one evening to watch for UFOs after a mass sighting. A feeling of warm camaraderie prevails as the crowd waits patiently for an encounter with an otherworldly reality. At last, two bright lights are seen approaching in the distance as one of the watchers displays a sign that reads "Stop and Be Friendly" as they anticipate a meeting with extraterrestrial visitors. As the lights approach more closely, however, they turn out not to be alien spaceships, but a pair of U.S. military helicopters that disperse the crowd with their rotor wash.

The helicopters are being used to create confusion in the minds of the witnesses by making them believe that the UFOs they had observed were nothing but military aircraft. In the film this operation is part of an effort to cover up the real contact with aliens, which will be conducted secretly by government officials. Later in the film helicopters are used to disperse a sleep-inducing gas to prevent unauthorized personnel from witnessing the dramatic first contact between humanity and extraterrestrials. The movie's screenplay does not explain exactly why our government is using military assets to conceal their clandestine collaboration with the aliens and to drug and intimidate ordinary citizens, but its plot does reflect a real-world connection between UFO abductees and what have been called "black helicopters."

These mystery aircraft first began to be reported in the late 1970s in connection with the so-called "cattle mutilation" phenomenon. Ranchers in the western United States began to find livestock that had been killed and certain body parts removed with surgical precision and their carcasses drained of blood. The mutilations were associated with the actions of unmarked helicopters that were seen in the vicinity of the animal victims. Some witnesses claimed that UFOs, not helicopters, were responsible for the mutilations. A number of alternative explanations for the phenomenon have been put forth, including the actions of predators, ritual killings by satanic cults, clandestine military operations and attacks by cryptids, but a connection between UFOs and mystery helicopters had been established in the public mind.

The aircraft were described as being machines used by the U.S. military such as the Bell UH-1 "Huey" copter used extensively in the Vietnam War. Colored black, gray or dark green, their common feature was a total lack of tail numbers, unit markings or insignia that could identify them. Over time, they would become associated with conspiracy theories about a military takeover of America by a secret cabal within our government or by the United Nations. Aside from their alleged participation in cattle mutilations and paranoid notions about secret military operations, the mystery helicopters have also been involved in the apparent harassment of abductees, and some researchers theorize that the Men in Black have traded in their black automobiles for black helicopters.

In his foreword to Raymond Fowler's 1990 book *The Watchers: The Secret Design behind UFO Abduction*, Whitley Strieber states, "Another odd and hitherto unpublished fact is that people who have the visitor experience very often observe unmarked helicopters over their homes in the months and years afterward. Indeed, this bizarre outcome is surprisingly consistent. A fair number of these witnesses have photographed the helicopters, and they can be identified as unmarked versions of common types."[1]

Abductee Betty Andreasson and her husband Bob Luca (who also claims to have been abducted) reported being plagued by flights of helicopters over their home, including an unmarked aircraft that descended and hovered right over Betty one day while she was working in her garden. Then, on June 8, 1978, at 5:35 p.m., Betty and her daughter were alone in their house in Ashburnham, Massachusetts, when they glanced out their front window to observe two odd-looking men in their driveway who seemed to be surveilling the house and grounds. One of the men was very tall and was dressed in a black suit. He had pale features, a severely high forehead and very dark, black hair.

The second man was short, was wearing a khaki-colored jacket, and walked behind his companion with a strange, shuffling gait.

Betty and her daughter were apprehensive as they watched the two strange figures, but hesitated to call the police. When cars drove by the house the two men concealed themselves behind some bushes, and when the traffic had passed by they walked behind a nearby stone wall and were lost from sight. A short while later Betty and Becky saw two cars that had been hidden from sight drive away, presumably with the two strange men inside.[2] This episode has all the earmarks of a classic MIB encounter, and there was perhaps a connection between the two men who paid a house call and the mysterious helicopters.

After the family had moved to Connecticut, Betty's husband Bob Luca became obsessed with the black, unmarked aircraft that were flying over their home at altitudes as low as 100 feet. He took hundreds of photographs of these machines, which had dark-tinted cockpit windows that prevented the pilots from being seen. Luca managed to track one of the helicopters to the Sikorsky Memorial Airport near Stratford, Connecticut, and was informed by the control tower that he had probably witnessed the routine Navy flight of a Sikorsky UH-60 Black Hawk helicopter.[3] Why a military chopper would be conducting harassing surveillance flights over the home of two abductees remains an open question.

Another prominent abductee, Debbie Jordan, who was the subject of Budd Hopkins' book *Intruders*, was also plagued by overflights of the mystery machines. In her book *Abducted: The Story of the Intruders Continues*. She writes, "These odd helicopters could be seen almost daily around our houses. They are so obvious about their flights it is almost comical. On occasions too numerous to even remember, they have hovered around my house, above my house, and above me for several minutes at a time, not trying to hide themselves or the fact that they are watching us…. They are completely without identification and are always low enough so that I could easily see the pilot…. But the windshields are smoky black, with a finish that makes it impossible to see inside."[4]

On one occasion Debbie was driving down a deserted country road with a friend when her car was buzzed by a black helicopter that hovered directly over her vehicle at an extremely low altitude. She claims that the black helicopters make a louder noise that is easily distinguishable from that of ordinary helicopters. Like the aircraft observed by Betty Andreasson, these copters sport dark-tinted canopies that conceal the identities of whoever (or whatever) is flying them.

The nature and mission of the black helicopters remains unknown. Are they being operated by the U.S. government as part of a deliberate effort to threaten and harass abductees? And, if so, what is the ultimate purpose? Is it to discredit their experiences, or merely to create confusion about the phenomenon as in the *Close Encounters* film? Note that identifying serial numbers, called tail numbers, are required to be displayed on all military aircraft as part of the Aircraft Visual Identification System, but the black machines lack these or any unit identification markings.

Are the black helicopters being operated by clandestine U.S. military units as part of what are referred to in government as "black ops"? Or is it possible that, like the MIB's mysterious black limousines, they are simulacra of earthly machines being flown by hybrid pilots? There have been sightings of unknown "aircraft" that seem to mimic various civil and military types, and analyses of some helicopter reports reveal that these "helicopters" lack tail assemblies, rotors, and are more circular than tubular, and make no noise, and are possibly screen memories of UFOs.

The black helicopter phenomenon is considered an aspect of what has been dubbed the "Darkside Hypothesis." This conspiracy theory posits that a relationship exists between the U.S. government (and possibly the United Nations) and the aliens, which supposedly dates back to a secret meeting between the two groups at Holloman Air Force Base in 1964. A treaty supposedly allows the aliens to abduct people with impunity in exchange for the aliens' advanced technology. Dire narratives tell of underground bases where military personnel work alongside the Grays conducting strange medical and genetic experiments on hapless abductees. While these notions may seem to be nothing more than a paranoid fantasy, there have been reports of abductees who have been re-abducted by humans wearing military uniforms and subjected to intrusive medical and psychological experiments.

One of the seminal cases of the military involvement scenario was the abduction of Myrna Hansen. On the night of May 5, 1980, Ms. Hansen and her six-year-old son were driving near the town of Cimarron, New Mexico, when they encountered two glowing UFOs and experienced a period of missing time. In subsequent hypnosis sessions, she recalled being transported inside one of the craft along with her son. She also witnessed a cow being taken up into the UFO and mutilated by Gray aliens.

After the usual medical procedures had been performed on the mother and son, they were approached by what appeared to be a tall man with a jaundiced, yellow complexion who was dressed in strange, anachronistic clothes. The man offered a sort of apology, saying that their abduction was a mistake and shouldn't have happened. By this time the UFO had landed somewhere in the New Mexican desert, and Hansen and her son were escorted to a hidden elevator that took them to a base concealed deep inside a mountain, where she observed Grays working alongside ordinary humans.

When she was separated from her son she panicked and ran from her captors. Wending her way through the facility she eventually entered a dimly-lit room where she came upon some large vats. Looking inside one of the vats she was horrified to see human body parts suspended in some kind of bubbling liquid. She collapsed in terror at the sight and was discovered by her abductors, who transported her to another room at the base, where several devices were implanted in her body. Afterward, she was reunited with her son and taken to another room where she was subjected to intense flashes of light that she believed were designed to erase her memories of the event. When their ordeal was ended, Hansen and her son were taken into another craft and returned to their car on the highway.[5]

This incident contains a number of themes that encapsulate the paranoid narrative features of the Darkside Hypothesis: UFO abduction, cattle mutilation, an underground base and humans working in collaboration with Gray aliens. The vat in which human body parts were stewing, however, seems like a plot element derived from a bad sci-fi horror film. In the ensuing years other researchers claimed that secret alien bases existed at several locations within the United States, including beneath the town of Dulce, New Mexico, and inside Mount Shasta in California.

As previously discussed, researcher Nick Redfern cites two well-known cases that he claims were orchestrated by U.S. Intelligence agencies. The 1958 Antonio Villas-Boas abduction was supposedly an elaborate hoax perpetrated by the CIA and the AID in an effort to create a bogus close encounter for the purpose of gauging the public's reaction to the alien presence on Earth. Powerful hallucinogenic drugs and a helicopter were allegedly used to simulate an alien abduction. Likewise, Redfern claims that the 1973 abduction of Hickson and Parker was another clandestine operation that employed psychedelic agents, a helicopter and elaborate costumes to create the illusion of an unearthly encounter, in this case to portray aliens in an unfavorable light during the 1973 wave of sightings and abductions. Redfern also implies, without citing specifics, that many other alleged abduction events were planned and executed by U.S. intelligence agencies. While the two cases examined by Redfern do not lend credence to this thesis, evidence seems to suggest that our government may be involved in re-abducting witnesses, perhaps in an effort to create confusion and uncertainty about the true nature of the phenomenon.

The CIA's involvement with the use of LSD and other mind-altering technologies during the 1960s has been well documented. Reports of MILABs by abductees seem to suggest that this type of human experimentation may still be continuing as covert "black projects" that are not subject to governmental oversight or review. Researchers have speculated that clandestine elements of the military/scientific complex may be gathering data about exotic technologies utilizing brain implants, virtual reality bio-chips, holographic image projection, cloaking devices, and other mind altering weapons.

Some reports seem to indicate a connection between MILAB personnel and MIBs. Researcher Jerome Clark reports on an event that took place on March 16, 1993, in the vicinity of Groom Lake, Nevada, also known as the infamous "Area 51," the highly classified military base where experimental aircraft are test-flown. Unsubstantiated accounts also claim that our government is testing captured UFO technology at the site. The witness was ufologist William F. Hamilton III, who was parked on a hill near the base with an anonymous lady friend hoping to observe UFO activity.

As they kept their vigil they watched as anomalous nocturnal lights approached their truck. The lights somehow resolved themselves into an automotive vehicle, and afterward the couple experienced a half hour of missing time. They both underwent regression hypnosis and recalled being abducted by a mixed group of Grays and military types. Hamilton was taken into an alien craft, while his companion was led into a white van where she was subjected to a number of intrusive medical procedures.

The woman's abductors were described as two men dressed completely in black wearing black baseball hats on their heads. She recalled seeing automatic rifles and electronic instruments inside the van. The men administered eye drops into her right eye and inserted an instrument into her left ear canal. When the procedures were completed, the men warned her not to speak about her experience. She does not remember how she was returned back to her same position in the truck after the ordeal was finished. This incident involved the combination of an abduction by Grays with a MILAB conducted by MIB-like military personnel. The procedures performed by the two military types seem more like a contrivance than some kind of genuine medical practices.[6]

In their 1996 book *Connections: Solving Our Alien Abduction Mystery*, co-authors Beth Collings and Anna Jamerson relate a complex account of an apparent MILAB experience. Ms. Collings was the main witness to the event, which transpired in April of 1993. She had been taking evening classes at a local community college and had departed the school at around 9:00 p.m. While driving home through Maryland back country roads to the horse farm the two women shared, she noticed that she was being followed by a pickup truck. The lone driver, who was not visible inside his vehicle, began pursuing her, driving practically bumper to bumper with her car while shining his bright headlights into her car in a harassing manner. She gave the driver several opportunities to pass her, but the truck stayed with her.

When Beth reached a crossroads at about 9:25 she noticed that the truck had disappeared, but now she saw lights from flares and the headlights of vehicles parked across the entire roadway forming a roadblock. She observed a couple of county police cruisers and uniformed state troopers at the roadblock, along with military jeeps and camouflaged Army trucks.

A man wearing plain clothes signaled for her to pull over and asked to see her driver's license. He inspected it and handed it back to her, but when she put her car in gear thinking she could leave, he ordered her to step out of her vehicle for no apparent reason. She was beginning to get apprehensive and asked to see the man's ID, but he replied that wasn't necessary and repeated his command for her to exit her car. At this point Beth remembered that the man backed up a few steps and waved her through the roadblock. On her way home the pickup truck reappeared and continued to harass her until she reached the farm. She felt exhausted and found that the clock read 11:00 p.m., indicating that she had experienced about an hour and a half of missing time.

Suspecting that she had been abducted, she tried to remember what happened during her amnesiac episode, but drew a blank until she was hypnotized by Anna. Under hypnosis, she recalled that she had been forcibly removed from her car by the man who had demanded her license and another man wearing a black coat. The men escorted her to a military truck with camouflage markings and put her in the back of the vehicle, where she was seated, tied up and blindfolded. Then the truck was driven to a building somewhere in the woods where Beth was carried out of the vehicle and taken inside.

Still tied and blindfolded she was placed on a chair and given an injection in the arm by her captors that served to make her groggy. Then she was taken to another building where she was placed on her back on a cot and subjected to a gynecological examination by a woman. She was asked some ambiguous questions which she did not answer clearly because of her groggy mental state. Another injection was administered and Beth, still blindfolded, was led back into the truck and driven back to the roadblock. The blindfold was removed and she was placed back inside her car and allowed to leave. On her way home she was harassed by the same pickup truck that followed her and only drove off when she had reached the entrance to the horse farm.

Beth remembered nothing from the time she had been ordered to step out of her car to when she was able to drive away, and the memory of her missing time was only recovered under hypnosis. To check the veracity of her account of being stopped at the roadblock, she had an associate travel to the site where he discovered evidence of burned flares in the exact location, indicating that the roadblock at least had been a real event. Beth called the local and state police to ascertain if they had been responsible for the roadblock and received negative replies. This case seems to have similarities with cases involving "phantom road workers" as discussed in a previous chapter.[7]

What was the purpose of this apparent MILAB operation? Were her abductors really military personnel or something else? Was the man in the black coat an MIB? Who was driving the mysterious pickup truck that had hounded Beth guiding her to the abduction site? Can our military induce missing time amnesia in a manner similar to the memory erasure techniques employed by the aliens? There are many questions, but no unambiguous answers.

One of the most bizarre experiences reported by abductees involves a procedure that has been termed the "breathing pool." David Jacobs describes this strange practice as follows: "In one common ancillary procedure, the aliens bring the abductee into a room with a large tank or even a small 'swimming pool' in it. The aliens tell her to get into the tank. The liquid is clear and at first glance looks like water, but it is not water. The abductee is told to submerge herself in the liquid and stay there…. She gets in over her head and then is told to breathe. She finds that she is able to breathe normally even though her head is under 'water.'"[8] Although the liquid resembles water, it is sometimes described as being heavier and more viscous than ordinary water. The purpose of this breathing pool procedure is unknown.

Researcher Helmut Lammer has investigated similar experiences conducted during MILABS. He cites the case of an abductee he refers to by the pseudonym "Lisa," who was kidnapped along with several others by military personnel and taken to an underground facility, where she observed naked humans floating inside large tubes. She and her fellow abductees were taken to a pool filled with a yellow, bubbly liquid and forced to submerge themselves in it and found that they could breathe while immersed in the liquid.[9]

Lammer compares these experiences with experiments into "fluid breathing" that were conducted by American scientists beginning in the 1960s. The experiments involved immersing animals in a fluid that had been saturated with oxygen at high temperatures that would enable them to breathe the fluid instead of air. The animals were able to survive for hours while breathing the super-saturated liquid. It was theorized that breathing liquid instead of air would revolutionize deep sea diving under high pressures. A sequence in James Cameron's 1989 alien-themed movie *The Abyss* shows an actual lab rat breathing while completely immersed in liquid as actor Ed Harris prepares for an ultra-deep dive. An attending scientist in the film remarks that "your body breathes fluid for the first nine months [in the womb]; your body will remember." Unlike Cameron's film, however, liquid breathing techniques have not been widely used for various physiological reasons.

In addition to deep sea diving, liquid breathing could be utilized during space travel to help the body withstand multiple G-forces during flight. Abduction researchers have theorized that these techniques are being used to enable ufonauts to survive the extreme gravitational forces during the extreme maneuvers performed by UFOs. Whether human technology has advanced far enough to enable fluid breathing as described by abductees during MILABs is an open question.

There is an alternative explanation for the confluence of techniques reported by abductees during alien abductions and MILABs, however. As David Jacobs explains, "Late-stage hybrids may also dress in military-like clothes such as one-piece jumpsuits that resemble flight suits. Because they look so human, it is easy to mistake them for American military personnel, and many abductees have linked military personnel to their abductions.... Hybrids will sometimes abduct people and bring them to abandoned military bases, or even to unused areas of active military bases.... All this, in conjunction with the long-standing and widespread suspicion of a 'coverup' by the American government has led many abductees and researchers to conclude that the government is secretly conspiring with the aliens."[10]

Whether MILABs are being conducted by the U.S. government or by hybrids posing as military personnel is still an open question. The only certainty is the confusion caused by this ambiguity, which may be the intent of both humans and aliens.

Conclusion

Whistling Past the Graveyard

Something is lurking on the edge of our collective consciousness. Something we don't want to look at. Something too terrifying to contemplate. Something humanity may be ignoring at its peril.

The notion of alien abduction is too fantastic for us to accept. It's mass hysteria, science fiction, space-age fantasy. It can't be, therefore it isn't. We can't handle the truth.

Folklorist and abduction researcher Eddie Bullard has written, "Abduction witnesses represent a normal cross-section of society ... [they] seem to be free of any psychological abnormalities which might predispose them to fantasize such a story ... if abductions are literally true, they are the greatest story of all time. If they are subjective, they offer a seldom-equaled opportunity to gain insight into the interaction of belief with experience and the social transmission of ideas."[1] After analyzing hundreds of abduction accounts, Bullard has pointed out that they do not significantly vary from each other in a manner that would suggest they are urban legends, but instead exhibit a similarity that supports their veracity as experiential events.

Jacques Vallee, among others, has stated that the solution to the UFO enigma may not be possible using the scientific method. J. Allen Hynek has reminded us that, while our current scientific paradigms do not encompass the UFO phenomenon, scientific advances of the future may someday enable us to do so. It's also possible that human science may never be able to comprehend the riddle of an alien presence on Earth.

From all indications there will never be open contact between the inhabitants of Earth and an advanced civilization on equal terms.

No invitation from a beneficent race to join a Galactic Federation of Worlds is forthcoming. Instead, we run the risk of becoming slaves to a race of beings possessing a technology beyond our comprehension and the ability to overwhelm and manipulate our minds. The aliens have shown themselves to be masters of deception. They staged the Occupant encounters of the 1950s and 1960s to deceive us into thinking they were scientists, astronauts or space tourists who were just visiting Earth in order to obscure their true motives. Then they commenced the real work of collecting our genetic material, gathering biological samples and probing the human psyche. A process of planetary acquisition appears to have been going on for many decades, if not longer. Imagine an invasion that could take a hundred years or even longer. As anomalist Charles Fort once declared, we are property.

Some skeptical viewpoints about the phenomenon rest on erroneous and outdated assumptions. For instance, skeptics ridiculed reports of UFOs chasing vehicles down deserted roads at night. Why, they wondered, would aliens travel trillions of miles through outer space just to play games with unfortunate motorists? This behavior makes sense, however, if it is seen as practice or training runs for subsequent highway abductions.

Skeptics also balk at reported alien medical techniques. Why, they ask, do the ufonauts persist in performing the same medical procedures over and over when they could more easily obtain this information about human physiology from reference books, medical schools, cadavers or hacking into the files of the Mayo Clinic? This question assumes that the aliens are actually conducting medical research into humans, but the answer is that they are not researching but are obtaining data on Earth's environmental pollution from living specimens. They are also harvesting genetic material and psychological information about human society from the abductees pursuant to their hybrid infiltration program.

The aliens' surgical skills are also called into question as being so unsophisticated as to leave scars and bruises all over the bodies of abductees, along with painful nasal implants. Once again, the abductors are not performing surgeries for therapeutic purposes, but are using the abductees as the equivalent of laboratory animals with little regard for the well-being of their human subjects.

Skeptics ask why abductees are never allowed to take away physical evidence of alien technology or are given any useful scientific knowledge that could enrich humanity? The answer is that the aliens go to great lengths to keep their agenda secret and are not interested in providing us with evidence of their existence or helping us in any way.

It's undeniably true that hard evidence of abductions is sorely lacking, but there have been some intriguing, if inconclusive clues. As mentioned in Chapter Six, Australian researcher Bill Chalker's book *Hair of the Alien* discusses a DNA analysis of an alleged hair obtained from a hybrid woman that was conducted by a team of biochemists who wished to remain anonymous. Forensic techniques employed by the FBI were used in the analysis, which was performed in 1998. The hair came from a Caucasian woman but lacked pigmentation in the manner of an albino individual. Only mitochondrial DNA (the mother's DNA) rather than nuclear DNA (from the father) was present in the sample. Small amounts of the DNA were amplified using the polymerase chain reaction (PCR) process.

The DNA from both the hair's shaft and root were analyzed. The DNA from the shaft was found to be a rare type from a person of Chinese/Mongolian ethnicity, while the hair's root indicated a Basque/Gaelic ancestry. The most interesting feature of the sample was the deletion of the CCR5 gene, which confers immunity to HIV, smallpox, and possibly other viral diseases, a quality that has potential advantages for hybrid beings engaged in infiltrating the human population.[2]

A case involving visits by alien beings was investigated by Jenny Randles and the British research journal *Flying Saucer Review*. The witness was a Manchester housewife named Cynthia Appleton, who experienced multiple encounters during 1957 and 1958 with an alien being who claimed to be from the planet "Gharnasvarn." Her main visitant was a tall, human-looking being with pale skin and long blond hair. During one of his visits the alien claimed that his finger was burned and asked Cynthia to provide him with a bowl of hot water to bathe his hand. He then injected himself with a substance from a tube and spread a jelly-like material over the wounded area, which healed the burn.

After the being left her home Cynthia discovered a small piece of skin that had been discarded in the washing bowl, which she dutifully preserved. She gave the skin sample to clinical psychologist Dr. John Dale, who submitted it to a chemist at a Manchester university for analysis where a scanning electron microscope was used to examine the sample. While nothing obviously extraterrestrial was discovered in the sample, it did not look like human skin but more closely resembled the epidermis of an animal, possibly that of a pig.[3]

In his book *The UFO Files*, researcher Jerome Clark cites an article in the December 25, 1986, issue of the science journal *Nature* entitled "Mystery Object Amid the Chromosomes." The article states that seven doctors from the genetics department of Churchill Hospital at Headington in Oxford, England, made a baffling discovery of a mysterious object in a female patient's amniotic fluid during an amniocentesis procedure. The tiny object resembled a section of a crossword puzzle with a grid of black and white squares that was nestled among the patient's chromosomes and appeared to be of artificial origin. The physicians admitted they were as intrigued as they were ignorant about the nature of the object and how it had gotten into the patient's amniotic fluid.

After the publication of the article a number of savants weighed in with opinions about the origin and nature of the object, including some writers who theorized that it was of extraterrestrial manufacture, but the authors of the article thought all these explanations were inadequate, but could offer no convincing theories about the object. Although there's nothing to indicate that the patient had been abducted, abductees report that the aliens conduct various amniocentesis-like procedures during their encounters.[4]

In spite of the hundreds of thousands of UFO sightings reported from 1947 to the present, a number of which are observed by pilots, scientists and other reliable witnesses, and the untold thousands of abduction cases (many of which go unreported), skeptics insist that the phenomenon is entirely a result of hallucination, illusion and delusion. Proponents of an alien presence on Earth are routinely dismissed as "true believers" and tinfoil hat conspiracy theorists with only a cursory examination of the evidence. While there are rumors of U.S. government involvement in procuring hard evidence of UFOs, this seems to be a low priority effort that is afforded minimal financial resources.

In his 1990 study of the phenomenon, *Out There*, journalist Howard Blum quotes from a paper entitled "UFO Hypothesis and Survival Questions" that was circulated between various U.S. intelligence agencies back in the 1980s: "If you are walking along a forest path and someone yells 'rattler,' your reaction would be immediate and defensive. You would not take time to speculate before you act. You would have to treat the alarm as if it were a real and immediate threat to your survival.... It would seem a little more of this survival attitude is called for in dealing with the UFO problem."[5] Members of the UFO research community have been sounding the alarm about this possible threat to the existence of humanity for decades, and it is hoped that these warnings will someday be heeded.

Chapter Notes

Introduction

1. Michael Mannion, *Project Mindshift: The Re-Education of the American Public Concerning Extraterrestrial Life, 1947–Present* (New York: M. Evans & Co., 1998), 122.

2. Nick Pope, *The Uninvited: An Exposé of the Alien Abduction Phenomenon* (London: Lume Books, 2020), ii.

Chapter One

1. J. Allen Hynek, *The Hynek UFO Report* (New York: Dell, 1977), 203–205.

2. Jim and Coral Lorenzen, *Encounters with UFO Occupants* (New York: Berkley Medallion, 1976), 143.

3. *Ibid.*, 116–118.

4. *Ibid.*, 125–126.

5. Hynek, *The Hynek UFO Report*, 223–229.

6. Charles Bowen, ed., *Encounter Cases from Flying Saucer Review* (New York: Signet, 1977), 57–71.

7. Raymond Fowler, *UFO Testament: Anatomy of an Abductee* (Lincoln: iUniverse, 2002), 179–181.

8. Bowen, *Encounter Cases*, 103–115.

9. Richard Hall, *Uninvited Guests: A Documented History of UFO Sightings, Alien Encounters and Coverups* (Santa Fe: Aurora Press, 1998), 274–275.

10. Budd Hopkins, *Missing Time: A Documented Study of UFO Abductions* (New York: Richard Marek, 1981), 34–50.

11. *Ibid.*, 47–48.

12. Hynek, *The Hynek UFO Report*, 206.

13. Hall, *Uninvited Guests*, 68–69.

Chapter Two

1. Michael Lindeman, ed., *UFOs and the Alien Presence: Six Viewpoints* (Santa Barbara: The 2020 Group, 1991), 135–136.

2. Jenny Randles, *Alien Abductions: The Mystery Solved* (New Brunswick: Inner Light Books, 1988), 75–76.

3. Kevin D. Randle, Russ Estes and William P. Cone, *The Abduction Enigma: The Truth Behind the Mass Alien Abductions of the Late Twentieth Century* (New York: Tom Doherty Associates, 1999), 30.

4. Lorenzens, *Encounters with UFO Occupants*, 61–87.

5. *Ibid.*, 374–375.

6. D. Scott Rogo, ed., *UFO Abductions: True Cases of Alien Kidnapping* (New York: Signet, 1980), 112–121.

7. Leonard Stringfield, *Situation Red: The UFO Siege* (New York: Fawcett Crest, 1977), 70.

8. John Spencer, *The UFO Encyclopedia* (New York: Avon Books, 1991), 180–181.

9. Raymond Fowler, *UFOs: The Ultimate Abduction* (Portsmouth, NH: Seacoast Press, 2020), 218.

10. David M. Jacobs, *Secret Life: First-hand Accounts of UFO Abductions* (New York: Simon & Schuster, 1992), 67.

11. Kevin D. Randle, *The October Scenario: UFO Abductions,Theories About Them and a Prediction of When They Will Return* (Iowa City: Middle Coast, 1988), 11–15.

12. *Ibid.*, 17–30.

13. Randles, *Alien Abductions*, 76–79.

14. Randle, *The October Scenario*, 31–44.

15. *Ibid.*, 45–52.

16. Fowler, *UFOs: The Ultimate Abduction*, 176–178.

17. Randles, *Alien Abductions*, 171–173.
18. Carl Nagaitis and Philip Mantle, *Without Consent: A Comprehensive Survey of Missing-Time and Abduction Phenomena* (New York: Marlowe and Company, 1994), 63–78.
19. Jim and Coral Lorenzen, *Abducted! Confrontations with Beings from Outer Space* (New York: Berkley Medallion, 1977), 38–51.
20. Stringfield, *Situation Red*, 228–243.
21. John G. Fuller, *The Interrupted Journey* (New York: Dell, 1967), 240.
22. Walter Web, *Encounter at Buff Ledge: A UFO Case History* (Chicago: Center for UFO Studies, 1994), 12.
23. Raymond Fowler, *The Allagash Abductions: Undeniable Evidence of Alien Intervention* (Tigard, OR: Wildflower Press, 1993), 57.

Chapter Three

1. David M. Jacobs, *The Threat: The Secret Agenda: What the Aliens Really Want ... and How They Plan to Get It* (New York: Simon & Schuster, 1998), 17–18.
2. Budd Hopkins, *Missing Time: A Documented Study of UFO Abductions* (New York: Richard Marek, 1981), 54–61.
3. Gary Smith, "Unspeakable Secret," *Washington Post*, January 3, 1988.
4. Hopkins, *Missing Time*, 217.
5. *Ibid.*, 179.
6. Budd Hopkins, *Intruders: The Strange Visitations at Copley Woods* (New York: Random House, 1987), 182.
7. *Ibid.*, 190.
8. Whitley Strieber, *Communion: A True Story* (New York: Avon, 1987), 174.
9. Budd Hopkins and Carol Rainey, *Sight Unseen: Science, UFO Invisibility and Transgenic Beings* (New York: Atria Books, 2003), 217.

Chapter Four

1. John E. Mack, *Abduction: Human Encounters with Aliens* (New York: Scribner's, 1994), 48–49.
2. Whitley Strieber, *Transformation: The Breakthrough* (New York: Beech Tree Books, 1998), 240.
3. *Ibid.*, 239.

4. Jacobs, *Secret Life*, 191.
5. Preston Dennett. *UFO Healings: True Accounts of People Healed by Extraterrestrials* (Mill Spring, NC: Wild Flower Press, 1996), xii.
6. Hopkins and Rainey, *Sight Unseen*, 355–356.
7. John G. Miller, MD, "Medical Procedural Differences: Alien vs. Human," in David Prichard, et al., eds., *Alien Discussions: Proceedings of the Abduction Conference at MIT* (Cambridge: North Cambridge Press, 1992), 59.
8. Jenny Randles, *Time Storms: Amazing Evidence for Time Warps, Space Riffs and Time Travel* (New York: Berkley Books, 2002), 54–55.
9. Jacobs, *The Threat*, 265.
10. Debbie Jordan and Kathy Mitchell, *Abducted: The Story of the Intruders Continues* (New York: Carroll & Graf, 1994), 3.
11. David M. Jacobs, *Walking Among Us: The Alien Plan to Control Humanity* (San Francisco: Disinformation Books, 2015), 216–219.
12. Stanton Friedman and Kathleen Marden, *Captured: The Betty and Barney Hill UFO Experience* (Franklin Lakes, NJ: New Page Books, 2007), 207.
13. Randles, *Alien Abductions: Mystery Solved*, 80.
14. Jordan and Mitchell, *Abducted*, 67–68.
15. Terry Lovelace, *Devil's Den: The Reckoning* (privately published, 2020), 276.
16. John Spencer, *The UFO Encyclopedia* (New York: Avon Books, 1991), 16.
17. Beth Collings and Anna Jamerson, *Connections: Solving Our Alien Abduction Mystery* (Newberg, OR: Wildflower Press, 1996), 102.
18. Friedman and Marden, *Captured*, 57–58.
19. Jordan and Mitchell, *Abducted*, 61–62.
20. Stringfield, *Situation Red*, 241.

Chapter Five

1. Jerome Clark, *The UFO Files: Tales of Alien Abductions, Extraterrestrial Visitations, Flying Saucers, and More* (Lincolnwood, IL: Publications International, 1996), 96.
2. Hopkins, *Missing Time*, 155–156.

3. Anne Druffel, *How to Defend Your-self Against Alien Abduction* (New York: Three Rivers Press, 1998), 24.
4. John E. Mack, *Abduction*, 70.
5. *Ibid.*, 221.
6. Clark, *UFO Files*, 103–104.
7. Jacobs, *Secret Life*, 287–288.
8. Kevin D. Randle, et al., *The Abduction Enigma*, 100.
9. Peter Brookesmith, *Alien Abductions* (New York: Barnes & Noble Books, 1998), 86–94.
10. Randle, *The Abduction Enigma*, 123.
11. Nick Redfern, *Top Secret Alien Abduction Files: What the Government Doesn't Want You to Know* (Newburyport, MA: Disinformation Books, 2018), 35–40.
12. *Ibid.*, 91–96.

Chapter Six

1. "Shane Kurz Abduction," thenightski. org.
2. Judith M. Gansberg and Alan L. Gansberg, *Direct Encounters: Personal Histories of UFO Abductees* (New York: Walker and Company, 1980), 19–22.
3. Hopkins, *Intruders*, 90–98.
4. Lovelace, *Devil's Den: The Reckoning*, 281–285.
5. Whitley Strieber and Anne Strieber, eds., *The Communion Letters* (New York: Harper Prism, 1997), 111–112.
6. Nick Pope, *The Uninvited*, 139–140.
7. *Ibid.*, 129–131.
8. Bill Chalker, *Hair of the Alien: DNA and Other Evidence of Alien Abduction* (New York: Paraview Pocket Books, 2005), 17, 22–38.
9. Hopkins and Rainey, *Sight Unseen*, 246–253.

Chapter Seven

1. John A. Keel, *The Mothman Prophecies* (New York: Tor Books, 1991), 89–94.
2. Randles, *Alien Abduction: Mystery Solved*, 116–120.
3. Fowler, *UFOs: The Ultimate Abduction*, 175.
4. Nomar Slevik, *Otherworldly Encounters: Evidence of UFO Sightings and Abductions* (Woodbury, MN: Llewellyn Publications, 2018), 263–270.

5. Randles, *Alien Abduction: Mystery Solved*, 8–22.
6. *Ibid.*, 131–133.
7. Jim Keith, *Casebook on the Men in Black* (Lilburn, GA: IllumiNet Press, 1997), 198–199.
8. Susan Michaels, *Sightings: UFOs* (New York: Fireside Books, 1997), 219–220.
9. Jenny Randles, *The Truth Behind Men in Black* (New York: St. Martin's, 1997), 174–176.
10. Keith, *Casebook on the Men in Black*, 193–195.
11. Nick Redfern, *True Stories of the Real Men in Black* (New York: Rosen Publishing Group, 2015), 128.
12. Terry Lovelace, *Incident at Devil's Den: A True Story* (privately published, 2018), 216–225.
13. Lovelace, *Devil's Den: The Reckoning*, 126.
14. Nick Pope, *The Uninvited*, 141–142.
15. Peter Hough and Moshe Kalman, *The Truth about Alien Abductions* (London: Blanford Books, 1997), 139.
16. *Ibid.*, 139–140.

Chapter Eight

1. Jacobs, *The Threat*, 186.
2. Hopkins and Rainey, *Sight Unseen*, 188–206.
3. *Ibid.*, 207–213.
4. *Ibid.*, 214–217.
5. Randles, *The Truth Behind Men in Black*, 21.
6. Bill Foster, Peggy Foster and Nadine Wheeler, *The Black Triangle Abduction* (Woodbridge, VA: The Invisible College Press, 2005), 21.
7. Carl Nagaitis and Philip Mantle, *Without Consent*, 18–25.
8. Foster, *The Black Triangle Abduction*, 37–38.
9. Philip J. Imbrogno and Marianne Horrigan, *Contact of the 5th Kind* (St. Paul: Llewellyn Publications, 1997), 77.
10. Bowen, *Encounter Cases from Flying Saucer Review*, 197–204.
11. Pope, *The Uninvited*, 157–167.
12. Peter Hough and Moshe Kalman, *The Truth about Alien Abductions*, 85.
13. *Ibid.*, 85–86.
14. Lovelace, *Devil's Den: The Reckoning*, 168–188.

15. *BUFORA Journal*, January 5, 1978.
16. Hopkins and Rainey, *Sight Unseen*, 259.
17. *Ibid.*, 259–275.

Chapter Nine

1. Raymond Fowler. *The Watchers: The Secret Design Behind UFO Abduction* (New York: Bantam Books, 1991), xii.
2. *Ibid.*, 35–38.
3. Nick Redfern, *Top Secret Alien Abduction Files*, 111.
4. Jordan, *Abducted*, 141.
5. Jerome Clark, *The UFO Book: Encyclopedia of the Extraterrestrial* (Detroit: Visible Ink Press, 1998), 147.
6. *Ibid.*, 383–384.

7. Collings and Jamerson, *Connections*, 319–339.
8. Jacobs, *Secret Life*, 187.
9. Helmut Lammer, "Military Abductions," at http://rense.com>ufo2>lammer.
10. Jacobs, *The Threat*, 187.

Conclusion

1. Hall, *Uninvited Guests*, 105–106.
2. Chalker, *Hair of the Alien*, 71–80.
3. Randles, *The Truth Behind Men in Black*, 66.
4. Clark, *The UFO Files*, 109–110.
5. Howard Blum, *Out There: The Government's Secret Quest for Extraterrestrials* (New York: Simon & Schuster, 1990), 81.

Bibliography

Adamski, George. *Inside the Flying Saucers.* New York: Paperback Library, 1955.

Baker, Alan. *The Encyclopedia of Alien Encounters.* New York: Checkmark Books, 2000.

Blum, Howard. *Out There: The Government's Secret Quest for Extraterrestrials.* New York: Simon & Schuster, 1990.

Bowen, Charles, ed. *Encounter Cases from Flying Saucer Review.* New York: Signet, 1977.

Brookesmith, Peter. *Alien Abductions.* New York: Barnes & Noble Books, 1998.

Bryan, C.D.B. *Close Encounters of the Fourth Kind: Alien Abduction, UFOs and the Conference at M.I.T.* New York: Alfred A. Knopf, 1995.

Bullard, Thomas E. *The Myth and Mystery of UFOs.* Lawrence: University Press of Kansas, 2010.

Chalker, Bill. *Hair of the Alien: DNA and Other Evidence of Alien Abduction.* New York: Paraview Pocket Books, 2005.

Clark, Jerome. *The UFO Book: Encyclopedia of the Extraterrestrial.* Detroit: Visible Ink Press, 1998.

_____. *The UFO Files: Tales of Alien Abductions, Extraterrestrial Visitations, Flying Saucers, and More.* Lincolnwood, IL: Publications International, 1996.

Collings, Beth, and Anna Jamerson. *Connections: Solving Our Alien Abduction Mystery.* Newberg, OR: Wildflower Press, 1996.

Cooper, Gordon. *Leap of Faith: An Astronaut's Journey into the Unknown.* New York: HarperCollins, 2001.

Dennett, Preston. *UFO Healings: True Accounts of People Healed by Extraterrestrials.* Mill Spring, NC: Wild Flower Press, 1996.

Dolan, Richard. *The Alien Agendas: A Speculative Analysis of Those Visiting Earth.* Rochester: Richard Dolan Press, 2020.

Donderi, *UFOs, ETs and Alien Abductions: A Scientist Looks at the Evidence.* Charlottesville: Hampton Roads, 2013.

Druffel, Ann. *How to Defend Yourself Against Alien Abduction.* New York: Three Rivers Press, 1998.

Druffel, Ann, and D. Scott Rogo. *The Tujunga Canyon Contacts.* New York: Signet, 1989.

Foster, Bill, Peggy Foster, and Nadine Wheeler. *The Black Triangle Abduction.* Woodbridge, VA: The Invisible College Press, 2005.

Fowler, Raymond E. *The Allagash Abductions: Undeniable Evidence of Alien Intervention.* Tigard, OR: Wildflower Press, 1993.

_____. *The Andreasson Affair.* New York: Bantam Books, 1980.

_____. *UFO Testament: Anatomy of an Abductee.* Lincoln: iUniverse, 2002.

_____. *UFOs: The Ultimate Abduction.* Portsmouth, NH: Seacoast Press, 2020.

_____. *The Watchers: The Secret Design Behind UFO Abduction.* New York: Bantam Books, 1991.

Friedman, Stanton, and Kathleen Marden. *Captured: The Betty and Barney Hill UFO Experience.* Franklin Lakes, NJ: New Page Books, 2007.

Fuller, John G. *The Interrupted Journey.* New York: Dell, 1967.

Gansberg, Judith M., and Alan L. Gansberg. *Direct Encounters: Personal Histories of UFO Abductees.* New York: Walker and Company, 1980.

Gray, Barker. *They Knew Too Much about*

Flying Saucers. New York: University Books, 1956.

Hall, Richard. *Unauthorized Guests: A Documented History of UFO Sightings, Alien Encounters and Coverups*. Santa Fe: Aurora Press, 1998.

Hickson, Charles, and William Mendez. *UFO Contact at Pascagoula*. Tucson: Wendelle C. Stevens, 1983.

Hopkins, Budd. *Intruders: The Strange Visitations at Copley Woods*. New York: Random House, 1987.

_____. *Missing Time: A Documented Study of UFO Abductions*. New York: Richard Marek, 1981.

Hopkins, Budd, and Carol Rainey. *Sight Unseen: Science, UFO Invisibility and Transgenic Beings*. New York: Atria Books, 2003.

Horsley, Sir Peter. *Sounds from Another Room: Memories of Planes, Princes and the Paranormal*. London: Pen and Sword Military, 1990.

Hough, Peter, and Jenny Randles. *Looking for the Aliens: A Psychological, Scientific and Imaginative Investigation*. London: Blanford Books, 1991.

Hough, Peter, and Moshe Kalman. *The Truth about Alien Abductions*. London: Blanford Books, 1997.

Hufford, David J. *The Terror that Comes in the Night: An Experience Centered Study of Supernatural Assault Traditions*. Philadelphia: University of Pennsylvania Press, 1982.

Hynek, J. Allen. *The Hynek UFO Report*. New York: Dell, 1977.

Hynek, J. Allen, and Jacques Vallee. *The Edge of Reality: A Progress Report on Unidentified Objects*. Chicago: Henry Regnery, 1975.

Imbrogno, Philip J., and Marianne Horrigan. *Contact of the 5th Kind*. St. Paul, MN: Llewellyn, 1997.

Jacobs, David M. *Secret Life: Firsthand Accounts of UFO Abductions*. New York: Simon & Schuster, 1992.

_____. *The Threat: The Secret Agenda: What the Aliens Really Want ... and How They Plan to Get It*. New York: Simon & Schuster, 1998.

_____. *The UFO Controversy in America*. New York: New American Library, 1976.

_____. *Walking Among Us: The Alien Plan to Control Humanity*. San Francisco: Disinformation Books, 2015.

Jordan, Debbie, and Kathy Mitchell. *Abducted: The Story of the Intruders Continues*. New York: Carroll & Graf, 1994.

Keel, John A. *The Mothman Prophecies*. New York: Tor Books, 1991.

Kieth, Jim. *Casebook on the Men in Black*. Lilburn, GA: IllumiNet Press, 1997.

Krapf, Phillip H. *The Challenge of Contact: A Mainstream Journalist's Report on Interplanetary Diplomacy*. Mt. Shasta, CA: Origin Press, 2001.

_____. *The Contact Has Begun: The True Story of a Journalist's Encounter with Alien Beings*. Carlsbad: Hay House, 1998.

Lindeman, Michael, ed. *UFOs and the Alien Presence: Six Viewpoints*. Santa Barbara: The 2020 Group, 1991.

Lorenzen, Coral, and Jim Lorenzen. *Abducted! Confrontations with Beings from Outer Space*. New York: Berkley Medallion, 1977.

_____. *Encounters with UFO Occupants*. New York: Berkley Medallion, 1976.

Lovelace, Terry. *Devil's Den: The Reckoning*. Privately published, 2020.

_____. *Incident at Devil's Den: A True Story*. Privately published, 2018.

Mack, John E. *Abduction: Human Encounters with Aliens*. New York: Scribner's, 1994.

_____. *Passport to the Cosmos: Human Transformation and Alien Encounters*. New York: Three Rivers Press, 1999.

Mannion, Michael. *Project Mindshift: The Re-education of the American Public Concerning Extraterrestrial Life, 1947–Present*. New York: M. Evans & Co., 1998.

Marden, Kathleen. *Forbidden Knowledge: A Personal Journey from Alien Abduction to Spiritual Transformation*. Privately published, 2022.

Marden, Kathleen, and Denise Stoner. *The Alien Abduction Files: The Most Startling Cases of Human-Alien Contact Ever Reported*. Pompton Plains, NJ: New Page Press, 2013.

Meehan, Paul. *Alien Abduction in the Cinema: A History from the 1950s to the Present*. Jefferson, NC: McFarland, 2023.

Menger, Howard. *From Outer Space to You*. New York: Pyramid Books, 1974.

Michaels, Susan. *Sightings: UFOs*. New York: Fireside Books, 1997.

Nagaitis, Carl, and Philip Mantle. *Without*

Consent: *A Comprehensive Survey of Missing-Time and Abduction Phenomena.* New York: Marlowe and Company, 1994.

Pope, Nick. *The Uninvited: An Exposé of the Alien Abduction Phenomenon.* London: Lume Books, 2020.

Prichard, David, et al., eds. *Alien Discussions: Proceedings of the Abduction Conference at MIT.* Cambridge: North Cambridge Press, 1992.

Randle, Kevin D. *The October Scenario: UFO Abductions, Theories About Them and a Prediction of When They Will Return.* Iowa City: Middle Coast, 1988.

Randle, Kevin D., Russ Estes and William P. Cone. *The Abduction Enigma: The Truth Behind the Mass Alien Abductions of the Late Twentieth Century.* New York: Tom Doherty Associates, 1999.

Randles, Jenny. *Alien Abductions: The Mystery Solved.* New Brunswick: Inner Light Books, 1988.

_____. *Time Storms: Amazing Evidence for Time Warps, Space Riffs and Time Travel.* New York: Berkley Books, 2002.

_____. *The Truth Behind Men in Black.* New York: St. Martin's, 1997.

Redfern, Nick. *Contactees: A History of Alien-Human Interaction.* Franklin Lakes, NJ: New Page Books, 2010.

_____. *Top Secret Alien Abduction Files: What the Government Doesn't Want You to Know.* Newburyport, MA: Disinformation Books, 2018.

_____. *True Stories of the Real Men in Black.* New York: Rosen Publishing Group, 2015.

Ring, Kenneth. *The Omega Project: Near Death Experiences, UFO Encounters and Mind at Large.* New York: William Morrow, 1992.

Rogo, D. Scott, ed. *UFO Abductions: True Cases of Alien Kidnapping.* New York: Signet, 1980.

Sagan, Carl. *The Dragons of Eden: Speculations on the Evolution of Human Intelligence.* New York: Ballantine, 1977.

Scully, Frank. *Behind the Flying Saucers.* New York: Popular Library, 1950.

Slevik, Nomar. *Otherworldly Encounters: Evidence of UFO Sightings and Abductions.* Woodbury, MN: Llewellyn Publications, 2018.

Spencer, John. *The UFO Encyclopedia.* New York: Avon Books, 1991.

Strieber, Whitley. *Communion: A True Story.* New York: Avon, 1987.

_____. *Transformation: The Breakthrough.* New York: Beech Tree Books, 1998.

Strieber, Whitley, and Anne Strieber, eds. *The Communion Letters.* New York: Harper Prism, 1997.

Stringfield, Leonard. *Situation Red: The UFO Siege.* New York: Fawcett Crest, 1977.

Swann, Ingo. *Penetration: The Question of Extraterrestrial and Human Telepathy.* Privately published, 1998.

Vallee, Jacques. *Passport to Magonia: From Folklore to Flying Saucers.* Chicago: Henry Regnery, 1969.

_____. *Messengers of Deception: UFO Contacts and Cults.* Berkeley: And/Or Press, 1979.

Walton, Travis. *The Walton Experience: The Incredible Account of One Man's Abduction by a UFO.* New York: Berkley Medallion, 1978.

Webb, Walter. *Encounter at Buff Ledge: A UFO Case History.* Chicago: Center for UFO Studies, 1994.

Index

www.ingramcontent.com/pod-product-compliance
Lightning Source LLC
Chambersburg PA
CBHW021141090426
42740CB00008B/884